ADVANCED COMPUTER ARCHITECTURE AND PARALLEL PROCESSING

ADVANCED COMPUTER ARCHITECTURE AND PARALLEL PROCESSING

Hesham El-Rewini
Southern Methodist University

Mostafa Abd-El-Barr
Kuwait University

WILEY-
INTERSCIENCE

A JOHN WILEY & SONS, INC PUBLICATION

Library of Congress Cataloging-in-Publication Data is available

ISBN 0-471-46740-5

To the memory of Abdel Wahab Motawe, who wiped away the tears of many people and cheered them up even when he was in immense pain. His inspiration and impact on my life and the lives of many others was enormous.
—*Hesham El-Rewini*

To my family members (Ebtesam, Muhammad, Abd-El-Rahman, Ibrahim, and Mai) for their support and love
—*Mostafa Abd-El-Barr*

■■■■■■ CONTENTS

Single processor supercomputers have achieved great speeds and have been pushing hardware technology to the physical limit of chip manufacturing. But soon this trend will come to an end, because there are physical and architectural bounds, which limit the computational power that can be achieved with a single processor system. In this book, we study advanced computer architectures that utilize parallelism via multiple processing units. While parallel computing, in the form of internally linked processors, was the main form of parallelism, advances in computer networks has created a new type of parallelism in the form of networked autonomous computers. Instead of putting everything in a single box and tightly couple processors to memory, the Internet achieved a kind of parallelism by loosely connecting everything outside of the box. To get the most out of a computer system with internal or external parallelism, designers and software developers must understand the interaction between hardware and software parts of the system. This is the reason we wrote this book. We want the reader to understand the power and limitations of multiprocessor systems. Our goal is to apprise the reader of both the beneficial and challenging aspects of advanced architecture and parallelism. The material in this book is organized in 10 chapters, as follows.

Chapter 1 is a survey of the field of computer architecture at an introductory level. We first study the evolution of computing and the changes that have led to obtaining high performance computing via parallelism. The popular Flynn's taxonomy of computer systems is provided. An introduction to single instruction multiple data (SIMD) and multiple instruction multiple data (MIMD) systems is also given. Both shared-memory and the message passing systems and their interconnection networks are introduced.

Chapter 2 navigates through a number of system configurations for multiprocessors. It discusses the different topologies used for interconnecting multiprocessors. Taxonomy for interconnection networks based on their topology is introduced. Dynamic and static interconnection schemes are also studied. The bus, crossbar, and multi-stage topology are introduced as dynamic interconnections. In the static interconnection scheme, three main mechanisms are covered. These are the hypercube topology, mesh topology, and k-ary n-cube topology. A number of performance aspects are introduced including cost, latency, diameter, node degree, and symmetry.

Chapter 3 is about performance. How should we characterize the performance of a computer system when, in effect, parallel computing redefines traditional measures such as million instructions per second (MIPS) and million floating-point operations per second (MFLOPS)? New measures of performance, such as speedup, are discussed. This chapter examines several versions of speedup, as well as other performance measures and benchmarks.

Chapters 4 and 5 cover shared memory and message passing systems, respectively. The main challenges of shared memory systems are performance degradation due to contention and the cache coherence problems. Performance of shared memory system becomes an issue when the interconnection network connecting the processors to global memory becomes a bottleneck. Local caches are typically used to alleviate the bottleneck problem. But scalability remains the main drawback of shared memory system. The introduction of caches has created consistency problem among caches and between memory and caches. In Chapter 4, we cover several cache coherence protocols that can be categorized as either snoopy protocols or directory based protocols. Since shared memory systems are difficult to scale up to a large number of processors, message passing systems may be the only way to efficiently achieve scalability. In Chapter 5, we discuss the architecture and the network models of message passing systems. We shed some light on routing and network switching techniques. We conclude with a contrast between shared memory and message passing systems.

Chapter 6 covers abstract models, algorithms, and complexity analysis. We discuss a shared-memory abstract model (PRAM), which can be used to study parallel algorithms and evaluate their complexities. We also outline the basic elements of a formal model of message passing systems under the synchronous model. We design and discuss the complexity analysis of algorithms described in terms of both models.

Chapters 7–10 discuss a number of issues related to network computing, in which the nodes are stand-alone computers that may be connected via a switch, local area network, or the Internet. Chapter 7 provides the basic concepts of network computing including client/server paradigm, cluster computing, and grid computing. Chapter 8 illustrates the parallel virtual machine (PVM) programming system. It shows how to write programs on a network of heterogeneous machines. Chapter 9 covers the message-passing interface (MPI) standard in which portable distributed parallel programs can be developed. Chapter 10 addresses the problem of allocating tasks to processing units. The scheduling problem in several of its variations is covered. We survey a number of solutions to this important problem. We cover program and system models, optimal algorithms, heuristic algorithms, scheduling versus allocation techniques, and homogeneous versus heterogeneous environments.

Students in Computer Engineering, Computer Science, and Electrical Engineering should benefit from this book. The book can be used to teach graduate courses in advanced architecture and parallel processing. Selected chapters can be used to offer special topic courses with different emphasis. The book can also be used as a comprehensive reference for practitioners working as engineers, programmers, and technologists. In addition, portions of the book can be used to teach short courses to practitioners. Different chapters might be used to offer courses with different flavors. For example, a one-semester course in Advanced Computer Architecture may cover Chapters 1–5, 7, and 8, while another one-semester course on Parallel Processing may cover Chapters 1–4, 6, 9, and 10.

This book has been class-tested by both authors. In fact, it evolves out of the class notes for the SMU's CSE8380 and CSE8383, University of Saskatchewan's (UofS) CMPT740 and KFUPM's COE520. These experiences have been incorporated into the present book. Our students corrected errors and improved the organization of the book. We would like to thank the students in these classes. We owe much to many students and colleagues, who have contributed to the production of this book. Chuck Mann, Yehia Amer, Habib Ammari, Abdul Aziz, Clay Breshears, Jahanzeb Faizan, Michael A. Langston, and A. Naseer read drafts of the book and all contributed to the improvement of the original manuscript. Ted Lewis has contributed to earlier versions of some chapters. We are indebted to the anonymous reviewers arranged by John Wiley for their suggestions and corrections. Special thanks to Albert Y. Zomaya, the series editor and to Val Moliere, Kirsten Rohstedt and Christine Punzo of John Wiley for their help in making this book a reality. Of course, responsibility for errors and inconsistencies rests with us.

Finally, and most of all, we want to thank our wives and children for tolerating all the long hours we spent on this book. Hesham would also like to thank Ted Lewis and Bruce Shriver for their friendship, mentorship and guidance over the years.

HESHAM EL-REWINI
MOSTAFA ABD-EL-BARR
May 2004

CHAPTER 1

Introduction to Advanced Computer Architecture and Parallel Processing

Computer architects have always strived to increase the performance of their computer architectures. High performance may come from fast dense circuitry, packaging technology, and parallelism. Single-processor supercomputers have achieved unheard of speeds and have been pushing hardware technology to the physical limit of chip manufacturing. However, this trend will soon come to an end, because there are physical and architectural bounds that limit the computational power that can be achieved with a single-processor system. In this book we will study advanced computer architectures that utilize parallelism via multiple processing units.

Parallel processors are computer systems consisting of multiple processing units connected via some interconnection network plus the software needed to make the processing units work together. There are two major factors used to categorize such systems: the processing units themselves, and the interconnection network that ties them together. The processing units can communicate and interact with each other using either shared memory or message passing methods. The interconnection network for shared memory systems can be classified as bus-based versus switch-based. In message passing systems, the interconnection network is divided into static and dynamic. Static connections have a fixed topology that does not change while programs are running. Dynamic connections create links on the fly as the program executes.

The main argument for using multiprocessors is to create powerful computers by simply connecting multiple processors. A multiprocessor is expected to reach faster speed than the fastest single-processor system. In addition, a multiprocessor consisting of a number of single processors is expected to be more cost-effective than building a high-performance single processor. Another advantage of a multiprocessor is fault tolerance. If a processor fails, the remaining processors should be able to provide continued service, albeit with degraded performance.

Advanced Computer Architecture and Parallel Processing, by H. El-Rewini and M. Abd-El-Barr
ISBN 0-471-46740-5 Copyright © 2005 John Wiley & Sons, Inc.

1.1   FOUR DECADES OF COMPUTING

Most computer scientists agree that there have been four distinct paradigms or eras of computing. These are: batch, time-sharing, desktop, and network. Table 1.1 is modified from a table proposed by Lawrence Tesler. In this table, major characteristics of the different computing paradigms are associated with each decade of computing, starting from 1960.

1.1.1   Batch Era

By 1965 the IBM System/360 mainframe dominated the corporate computer centers. It was the typical batch processing machine with punched card readers, tapes and disk drives, but no connection beyond the computer room. This single mainframe established large centralized computers as the standard form of computing for decades. The IBM System/360 had an operating system, multiple programming languages, and 10 megabytes of disk storage. The System/360 filled a room with metal boxes and people to run them. Its transistor circuits were reasonably fast. Power users could order magnetic core memories with up to one megabyte of 32-bit words. This machine was large enough to support many programs in memory at the same time, even though the central processing unit had to switch from one program to another.

1.1.2   Time-Sharing Era

The mainframes of the batch era were firmly established by the late 1960s when advances in semiconductor technology made the solid-state memory and integrated circuit feasible. These advances in hardware technology spawned the minicomputer era. They were small, fast, and inexpensive enough to be spread throughout the company at the divisional level. However, they were still too expensive and difficult

TABLE 1.1   Four Decades of Computing

Feature	Batch	Time-Sharing	Desktop	Network
Decade	1960s	1970s	1980s	1990s
Location	Computer room	Terminal room	Desktop	Mobile
Users	Experts	Specialists	Individuals	Groups
Data	Alphanumeric	Text, numbers	Fonts, graphs	Multimedia
Objective	Calculate	Access	Present	Communicate
Interface	Punched card	Keyboard and CRT	See and point	Ask and tell
Operation	Process	Edit	Layout	Orchestrate
Connectivity	None	Peripheral cable	LAN	Internet
Owners	Corporate computer centers	Divisional IS shops	Departmental end-users	Everyone

LAN, local area network.

to use to hand over to end-users. Minicomputers made by DEC, Prime, and Data General led the way in defining a new kind of computing: time-sharing. By the 1970s it was clear that there existed two kinds of commercial or business computing: (1) centralized data processing mainframes, and (2) time-sharing minicomputers. In parallel with small-scale machines, supercomputers were coming into play. The first such supercomputer, the CDC 6600, was introduced in 1961 by Control Data Corporation. Cray Research Corporation introduced the best cost/performance supercomputer, the Cray-1, in 1976.

1.1.3 Desktop Era

Personal computers (PCs), which were introduced in 1977 by Altair, Processor Technology, North Star, Tandy, Commodore, Apple, and many others, enhanced the productivity of end-users in numerous departments. Personal computers from Compaq, Apple, IBM, Dell, and many others soon became pervasive, and changed the face of computing.

Local area networks (LAN) of powerful personal computers and workstations began to replace mainframes and minis by 1990. The power of the most capable big machine could be had in a desktop model for one-tenth of the cost. However, these individual desktop computers were soon to be connected into larger complexes of computing by wide area networks (WAN).

1.1.4 Network Era

The fourth era, or network paradigm of computing, is in full swing because of rapid advances in network technology. Network technology outstripped processor technology throughout most of the 1990s. This explains the rise of the network paradigm listed in Table 1.1. The surge of network capacity tipped the balance from a processor-centric view of computing to a network-centric view.

The 1980s and 1990s witnessed the introduction of many commercial parallel computers with multiple processors. They can generally be classified into two main categories: (1) shared memory, and (2) distributed memory systems. The number of processors in a single machine ranged from several in a shared memory computer to hundreds of thousands in a massively parallel system. Examples of parallel computers during this era include Sequent Symmetry, Intel iPSC, nCUBE, Intel Paragon, Thinking Machines (CM-2, CM-5), MsPar (MP), Fujitsu (VPP500), and others.

1.1.5 Current Trends

One of the clear trends in computing is the substitution of expensive and specialized parallel machines by the more cost-effective clusters of workstations. A cluster is a collection of stand-alone computers connected using some interconnection network. Additionally, the pervasiveness of the Internet created interest in network computing and more recently in grid computing. Grids are geographically distributed platforms of computation. They should provide dependable, consistent, pervasive, and inexpensive access to high-end computational facilities.

1.2 FLYNN'S TAXONOMY OF COMPUTER ARCHITECTURE

The most popular taxonomy of computer architecture was defined by Flynn in 1966. Flynn's classification scheme is based on the notion of a stream of information. Two types of information flow into a processor: instructions and data. The instruction stream is defined as the sequence of instructions performed by the processing unit. The data stream is defined as the data traffic exchanged between the memory and the processing unit. According to Flynn's classification, either of the instruction or data streams can be single or multiple. Computer architecture can be classified into the following four distinct categories:

- single-instruction single-data streams (SISD);
- single-instruction multiple-data streams (SIMD);
- multiple-instruction single-data streams (MISD); and
- multiple-instruction multiple-data streams (MIMD).

Conventional single-processor von Neumann computers are classified as SISD systems. Parallel computers are either SIMD or MIMD. When there is only one control unit and all processors execute the same instruction in a synchronized fashion, the parallel machine is classified as SIMD. In a MIMD machine, each processor has its own control unit and can execute different instructions on different data. In the MISD category, the same stream of data flows through a linear array of processors executing different instruction streams. In practice, there is no viable MISD machine; however, some authors have considered pipelined machines (and perhaps systolic-array computers) as examples for MISD. Figures 1.1, 1.2, and 1.3 depict the block diagrams of SISD, SIMD, and MIMD, respectively.

An extension of Flynn's taxonomy was introduced by D. J. Kuck in 1978. In his classification, Kuck extended the instruction stream further to single (scalar and array) and multiple (scalar and array) streams. The data stream in Kuck's classification is called the *execution stream* and is also extended to include single

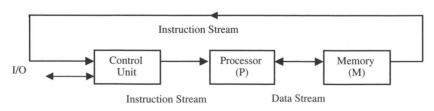

Figure 1.1   SISD architecture.

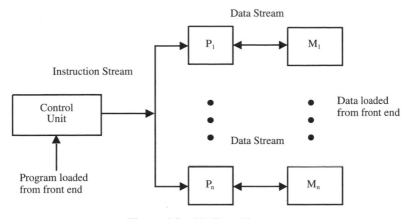

Figure 1.2   SIMD architecture.

(scalar and array) and multiple (scalar and array) streams. The combination of these streams results in a total of 16 categories of architectures.

1.3   SIMD ARCHITECTURE

The SIMD model of parallel computing consists of two parts: a front-end computer of the usual von Neumann style, and a processor array as shown in Figure 1.4. The processor array is a set of identical synchronized processing elements capable of simultaneously performing the same operation on different data. Each processor in the array has a small amount of local memory where the distributed data resides while it is being processed in parallel. The processor array is connected to the memory bus of the front end so that the front end can randomly access the local

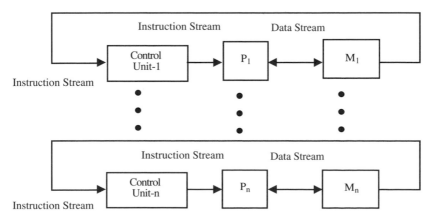

Figure 1.3   MIMD architecture.

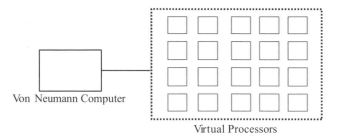

Figure 1.4   SIMD architecture model.

processor memories as if it were another memory. Thus, the front end can issue special commands that cause parts of the memory to be operated on simultaneously or cause data to move around in the memory. A program can be developed and executed on the front end using a traditional serial programming language. The application program is executed by the front end in the usual serial way, but issues commands to the processor array to carry out SIMD operations in parallel. The similarity between serial and data parallel programming is one of the strong points of data parallelism. Synchronization is made irrelevant by the lock–step synchronization of the processors. Processors either do nothing or exactly the same operations at the same time. In SIMD architecture, parallelism is exploited by applying simultaneous operations across large sets of data. This paradigm is most useful for solving problems that have lots of data that need to be updated on a wholesale basis. It is especially powerful in many regular numerical calculations.

There are two main configurations that have been used in SIMD machines (see Fig. 1.5). In the first scheme, each processor has its own local memory. Processors can communicate with each other through the interconnection network. If the interconnection network does not provide direct connection between a given pair of processors, then this pair can exchange data via an intermediate processor. The ILLIAC IV used such an interconnection scheme. The interconnection network in the ILLIAC IV allowed each processor to communicate directly with four neighboring processors in an 8×8 matrix pattern such that the ith processor can communicate directly with the $(i - 1)^{\text{th}}$, $(i + 1)^{\text{th}}$, $(i - 8)^{\text{th}}$, and $(i + 8)^{\text{th}}$ processors. In the second SIMD scheme, processors and memory modules communicate with each other via the interconnection network. Two processors can transfer data between each other via intermediate memory module(s) or possibly via intermediate processor(s). The BSP (Burroughs' Scientific Processor) used the second SIMD scheme.

1.4 MIMD ARCHITECTURE

Multiple-instruction multiple-data streams (MIMD) parallel architectures are made of multiple processors and multiple memory modules connected together via some

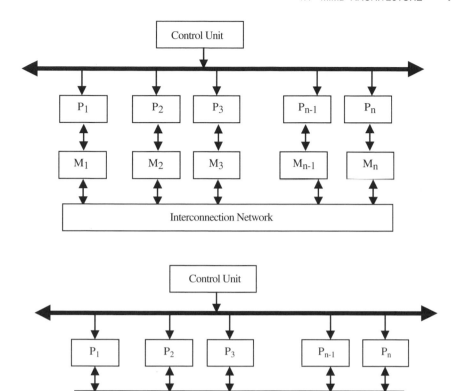

Figure 1.5 Two SIMD schemes.

interconnection network. They fall into two broad categories: shared memory or message passing. Figure 1.6 illustrates the general architecture of these two categories. Processors exchange information through their central shared memory in shared memory systems, and exchange information through their interconnection network in message passing systems.

A *shared memory system* typically accomplishes interprocessor coordination through a global memory shared by all processors. These are typically server systems that communicate through a bus and cache memory controller. The bus/ cache architecture alleviates the need for expensive multiported memories and interface circuitry as well as the need to adopt a message-passing paradigm when developing application software. Because access to shared memory is balanced, these systems are also called SMP (symmetric multiprocessor) systems. Each processor has equal opportunity to read/write to memory, including equal access speed.

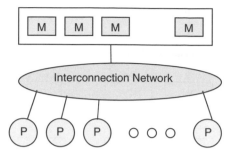

Shared Memory MIMD Architecture

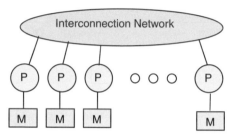

Message Passing MIMD Architecture

Figure 1.6 Shared memory versus message passing architecture.

Commercial examples of SMPs are Sequent Computer's Balance and Symmetry, Sun Microsystems multiprocessor servers, and Silicon Graphics Inc. multiprocessor servers.

A *message passing system* (also referred to as distributed memory) typically combines the local memory and processor at each node of the interconnection network. There is no global memory, so it is necessary to move data from one local memory to another by means of message passing. This is typically done by a Send/Receive pair of commands, which must be written into the application software by a programmer. Thus, programmers must learn the message-passing paradigm, which involves data copying and dealing with consistency issues. Commercial examples of message passing architectures c. 1990 were the nCUBE, iPSC/2, and various Transputer-based systems. These systems eventually gave way to Internet connected systems whereby the processor/memory nodes were either Internet servers or clients on individuals' desktop.

It was also apparent that distributed memory is the only way efficiently to increase the number of processors managed by a parallel and distributed system. If scalability to larger and larger systems (as measured by the number of processors) was to continue, systems had to use distributed memory techniques. These two forces created a conflict: programming in the shared memory model was easier, and designing systems in the message passing model provided scalability. The *distributed-shared memory* (DSM) architecture began to appear in systems like the SGI Origin2000, and others. In such systems, memory is physically distributed; for example, the hardware architecture follows the message passing school of design, but the programming model follows the shared memory school of thought. In effect, software covers up the hardware. As far as a programmer is concerned, the architecture looks and behaves like a shared memory machine, but a message passing architecture lives underneath the software. Thus, the DSM machine is a hybrid that takes advantage of both design schools.

1.4.1 Shared Memory Organization

A shared memory model is one in which processors communicate by reading and writing locations in a shared memory that is equally accessible by all processors. Each processor may have registers, buffers, caches, and local memory banks as additional memory resources. A number of basic issues in the design of shared memory systems have to be taken into consideration. These include access control, synchronization, protection, and security. Access control determines which process accesses are possible to which resources. Access control models make the required check for every access request issued by the processors to the shared memory, against the contents of the access control table. The latter contains flags that determine the legality of each access attempt. If there are access attempts to resources, then until the desired access is completed, all disallowed access attempts and illegal processes are blocked. Requests from sharing processes may change the contents of the access control table during execution. The flags of the access control with the synchronization rules determine the system's functionality. Synchronization constraints limit the time of accesses from sharing processes to shared resources. Appropriate synchronization ensures that the information flows properly and ensures system functionality. Protection is a system feature that prevents processes from making arbitrary access to resources belonging to other processes. Sharing and protection are incompatible; sharing allows access, whereas protection restricts it.

The simplest shared memory system consists of one memory module that can be accessed from two processors. Requests arrive at the memory module through its two ports. An arbitration unit within the memory module passes requests through to a memory controller. If the memory module is not busy and a single request arrives, then the arbitration unit passes that request to the memory controller and the request is granted. The module is placed in the busy state while a request is being serviced. If a new request arrives while the memory is busy servicing a previous request, the requesting processor may hold its request on the line until the memory becomes free or it may repeat its request sometime later.

Depending on the interconnection network, a shared memory system leads to systems can be classified as: uniform memory access (UMA), nonuniform memory access (NUMA), and cache-only memory architecture (COMA). In the UMA system, a shared memory is accessible by all processors through an interconnection network in the same way a single processor accesses its memory. Therefore, all processors have equal access time to any memory location. The interconnection network used in the UMA can be a single bus, multiple buses, a crossbar, or a multiport memory. In the NUMA system, each processor has part of the shared memory attached. The memory has a single address space. Therefore, any processor could access any memory location directly using its real address. However, the access time to modules depends on the distance to the processor. This results in a nonuniform memory access time. A number of architectures are used to interconnect processors to memory modules in a NUMA. Similar to the NUMA, each processor has part of the shared memory in the COMA. However, in this case the shared memory consists of cache memory. A COMA system requires that data be migrated to the processor requesting it. Shared memory systems will be discussed in more detail in Chapter 4.

1.4.2 Message Passing Organization

Message passing systems are a class of multiprocessors in which each processor has access to its own local memory. Unlike shared memory systems, communications in message passing systems are performed via send and receive operations. A *node* in such a system consists of a processor and its local memory. Nodes are typically able to store messages in buffers (temporary memory locations where messages wait until they can be sent or received), and perform send/receive operations at the same time as processing. Simultaneous message processing and problem calculating are handled by the underlying operating system. Processors do not share a global memory and each processor has access to its own address space. The processing units of a message passing system may be connected in a variety of ways ranging from architecture-specific interconnection structures to geographically dispersed networks. The message passing approach is, in principle, scalable to large proportions. By scalable, it is meant that the number of processors can be increased without significant decrease in efficiency of operation.

Message passing multiprocessors employ a variety of static networks in local communication. Of importance are hypercube networks, which have received special attention for many years. The nearest neighbor two-dimensional and three-dimensional mesh networks have been used in message passing systems as well. Two important design factors must be considered in designing interconnection networks for message passing systems. These are the link *bandwidth* and the network *latency*. The link bandwidth is defined as the number of bits that can be transmitted per unit time (bits/s). The network latency is defined as the time to complete a message transfer. Wormhole routing in message passing was introduced in 1987 as an alternative to the traditional store-and-forward routing in order to reduce the size of the required buffers and to decrease the message latency. In *wormhole routing*, a packet is divided into smaller units that are called *flits* (flow control bits) such that *flits* move in a pipeline fashion with the header *flit* of the packet leading the way to the destination node. When the header flit is blocked due to network congestion, the remaining flits are blocked as well. More details on message passing will be introduced in Chapter 5.

1.5   INTERCONNECTION NETWORKS

Multiprocessors interconnection networks (INs) can be classified based on a number of criteria. These include (1) mode of operation (synchronous versus asynchronous), (2) control strategy (centralized versus decentralized), (3) switching techniques (circuit versus packet), and (4) topology (static versus dynamic).

1.5.1   Mode of Operation

According to the mode of operation, INs are classified as *synchronous* versus *asynchronous*. In synchronous mode of operation, a single global clock is used by all components in the system such that the whole system is operating in a lock–step manner. Asynchronous mode of operation, on the other hand, does not require a global clock. Handshaking signals are used instead in order to coordinate the operation of asynchronous systems. While synchronous systems tend to be slower compared to asynchronous systems, they are race and hazard-free.

1.5.2   Control Strategy

According to the control strategy, INs can be classified as *centralized* versus *decentralized*. In centralized control systems, a single central control unit is used to oversee and control the operation of the components of the system. In decentralized control, the control function is distributed among different components in the system. The function and reliability of the central control unit can become the bottleneck in a centralized control system. While the crossbar is a centralized system, the multistage interconnection networks are decentralized.

1.5.3   Switching Techniques

Interconnection networks can be classified according to the switching mechanism as *circuit* versus *packet switching* networks. In the circuit switching mechanism, a complete path has to be established prior to the start of communication between a source and a destination. The established path will remain in existence during the whole communication period. In a packet switching mechanism, communication between a source and destination takes place via messages that are divided into smaller entities, called packets. On their way to the destination, packets can be sent from a node to another in a store-and-forward manner until they reach their destination. While packet switching tends to use the network resources more efficiently compared to circuit switching, it suffers from variable packet delays.

1.5.4   Topology

An *interconnection network topology* is a mapping function from the set of processors and memories onto the same set of processors and memories. In other words, the topology describes how to connect processors and memories to other processors and memories. A fully connected topology, for example, is a mapping in which each processor is connected to all other processors in the computer. A ring topology is a mapping that connects processor k to its neighbors, processors $(k - 1)$ and $(k + 1)$.

In general, interconnection networks can be classified as *static* versus *dynamic* networks. In static networks, direct fixed links are established among nodes to form a fixed network, while in dynamic networks, connections are established as needed. Switching elements are used to establish connections among inputs and outputs. Depending on the switch settings, different interconnections can be established. Nearly all multiprocessor systems can be distinguished by their interconnection network topology. Therefore, we devote Chapter 2 of this book to study a variety of topologies and how they are used in constructing a multiprocessor system. However, in this section, we give a brief introduction to interconnection networks for shared memory and message passing systems.

Shared memory systems can be designed using bus-based or switch-based INs. The simplest IN for shared memory systems is the bus. However, the bus may get saturated if multiple processors are trying to access the shared memory (via the bus) simultaneously. A typical bus-based design uses caches to solve the bus contention problem. Other shared memory designs rely on switches for interconnection. For example, a crossbar switch can be used to connect multiple processors to multiple memory modules. A crossbar switch, which will be discussed further in Chapter 2, can be visualized as a mesh of wires with switches at the points of intersection. Figure 1.7 shows (*a*) bus-based and (*b*) switch-based shared memory systems. Figure 1.8 shows bus-based systems when a single bus is used versus the case when multiple buses are used.

Message passing INs can be divided into static and dynamic. Static networks form all connections when the system is designed rather than when the connection is needed. In a static network, messages must be routed along established links.

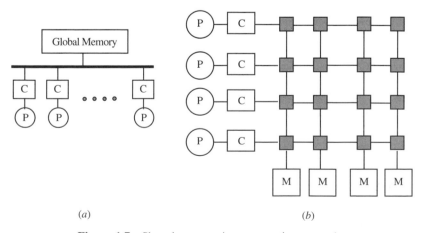

(a)   (b)

Figure 1.7   Shared memory interconnection networks.

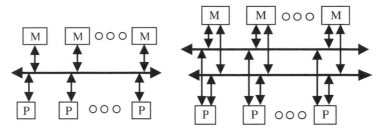

Figure 1.8 Single bus and multiple bus systems.

Dynamic INs establish a connection between two or more nodes on the fly as messages are routed along the links. The *number of hops* in a path from source to destination node is equal to the number of point-to-point links a message must traverse to reach its destination. In either static or dynamic networks, a single message may have to *hop* through intermediate processors on its way to its destination. Therefore, the ultimate performance of an interconnection network is greatly influenced by the number of hops taken to traverse the network. Figure 1.9 shows a number of popular static topologies: (*a*) linear array, (*b*) ring, (*c*) mesh, (*d*) tree, (*e*) hypercube.

Figure 1.10 shows examples of dynamic networks. The single-stage interconnection network of Figure 1.10*a* is a simple dynamic network that connects each of the inputs on the left side to some, but not all, outputs on the right side through a single layer of binary switches represented by the rectangles. The binary switches can direct the message on the left-side input to one of two possible outputs on the right side. If we cascade enough single-stage networks together, they form a completely connected multistage interconnection network (MIN), as shown in Figure 1.10*b*. The *omega MIN* connects eight sources to eight destinations. The connection from the source 010 to the destination 010 is shown as a bold path in Figure 1.10*b*. These are dynamic INs because the connection is made on the fly, as needed. In order to connect a source to a destination, we simply use a function of the bits of the source and destination addresses as instructions for dynamically selecting a path through the switches. For example, to connect source 111 to destination 001 in the omega network, the switches in the first and second stage must be set to connect to the upper output port, while the switch at the third stage must be set

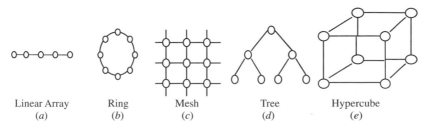

Linear Array	Ring	Mesh	Tree	Hypercube
(*a*)	(*b*)	(*c*)	(*d*)	(*e*)

Figure 1.9 Examples of static topologies.

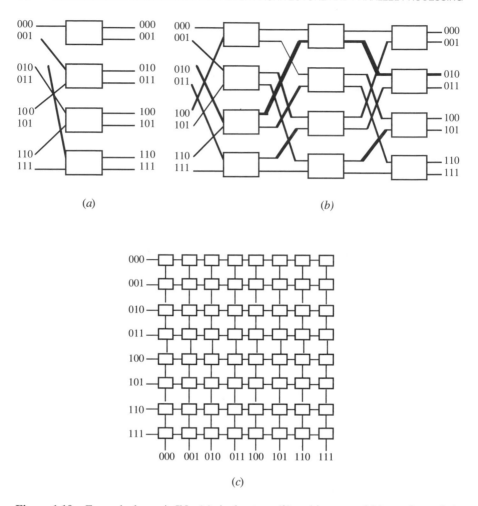

Figure 1.10   Example dynamic INs: (*a*) single-stage, (*b*) multistage, and (*c*) crossbar switch.

to connect to the lower output port (001). Similarly, the crossbar switch of Figure 1.10*c* provides a path from any input or source to any other output or destination by simply selecting a direction on the fly. To connect row 111 to column 001 requires only one binary switch at the intersection of the 111 input line and 011 output line to be set.

The crossbar switch clearly uses more binary switching components; for example, N^2 components are needed to connect $N \times N$ source/destination pairs. The omega MIN, on the other hand, connects $N \times N$ pairs with $N/2$ (log N) components. The major advantage of the crossbar switch is its potential for speed. In one clock, a connection can be made between source and destination. The diameter of the crossbar is one. (Note: Diameter, D, of a network having N nodes is defined as the maximum shortest paths between any two nodes in the network.) The omega

TABLE 1.2   Performance Comparison of Some Dynamic INs

Network	Delay	Cost (Complexity)
Bus	$O(N)$	$O(1)$
Multiple-bus	$O(mN)$	$O(m)$
MINs	$O(\log N)$	$O(N \log N)$

MIN, on the other hand requires log N clocks to make a connection. The diameter of the omega MIN is therefore log N. Both networks limit the number of alternate paths between any source/destination pair. This leads to limited fault tolerance and network traffic congestion. If the single path between pairs becomes faulty, that pair cannot communicate. If two pairs attempt to communicate at the same time along a shared path, one pair must wait for the other. This is called *blocking*, and such MINs are called *blocking networks*. A network that can handle all possible connections without blocking is called a *nonblocking network*.

Table 1.2 shows a performance comparison among a number of different dynamic INs. In this table, m represents the number of multiple buses used, while N represents the number of processors (memory modules) or input/output of the network.

Table 1.3 shows a performance comparison among a number of static INs. In this table, the degree of a network is defined as the maximum number of links (channels) connected to any node in the network. The diameter of a network is defined as the maximum path, p, of the shortest paths between any two nodes. Degree of a node, d, is defined as the number of channels incident on the node. Performance measures will be discussed in more detail in Chapter 3.

1.6   CHAPTER SUMMARY

In this chapter, we have gone over a number of concepts and system configurations related to obtaining high-performance computing via parallelism. In particular, we have provided the general concepts and terminology used in the context of multiprocessors. The popular Flynn's taxonomy of computer systems has been provided. An introduction to SIMD and MIMD systems was given. Both shared-memory and the message passing systems and their interconnection networks were introduced. The

TABLE 1.3   Performance Characteristics of Static INs

Network	Degree	Diameter	Cost (#links)
Linear array	2	$N - 1$	$N - 1$
Binary tree	3	$2([\log_2 N] - 1)$	$N - 1$
n-cube	$\log_2 N$	$\log_2 N$	$nN/2$
2D-mesh	4	$2(n - 1)$	$2(N - n)$

rest of the book is organized as follows. In Chapter 2 interconnection networks will be covered in detail. We will study performance metrics in Chapter 3. Shared-memory and message passing architectures are explained in Chapters 4 and 5, respectively. We cover abstract models to study shared memory and message passing systems in Chapter 6. We then study network computing in Chapter 7. Chapters 8 and 9 are dedicated to the parallel virtual machine (PVM) and message passing interface (MPI), respectively. The last chapter gives a comprehensive coverage of the challenging problem of task scheduling and task allocation.

PROBLEMS

1. What has been the trend in computing from the following points of views:
   (a) cost of hardware;
   (b) size of memory;
   (c) speed of hardware;
   (d) number of processing elements; and
   (e) geographical locations of system components.
2. Given the trend in computing in the last 20 years, what are your predictions for the future of computing?
3. What is the difference between cluster computing and grid computing?
4. Assume that a switching component such as a transistor can switch in zero-time. We propose to construct a disk-shaped computer chip with such a component. The only limitation is the time it takes to send electronic signals from one edge of the chip to the other. Make the simplifying assumption that electronic signals can travel at 300,000 km/s. What is the limitation on the diameter of a round chip so that any computation result can by used anywhere on the chip at a clock rate of 1 GHz? What are the diameter restrictions if the whole chip should operate at 1 THz $= 10^{12}$ Hz? Is such a chip feasible?
5. Compare uniprocessor systems with multiprocessor systems for the following aspects:
   (a) ease of programming;
   (b) the need for synchronization;
   (c) performance evaluation; and
   (d) run time system.
6. Provide a list of the main advantages and disadvantages of SIMD and MIMD machines.
7. Provide a list of the main advantages and disadvantages of shared-memory and message-passing paradigm.
8. List three engineering applications, with which you are familiar, for which SIMD is most efficient to use, and another three for which MIMD is most efficient to use.

9. Assume that a simple addition of two elements requires a unit time. You are required to compute the execution time needed to perform the addition of a 40×40 elements array using each of the following arrangements:

   (a) A SIMD system having 64 processing elements connected in nearest-neighbor fashion. Consider that each processor has only its local memory.

   (b) A SIMD system having 64 processing elements connected to a shared memory through an interconnection network. Ignore the communication time.

   (c) A MIMD computer system having 64 independent elements accessing a shared memory through an interconnection network. Ignore the communication time.

   (d) Repeat (b) and (c) above if the communication time takes two time units.

10. Conduct a comparative study between the following interconnection networks in their cost, performance, and fault tolerance:

    (a) bus;

    (b) hypercube;

    (c) mesh;

    (d) fully connected;

    (e) multistage dynamic network;

    (f) crossbar switch.

REFERENCES

Abraham, S. and Padmanabhan, K. Performance of the direct binary n-cube network for multiprocessors. *IEEE Transactions on Computers*, 38 (7), 1000–1011 (1989).

Agrawal, P., Janakiram, V. and Pathak, G. Evaluating the performance of multicomputer configurations. *IEEE Transaction on Computers*, 19 (5), 23–27 (1986).

Almasi, G. and Gottlieb, A. *Highly Parallel Computing*, Benjamin Cummings, 1989.

Al-Tawil, K., Abd-El-Barr, M. and Ashraf, F. A survey and comparison of wormhole routing techniques in mesh networks. *IEEE Network*, March/April 1997, 38–45 (1997).

Bhuyan, L. N. (ed.) Interconnection networks for parallel and distributed processing. *Computer* (Special issue), 20 (6), 9–75 (1987).

Bhuyan, L. N., Yang, Q. and Agrawal, D. P. Performance of multiprocessor interconnection networks. *Computer*, 22 (2), 25–37 (1989).

Chen, W.-T. and Sheu, J.-P. Performance analysis of multiple bus interconnection networks with hierarchical requesting model. *IEEE Transactions on Computers*, 40 (7), 834–842 (1991).

Dasgupta, S. *Computer Architecture: A Modern Synthesis*, vol. 2; Advanced Topics, John Wiley, 1989.

Decegama, A. *The Technology of Parallel Processing: Parallel Processing Architectures and VLSI Hardware*, Vol. 1, Prentice-Hall, 1989.

Dongarra, J. *Experimental Parallel Computing Architectures*, North-Holland, 1987.

Duncan, R. A survey of parallel computer architectures. *Computer*, 23 (2), 5–16 (1990).

El-Rewini, H. and Lewis, T. G. *Distributed and Parallel Computing*, Manning & Prentice Hall, 1998.

Flynn. *Computer Architecture: Pipelined and Parallel Processor Design*, Jones and Bartlett, 1995.

Goodman, J. R. Using cache memory to reduce processor-memory traffic. *Proceedings 10th Annual Symposium on Computer Architecture*, June 1983, pp. 124–131.

Goyal, A. and Agerwala, T. Performance analysis of future shared storage systems. *IBM Journal of Research and Development*, 28 (1), 95–107 (1984).

Hennessy, J. and Patterson, D. *Computer Architecture: A Quantitative Approach*, Morgan Kaufmann, 1990.

Hwang, K. and Briggs, F. A. *Computer Architecture and Parallel Processing*, McGraw-Hill, 1984.

Ibbett, R. N. and Topham, N. P. *Architecture of High Performance Computers II*, Springer-Verlag, 1989.

Juang, J.-Y. and Wah, B. A contention-based bus-control scheme for multiprocessor systems. *IEEE Transactions on Computers*, 40 (9), 1046–1053 (1991).

Lewis, T. G. and El-Rewini, H. *Introduction to Parallel Computing*, Prentice-Hall, 1992.

Linder, D. and Harden, J. An adaptive and fault tolerant wormhole routing strategy for *k*-ary *n*-cubes. *IEEE Transactions on Computers*, 40 (1), 2–12 (1991).

Moldovan, D. *Parallel Processing, from Applications to Systems*, Morgan Kaufmann Publishers, 1993.

Ni, L. and McKinely, P. A survey of wormhole routing techniques in direct networks. *IEEE Computer*, February 1993, 62–76 (1993).

Patel, J. Performance of processor–memory interconnections for multiprocessor computer systems. *IEEE Transactions*, 28 (9), 296–304 (1981).

Reed, D. and Fujimoto, R. *Multicomputer Networks*: *Message-Based Parallel Processing*, MIT Press, 1987.

Serlin, O. *The Serlin Report On Parallel Processing*, No. 54, pp. 8–13, November 1991.

Sima, E., Fountain, T. and Kacsuk, P. *Advanced Computer Architectures: A Design Space Approach*, Addison-Wesley, 1996.

Stone, H. *High-Performance Computer Architecture*, 3rd ed., Addison-Wesley, 1993.

The Accelerated Strategic Computing Initiative Report, Lawrence Livermore National Laboratory, 1996.

Wilkinson, B. *Computer Architecture: Design and Performance*, 2nd ed., Prentice-Hall, 1996.

Yang, Q. and Zaky, S. Communication performance in multiple-bus systems. *IEEE Transactions on Computers*, 37 (7), 848–853 (1988).

Youn, H. and Chen, C. A comprehensive performance evaluation of crossbar networks. *IEEE Transactions on Parallel and Distribute Systems*, 4 (5), 481–489 (1993).

Zargham, M. *Computer Architecture: Single and Parallel Systems*, Prentice-Hall, 1996.

CHAPTER 2

Multiprocessors Interconnection Networks

As we have seen in Chapter 1, a multiprocessor system consists of multiple processing units connected via some interconnection network plus the software needed to make the processing units work together. There are two major factors used to categorize such systems: the processing units themselves, and the interconnection network that ties them together. A number of communication styles exist for multiprocessing networks. These can be broadly classified according to the communication model as shared memory (single address space) versus message passing (multiple address spaces). Communication in shared memory systems is performed by writing to and reading from the global memory, while communication in message passing systems is accomplished via send and receive commands. In both cases, the interconnection network plays a major role in determining the communication speed. In this chapter, we introduce the different topologies used for interconnecting multiple processors and memory modules. Two schemes are introduced, namely static and dynamic interconnection networks. Static networks form all connections when the system is designed rather than when the connection is needed. In a static network, messages must be routed along established links. Dynamic interconnection networks establish connections between two or more nodes on the fly as messages are routed along the links. The hypercube, mesh, and k-ary n-cube topologies are introduced as examples for static networks. The bus, crossbar, and multistage interconnection topologies are introduced as examples for dynamic interconnection networks. Our coverage in this chapter will conclude with a section on performance evaluation and analysis of the different interconnection networks.

2.1 INTERCONNECTION NETWORKS TAXONOMY

In this section, we introduce a topology-based taxonomy for interconnection networks (INs). An interconnection network could be either static or dynamic. Connections in a static network are fixed links, while connections in a dynamic network

Advanced Computer Architecture and Parallel Processing, by H. El-Rewini and M. Abd-El-Barr
ISBN 0-471-46740-5   Copyright © 2005 John Wiley & Sons, Inc.

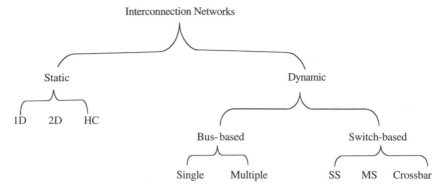

Figure 2.1 A topology-based taxonomy for interconnection networks.

are established on the fly as needed. Static networks can be further classified according to their interconnection pattern as one-dimension (1D), two-dimension (2D), or hypercube (HC). Dynamic networks, on the other hand, can be classified based on interconnection scheme as bus-based versus switch-based. Bus-based networks can further be classified as single bus or multiple buses. Switch-based dynamic networks can be classified according to the structure of the interconnection network as single-stage (SS), multistage (MS), or crossbar networks. Figure 2.1 illustrate this taxonomy. In the following sections, we study the different types of dynamic and static interconnection networks.

2.2 BUS-BASED DYNAMIC INTERCONNECTION NETWORKS

2.2.1 Single Bus Systems

A single bus is considered the simplest way to connect multiprocessor systems. Figure 2.2 shows an illustration of a single bus system. In its general form, such a system consists of N processors, each having its own cache, connected by a

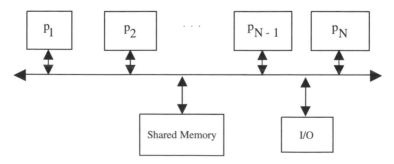

Figure 2.2 Example single bus system.

shared bus. The use of local caches reduces the processor–memory traffic. All processors communicate with a single shared memory. The typical size of such a system varies between 2 and 50 processors. The actual size is determined by the traffic per processor and the bus bandwidth (defined as the maximum rate at which the bus can propagate data once transmission has started). The single bus network complexity, measured in terms of the number of buses used, is $O(1)$, while the time complexity, measured in terms of the amount of input to output delay is $O(N)$.

Although simple and easy to expand, single bus multiprocessors are inherently limited by the bandwidth of the bus and the fact that only one processor can access the bus, and in turn only one memory access can take place at any given time. The characteristics of some commercially available single bus computers are summarized in Table 2.1.

2.2.2 Multiple Bus Systems

The use of multiple buses to connect multiple processors is a natural extension to the single shared bus system. A multiple bus multiprocessor system uses several parallel buses to interconnect multiple processors and multiple memory modules. A number of connection schemes are possible in this case. Among the possibilities are the multiple bus with full bus–memory connection (MBFBMC), multiple bus with single bus memory connection (MBSBMC), multiple bus with partial bus–memory connection (MBPBMC), and multiple bus with class-based memory connection (MBCBMC). Illustrations of these connection schemes for the case of $N = 6$ processors, $M = 4$ memory modules, and $B = 4$ buses are shown in Figure 2.3. The multiple bus with full bus–memory connection has all memory modules connected to all buses. The multiple bus with single bus–memory connection has each memory module connected to a specific bus. The multiple bus with partial bus–memory connection has each memory module connected to a subset of buses. The multiple bus with class-based memory connection has memory modules grouped into classes whereby each class is connected to a specific subset of buses. A class is just an arbitrary collection of memory modules.

One can characterize those connections using the number of connections required and the load on each bus as shown in Table 2.2. In this table, k represents the number of classes; g represents the number of buses per group, and M_j represents the number of memory modules in class j.

TABLE 2.1 Characteristics of Some Commercially Available Single Bus Systems

Machine Name	Maximum No. of Processors	Processor	Clock Rate	Maximum Memory	Bandwidth
HP 9000 K640	4	PA-8000	180 MHz	4,096 MB	960 MB/s
IBM RS/6000 R40	8	PowerPC 604	112 MHz	2,048 MB	1,800 MB/s
Sun Enterprise 6000	30	UltraSPARC 1	167 MHz	30,720 MB	2,600 MB/s

In general, multiple bus multiprocessor organization offers a number of desirable features such as high reliability and ease of incremental growth. A single bus failure will leave $(B - 1)$ distinct fault-free paths between the processors and the memory modules. On the other hand, when the number of buses is less than the number of memory modules (or the number of processors), bus contention is expected to increase.

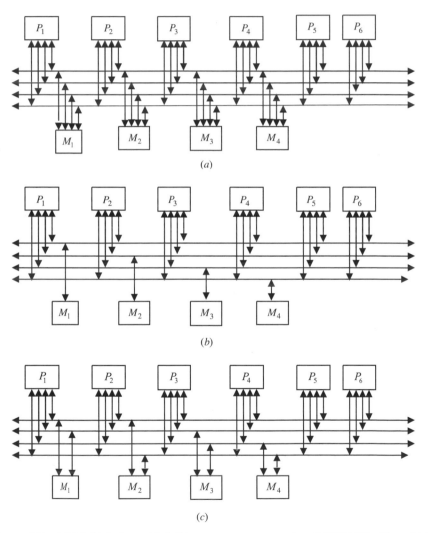

Figure 2.3 (*a*) Multiple bus with full bus–memory connection (MBFBMC); (*b*) multiple bus with single bus-memory connection (MBSBMC); (*c*) multiple bus with partial bus–memory connection (MBPBMC); and (*d*) multiple bus with class-based memory connection (MBCBMC).

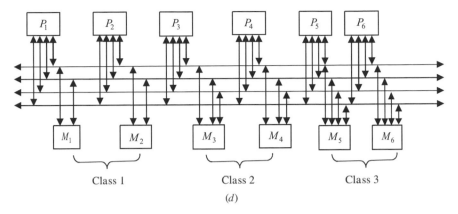

Figure 2.3 *Continued.*

2.2.3 Bus Synchronization

A bus can be classified as *synchronous* or *asynchronous*. The time for any transaction over a synchronous bus is known in advance. In accepting and/or generating
information over the bus, devices take the transaction time into account. Asynchronous bus, on the other hand, depends on the availability of data and the readiness of
devices to initiate bus transactions.

In a single bus multiprocessor system, bus arbitration is required in order to
resolve the bus contention that takes place when more than one processor competes
to access the bus. In this case, processors that want to use the bus submit their
requests to bus *arbitration logic*. The latter decides, using a certain priority
scheme, which processor will be granted access to the bus during a certain time
interval (bus master). The process of passing bus mastership from one processor
to another is called *handshaking* and requires the use of two control signals: *bus
request* and *bus grant*. The first indicates that a given processor is requesting mastership of the bus, while the second indicates that bus mastership is granted. A third
signal, called *bus busy*, is usually used to indicate whether or not the bus is currently
being used. Figure 2.4 illustrates such a system.

In deciding which processor gains control of the bus, the bus arbitration logic
uses a predefined priority scheme. Among the priority schemes used are random

TABLE 2.2 Characteristics of Multiple Bus Architectures

Connection Type	No. of Connections	Load on Bus i
MBFBMC	$B(N + M)$	$N + M$
MBSBMC	$BN + M$	$N + M_j$
MBPBMC	$B(N + M/g)$	$N + M/g$
MBCBMC	$BN + \sum_{j=1}^{k} M_j(j + B - k)$	$N + \sum_{j=\max(i+k-B,1)}^{k} M_j, 1 \leq i \leq B$

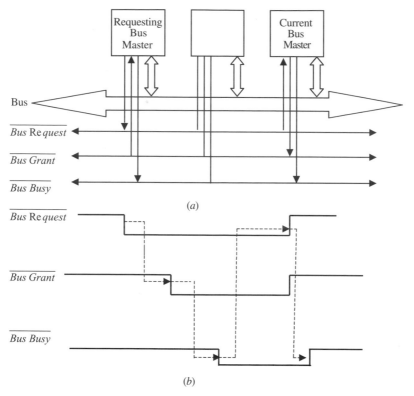

Figure 2.4 Bus handshaking mechanism (*a*) the scheme; and (*b*) the timing.

priority, simple rotating priority, equal priority, and least recently used (LRU) priority. After each arbitration cycle, in simple rotating priority, all priority levels are reduced one place, with the lowest priority processor taking the highest priority. In equal priority, when two or more requests are made, there is equal chance of any one request being processed. In the LRU algorithm, the highest priority is given to the processor that has not used the bus for the longest time.

2.3 SWITCH-BASED INTERCONNECTION NETWORKS

In this type of network, connections among processors and memory modules are made using simple switches. Three basic interconnection topologies exist: *crossbar*, *single-stage*, and *multistage*.

2.3.1 Crossbar Networks

A *crossbar network* represents the other extreme to the limited single bus network. While the single bus can provide only a single connection, the crossbar can provide simultaneous connections among all its inputs and all its outputs. The crossbar contains a switching element (SE) at the intersection of any two lines extended horizontally or vertically inside the switch. Consider, for example the 8×8 crossbar network shown in Figure 2.5. In this case, an SE (also called a cross-point) is provided at each of the 64 intersection points (shown as small squares in Fig. 2.5). The figure illustrates the case of setting the SEs such that simultaneous connections between P_i and M_{8-i+1} for $1 \le i \le 8$ are made. The two possible settings of an SE in the crossbar (straight and diagonal) are also shown in the figure.

As can be seen from the figure, the number of SEs (switching points) required is 64 and the message delay to traverse from the input to the output is constant, regardless of which input/output are communicating. In general for an $N \times N$ crossbar, the network complexity, measured in terms of the number of switching points, is $O(N^2)$ while the time complexity, measured in terms of the input to output delay, is $O(1)$. It should be noted that the complexity of the crossbar network pays off in the form of reduction in the time complexity. Notice also that the crossbar is a *nonblocking* network that allows a multiple input–output connection pattern (permutation) to be achieved simultaneously. However, for a large multiprocessor system the complexity of the crossbar can become a dominant financial factor.

2.3.2 Single-Stage Networks

In this case, a single stage of switching elements (SEs) exists between the inputs and the outputs of the network. The simplest switching element that can be used is the

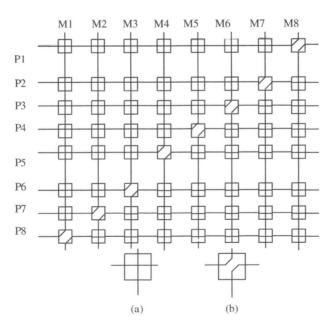

(a)   (b)

Figure 2.5   An 8×8 crossbar network (*a*) straight switch setting; and (*b*) diagonal switch setting.

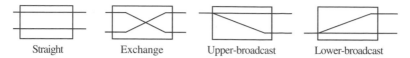

Figure 2.6 The different settings of the 2 × 2 SE.

2 × 2 switching element (SE). Figure 2.6 illustrates the four possible settings that an SE can assume. These settings are called *straight, exchange, upper-broadcast*, and *lower-broadcast*. In the straight setting, the upper input is transferred to the upper output and the lower input is transferred to the lower output. In the exchange setting the upper input is transferred to the lower output and the lower input is transferred to the upper output. In the upper-broadcast setting the upper input is broadcast to both the upper and the lower outputs. In the lower-broadcast the lower input is broadcast to both the upper and the lower outputs.

To establish communication between a given input (source) to a given output (destination), data has to be circulated a number of times around the network. A well-known connection pattern for interconnecting the inputs and the outputs of a single-stage network is the *Shuffle–Exchange*. Two operations are used. These can be defined using an m bit-wise address pattern of the inputs, $p_{m-1}p_{m-2} \ldots p_1p_0$, as follows:

$$S(p_{m-1}p_{m-2} \ldots p_1p_0) = p_{m-2}p_{m-3} \ldots p_1p_0p_{m-1}$$
$$E(p_{m-1}p_{m-2} \ldots p_1p_0) = p_{m-1}p_{m-2} \ldots p_1\overline{p_0}$$

With shuffle (S) and exchange (E) operations, data is circulated from input to output until it reaches its destination. If the number of inputs, for example, processors, in a single-stage IN is N and the number of outputs, for example, memories, is N, the number of SEs in a stage is $N/2$. The maximum length of a path from an input to an output in the network, measured by the number of SEs along the path, is $\log_2 N$.

Example   In an 8-input single stage *Shuffle–Exchange* if the source is 0 (000) and the destination is 6 (110), then the following is the required sequence of *Shuffle/ Exchange* operations and circulation of data:

$$E(000) \to 1(001) \to S(001) \to 2(010) \to E(010) \to 3(011) \to S(011) \to 6(110)$$

The network complexity of the single-stage interconnection network is $O(N)$ and the time complexity is $O(N)$.

In addition to the shuffle and the exchange functions, there exist a number of other interconnection patterns that are used in forming the interconnections among stages in interconnection networks. Among these are the *Cube* and the *Plus-Minus* 2^i(*PM2I*) networks. These are introduced below.

The Cube Network   The interconnection pattern used in the cube network is defined as follows:

$$C_i(p_{m-1}p_{m-2}\cdots p_{i+1}p_i p_{i-1}\cdots p_1 p_0) = p_{m-1}p_{m-2}\cdots p_{i+1}\overline{p_i}p_{i-1}\cdots p_1 p_0$$

Consider a 3-bit address ($N = 8$), then we have $C_2(6) = 2$, $C_1(7) = 5$ and $C_0(4) = 5$. Figure 2.7 shows the cube interconnection patterns for a network with $N = 8$.

The network is called the cube network due to the fact that it resembles the interconnection among the corners of an n-dimensional cube ($n = \log_2 N$) (see Fig. 2.16e, later).

The Plus–Minus 2^i (PM2I) Network   The PM2I network consists of $2k$ interconnection functions defined as follows:

$$PM2_{+i}(P) = P + 2^i \bmod N(0 \le i < k)$$

$$PM2_{-i}(P) = P - 2^i \bmod N(0 \le i < k)$$

For example, consider the case $N = 8$, $PM2_{+1}(4) = 4 + 2^1 \bmod 8 = 6$. Figure 2.8 shows the PM2I for $N = 8$. It should be noted that $PM2_{+(k-1)}(P) = PM2_{-(k-1)}(P) \forall P$, $0 \le P < N$. It should also be noted that $PM2_{+2} = C_2$. This last observation indicates that it should be possible to use the PM2I network to perform at least part of the connections that are parts of the Cube network (simulating the Cube network using the PM2I network) and the reverse is also possible. Table 2.3 provides the lower and the upper bounds on network simulation times for the three networks PM2I, Cube, and Shuffle–Exchange. In this table the entries at the intersection of a given row and a given column are the lower and the upper

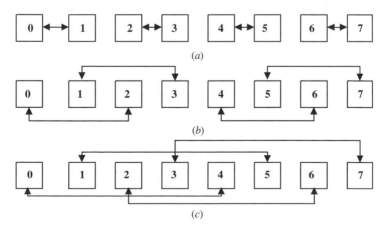

(a)

(b)

(c)

Figure 2.7   The cube network for $N = 8$ (a) C_0; (b) C_1; and (c) C_2.

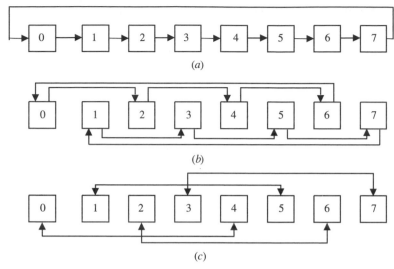

Figure 2.8   The PM2I network for $N = 8$ (a), $PM2_{+0}$ for $N = 8$; (b) $PM2_{+1}$ for $N = 8$; and (c) $PM2_{+2}$ for $N = 8$.

bounds on the time required for the network in the row to simulate the network in the column (see the exercise at the end of the chapter).

The Butterfly Function   The interconnection pattern used in the butterfly network is defined as follows:

$$B(p_{m-1}p_{m-2}\cdots p_1p_0) = p_0p_{m-2}\cdots p_1p_{m-1}$$

Consider a 3-bit address ($N = 8$), the following is the butterfly mapping:

B(000) = 000
B(001) = 100

TABLE 2.3   Network Simulation Time for Three Networks

	Simulation Time	PM2I	Cube	Shuffle–Exchange
PM2I	Lower	1	2	k
	Upper	1	2	$k + 1$
Cube	Lower	k	1	k
	Upper	k	1	k
Shuffle–Exchange	Lower	$2k - 1$	$k + 1$	1
	Upper	$2k$	$k + 1$	1

B(010) = 010
B(011) = 110
B(100) = 001
B(101) = 101
B(110) = 011
B(111) = 111

2.3.3 Multistage Networks

Multistage interconnection networks (MINs) were introduced as a means to improve some of the limitations of the single bus system while keeping the cost within an affordable limit. The most undesirable single bus limitation that MINs is set to improve is the availability of only one single path between the processors and the memory modules. Such MINs provide a number of simultaneous paths between the processors and the memory modules.

As shown in Figure 2.9, a general MIN consists of a number of stages each consisting of a set of 2×2 switching elements. Stages are connected to each other using Inter-stage Connection (ISC) Pattern. These patterns may follow any of the routing functions such as Shuffle–Exchange, Butterfly, Cube, and so on.

Figure 2.10 shows an example of an 8×8 MIN that uses the 2×2 SEs described before. This network is known in the literature as the *Shuffle–Exchange network* (SEN). The settings of the SEs in the figure illustrate how a number of paths can be established simultaneously in the network. For example, the figure shows how three simultaneous paths connecting the three pairs of input/output $000 \rightarrow 101$, $101 \rightarrow 011$, and $110 \rightarrow 010$ can be established. It should be noted that the interconnection pattern among stages follows the *shuffle* operation.

In MINs, the routing of a message from a given source to a given destination is based on the destination address (*self-routing*). There exist $\log_2 N$ stages in an

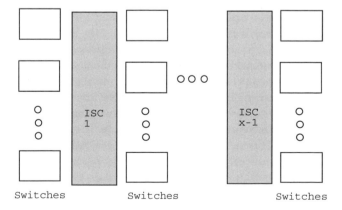

Figure 2.9 Multistage interconnection network.

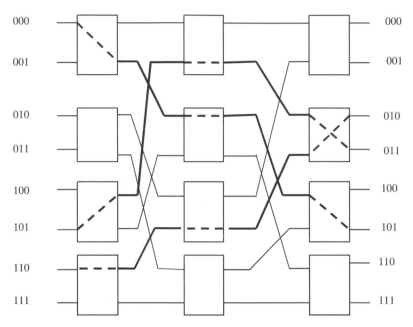

Figure 2.10   An example 8 × 8 Shuffle–Exchange network (SEN).

$N \times N$ MIN. The number of bits in any destination address in the network is $\log_2 N$. Each bit in the destination address can be used to route the message through one stage. The destination address bits are scanned from left to right and the stages are traversed from left to right. The first (most significant bit) is used to control the routing in the first stage; the next bit is used to control the routing in the next stage, and so on. The convention used in routing messages is that if the bit in the destination address controlling the routing in a given stage is 0, then the message is routed to the upper output of the switch. On the other hand if the bit is 1, the message is routed to the lower output of the switch. Consider, for example, the routing of a message from source input 101 to destination output 011 in the 8 × 8 SEN shown in Figure 2.10. Since the first bit of the destination address is 0, therefore the message is first routed to the upper output of the switch in the first (leftmost) stage. Now, the next bit in the destination address is 1, thus the message is routed to the lower output of the switch in the middle stage. Finally, the last bit is 1, causing the message to be routed to the lower output in the switch in the last stage. This sequence causes the message to arrive at the correct output (see Fig. 2.10). Ease of message routing in MINs is one of the most desirable features of these networks.

The Banyan Network   A number of other MINs exist, among these the Banyan network is well known. Figure 2.11 shows an example of an 8 × 8 Banyan network. The reader is encouraged to identify the basic features of the Banyan network.

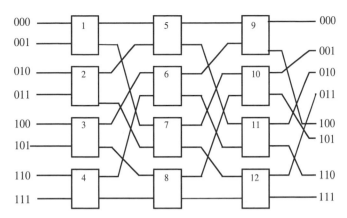

Figure 2.11   An 8 × 8 Banyan network.

If the number of inputs, for example, processors, in an MIN is N and the number of outputs, for example, memory modules, is N, the number of MIN stages is $\log_2 N$ and the number of SEs per stage is $N/2$, and hence the network complexity, measured in terms of the total number of SEs is $O(N \times \log_2 N)$. The number of SEs along the path is usually taken as a measure of the delay a message has to encounter as it finds its way from a source input to a destination output. The time complexity, measured by the number of SEs along the path from input to output, is $O(\log_2 N)$. For example, in a 16 × 16 MIN, the length of the path from input to output is 4. The total number of SEs in the network is usually taken as a measure for the total area of the network. The total area of a 16 × 16 MIN is 32 SEs.

The Omega Network   The Omega Network represents another well-known type of MINs. A size N *omega network* consists of n ($n = \log_2 N$ single-stage) Shuffle–Exchange networks. Each stage consists of a column of $N/2$, two-input switching elements whose input is a shuffle connection. Figure 2.12 illustrates the case of an $N = 8$ Omega network. As can be seen from the figure, the inputs to each stage follow the shuffle interconnection pattern. Notice that the connections are identical to those used in the 8 × 8 Shuffle–Exchange network (SEN) shown in Figure 2.10.

Owing to its versatility, a number of university projects as well as commercial MINs have been built. These include the *Texas Reconfigurable Array Computer* (TRAC) at the University of Texas at Austin, the *Cedar* at the University of Illinois at Urbana-Champaign, the *RP3* at IBM, the *Butterfly* by BBN Laboratories, and the NYU Ultracomputer at New York University. The NYU Ultracomputer is an experimental shared memory MIMD architecture that could have as many as 4096 processors connected through an Omega MIN to 4096 memory modules. The MIN is an enhanced network that can combine two or more requests bound for the same memory address. The network interleaves consecutive memory addresses across the memory modules in order to reduce conflicts in accessing different data

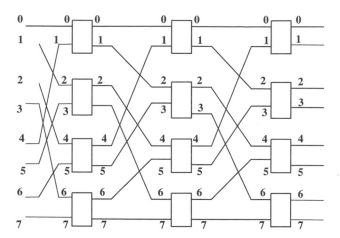

Figure 2.12   The Omega network for $N = 8$.

elements. The switch nodes in the NYU Ultracomputer are provided with queues (queue lengths of 8 to 10 messages) to handle messages collision at the switch. The system achieves one-cycle processor to memory access.

2.3.4   Blockage in Multistage Interconnection Networks

A number of classification criteria exist for MINs. Among these criteria is the criterion of *blockage*. According to this criterion, MINs are classified as follows.

Blocking Networks   Blocking networks possess the property that in the presence of a currently established interconnection between a pair of input/output, the arrival of a request for a new interconnection between two arbitrary unused input and output may or may not be possible. Examples of blocking networks include *Omega*, *Banyan*, *Shuffle–Exchange*, and *Baseline*. Consider, for example the SEN shown in Figure 2.10. In the presence of a connection between input 101 and output 011, a connection between input 100 and output 001 is not possible. This is because the connection 101 to 011 uses the upper output of the third switch from the top in the first stage. This same output will be needed by the requested connection 100 to 001. This contention will lead to the inability to satisfy the connection 100 to 001, that is, *blocking*. Notice however that while connection 101 to 011 is established, the arrival of a request for a connection such as 100 to 110 can be satisfied.

Rearrangeable Networks   Rearrangeable networks are characterized by the property that it is always possible to rearrange already established connections in order to make allowance for other connections to be established simultaneously. The *Benes* is a well-known example of *rearrangeable* networks. Figure 2.13 shows an example 8 × 8 Benes network. Two simultaneous connections are shown established in the network. These are $110 \rightarrow 100$ and $010 \rightarrow 110$. In the presence of the

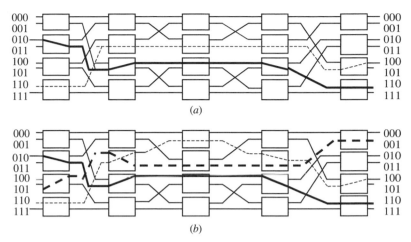

(a)

(b)

Figure 2.13 Illustration of the rearrangeability of the Benes network (a) Benes network with two simulataneously established paths; and (b) the rearrangement of connection $110 \rightarrow 100$ in order to satisfy connection $101 \rightarrow 001$.

connection $110 \rightarrow 100$, it will not be possible to establish the connection $101 \rightarrow 001$ unless the connection $110 \rightarrow 100$ is rearranged as shown in part (b) of the figure.

Nonblocking Networks Nonblocking networks are characterized by the property that in the presence of a currently established connection between any pair of input/output, it will always be possible to establish a connection between any arbitrary unused pair of input/output. The *Clos* is a well-known example of nonblocking networks. It consists of $r_1 n_1 \times m$ input crossbar switches (r_1 is the number of input crossbars, and $n_1 \times m$ is the size of each input crossbar), $m r_1 \times r_2$ middle crossbar switches (m is the number of middle crossbars, and $r_1 \times r_2$ is the size of each middle crossbar), and $r_2 m \times n_2$ output crossbar switches (r_2 is the number of output crossbars and $m \times n_2$ is the size of each output crossbar). The *Clos* network is not blocking if the following inequality is satisfied $m \geq n_1 + n_2 - 1$.

A three-stage *Clos* network is shown in Figure 2.14. The network has the following parameters: $r_1 = 4, n_1 = 2, m = 4, r_2 = 4$, and $n_2 = 2$. The reader is encouraged to ascertain the nonblocking feature of the network shown in Figure 2.14 by working out some example simultaneous connections. For example show that in the presence of a connection such as 110 to 010, any other connection will be possible. Note that Clos networks will be discussed again in Chapter 7.

2.4 STATIC INTERCONNECTION NETWORKS

Static (fixed) interconnection networks are characterized by having fixed paths, unidirectional or bidirectional, between processors. Two types of static networks can be identified. These are *completely connected networks* (CCNs) and *limited connection networks* (LCNs).

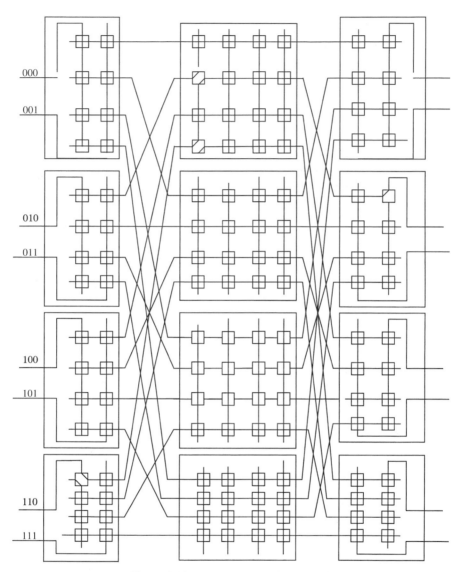

Figure 2.14 A three-stage *Clos* network.

2.4.1 Completely Connected Networks

In a completely connected network (CCN) each node is connected to all other nodes in the network. Completely connected networks guarantee fast delivery of messages from any source node to any destination node (only one link has to be traversed). Notice also that since every node is connected to every other node in the network, routing of messages between nodes becomes a straightforward task. Completely connected networks are, however, expensive in terms of the number of links needed for their construction. This disadvantage becomes more and more apparent for higher values of N. It should be noted that the number of links in a completely connected network is given by $N(N - 1)/2$, that is, $O(N^2)$. The delay complexity of CCNs, measured in terms of the number of links traversed as messages are routed from any source to any destination is constant, that is, $O(1)$. An example having $N = 6$ nodes is shown in Figure 2.15. A total of 15 links are required in order to satisfy the complete interconnectivity of the network.

2.4.2 Limited Connection Networks

Limited connection networks (LCNs) do not provide a direct link from every node to every other node in the network. Instead, communications between some nodes have to be routed through other nodes in the network. The length of the path between nodes, measured in terms of the number of links that have to be traversed, is expected to be longer compared to the case of CCNs. Two other conditions seem to have been imposed by the existence of limited interconnectivity in LCNs. These are: the need for a pattern of interconnection among nodes and the need for a mechanism for routing messages around the network until they reach their destinations. These two items are discussed below.

A number of regular interconnection patterns have evolved over the years for LCNs These patterns include:

- linear arrays;
- ring (loop) networks;
- two-dimensional arrays (nearest-neighbor mesh);
- tree networks; and
- cube networks.

Simple examples for these networks are shown in Figure 2.16.

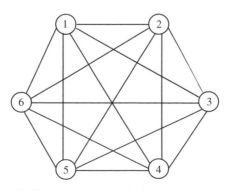

Figure 2.15 Example completely connected network.

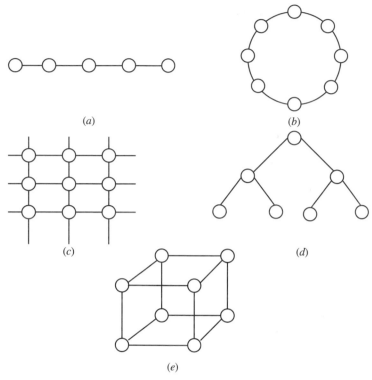

Figure 2.16 Examples of static limited connected networks (*a*) a linear array network; (*b*) a ring network; (*c*) a two-dimensional array (mesh) network; (*d*) a tree network; and (*e*) a three-cube network.

In a linear array, each node is connected to its two immediate neighboring nodes. The two nodes at the extreme ends of the array are connected to their single immediate neighbor. If node i needs to communicate with node $j, j > i$, then the message from node i has to traverse nodes $i + 1, i + 2, \ldots, j - i$. Similarly, when node i needs to communicate with node j, where $i > j$, then the message from node i has to traverse nodes $i - 1, i - 2, \ldots, i - j$. In the worst possible case, when node 1 has to send a message to node N, the message has to traverse a total of $N-1$ nodes before it can reach its destination. Therefore, although linear arrays are simple in their architecture and have simple routing mechanisms, they tend to be slow. This is particularly true when the number of nodes N is large. The network complexity of the linear array is $O(N)$ and its time complexity is $O(N)$. If the two nodes at the extreme ends of a linear array network are connected, then the resultant network has *ring* (*loop*) architecture.

In a tree network, of which the binary tree (shown in Fig. 2.16*d*) is a special case, if a node at level i (assuming that the root node is at level 0) needs to communicate with a node at level j, where $i > j$ and the destination node belongs to the same root's child subtree, then it will have to send its message up the tree traversing nodes at levels $i-1, i-2, \ldots, j+1$ until it reaches the destination node. If a node at level i needs to communicate with another node at the same level i (or with node at level $j \neq i$ where the destination node belongs to a different root's child subtree), it will have to send its message up the tree until the message reaches the root node at level 0. The message will have to be then sent down from the root nodes until it reaches its destination. It should be noted that the number of nodes (processors) in a binary tree system having k levels can be calculated as:

$$N(k) = 2^0 + 2^1 + 2^2 + \cdots + 2^k$$
$$= \frac{(2^k - 1)}{2 - 1} = 2^k - 1$$

Notice also that the maximum depth of a binary tree system is $\lceil \log_2 N \rceil$, where N is the number of nodes (processors) in the network. Therefore, the network complexity is $O(2^k)$ and the time complexity is $O(\log_2 N)$.

The cube-connected and the mesh-connected networks have been receiving increasing interest and, therefore, we discuss them in more detail in the following subsections.

2.4.3 Cube-Connected Networks

Cube-connected networks are patterned after the *n-cube* structure. An *n-cube* (hypercube of order *n*) is defined as an undirected graph having 2^n vertices labeled 0 to $2^n - 1$ such that there is an edge between a given pair of vertices if and only if the binary representation of their addresses differs by one and only one bit. A 4-cube is shown in Figure 2.17. In a cube-based multiprocessor system, processing elements are positioned at the vertices of the graph. Edges of the graph represent the point-to-point communication links between processors. As can be seen from the figure, each

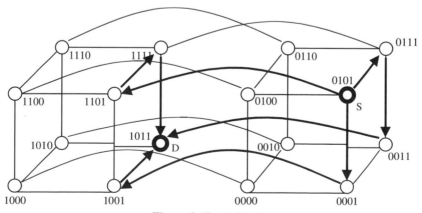

Figure 2.17   A 4-cube.

processor in a 4-cube is connected to four other processors. In an *n-cube*, each processor has communication links to *n* other processors. Recall that in a hypercube, there is an edge between a given pair of nodes if and only if the binary representation of their addresses differs by one and only one bit. This property allows for a simple message routing mechanism. The route of a message originating at node *i* and destined for node *j* can be found by XOR-ing the binary address representation of *i* and *j*. If the XOR-ing operation results in a 1 in a given bit position, then the message has to be sent along the link that spans the corresponding dimension. For example, if a message is sent from source (S) node 0101 to destination (D) node 1011, then the XOR operation results in 1110. That will mean that the message will be sent only along dimensions 2, 3, and 4 (counting from right to left) in order to arrive at the destination. The order in which the message traverses the three dimensions is not important. Once the message traverses the three dimensions in any order it will reach its destination. The three possible disjoint routes that can be taken by the message in this example are shown in bold in Figure 2.17. Disjoint routes do not share any common links among them.

In an *n-cube*, each node has a degree *n*. The degree of a node is defined as the number of links incident on the node. The upper limit on the number of disjoint paths in an *n-cube* is *n*. The hypercube is referred to as a *logarithmic* architecture. This is because the maximum number of links a message has to traverse in order to reach its destination in an *n-cube* containing $N = 2^n$ nodes is $\log_2 N = n$ links. One of the desirable features of hypercube networks is the recursive nature of their constructions. An *n*-cube can be constructed from two subcubes each having an $(n - 1)$ degree by connecting nodes of similar addresses in both subcubes. Notice that the 4-cube shown in Figure 2.17 is constructed from two subcubes each of degree three. Notice that the construction of the 4-cube out of the two 3-cubes requires an increase in the degree of each node. It is worth mentioning that the Intel *iPSC* is an example of hypercube-based commercial multiprocessor systems. A number of performance issues of hypercube multiprocessors will be discussed in Section 2.5.

A number of variations to the basic hypercube interconnection have been proposed. Among these is the *cube-connected cycle* architecture. In this architecture, 2^{n+r} nodes are connected in an *n-cube* fashion such that groups of *r* nodes each form cycles (loops) at the vertices of the cube. For example, a 3-cube connected cycle network with $r = 3$ will have three nodes (processors) forming a loop (ring) at each vertex of the 3-cube. The idea of cube-connected cycles has not been widely used.

2.4.4 Mesh-Connected Networks

An *n*-dimensional mesh can be defined as an interconnection structure that has $K_0 \times K_1 \times \cdots \times K_{n-1}$ nodes where *n* is the number of dimensions of the network and K_i is the radix of dimension *i*. Figure 2.18 shows an example of a $3 \times 3 \times 2$ mesh network. A node whose position is (i, j, k) is connected to its neighbors at dimensions $i \pm 1, j \pm 1$, and $k \pm 1$. Mesh architecture with wrap around connections forms a

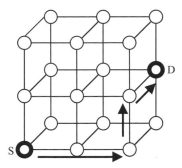

Figure 2.18   A $3 \times 3 \times 2$ mesh network.

torus. A number of routing mechanisms have been used to route messages around meshes. One such routing mechanism is known as the *dimension-ordering routing.* Using this technique, a message is routed in one given dimension at a time, arriving at the proper coordinate in each dimension before proceeding to the next dimension. Consider, for example, a 3D mesh. Since each node is represented by its position (i, j, k), then messages are first sent along the i dimension, then along the j dimension, and finally along the k dimension. At most two turns will be allowed and these turns will be from i to j and then from j to k. In Figure 2.18 we show the route of a message sent from node S at position $(0, 0, 0)$ to node D at position $(2, 1, 1)$. Other routing mechanisms in meshes have been proposed. These include *dimension reversal routing*, the *turn model routing*, and *node labeling routing*. Readers are referred to the bibliography for more information on those, and other routing mechanisms. It should be noted that for a mesh interconnection network with N nodes, the longest distance traveled between any two arbitrary nodes is $O(\sqrt{N})$.

Multiprocessors with mesh interconnection networks are able to support many scientific computations very efficiently. It is also known that n-dimensional meshes can be laid out in n dimensions using only short wires and built using identical boards, each requiring only a small number of pins for connections to other boards. Another advantage of mesh interconnection networks is that they are scalable. Larger meshes can be obtained from smaller ones without changing the node degree (a node degree is defined as the number of links incident on the node). Because of these features, a large number of distributed memory parallel computers utilize mesh interconnection networks. Examples include MPP from Goodyear Aerospace, Paragon from Intel, and J-Machine from MIT.

2.4.5   The *k*-ary *n*-Cube Networks

The k-ary n-cube network is a radix k cube with n dimensions. The radix implies that there are k nodes in each dimension. An 8-ary 1-cube is simply an eight node ring, while an 8-ary 2-cube is eight 8-node rings connected such that nodes are connected to all nodes with an address that differs in only one digit (see

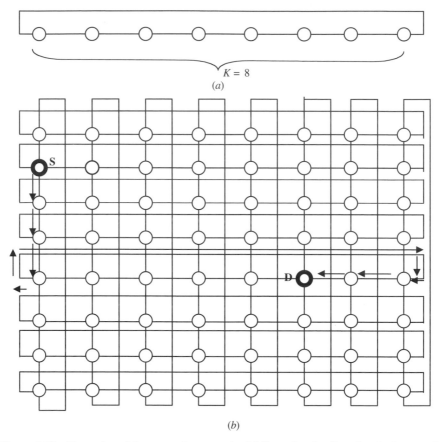

Figure 2.19   Examples of k-ary n-cube networks (a) 8-ary 1-cube (8 nodes ring) network; and (b) 8-ary 2-cube (eight 8-node rings) network.

Fig. 2.19). It should be noted that the number of nodes in a k-ary n-cube is $N = k^n$ nodes and that when $k = 2$, the architecture becomes a binary n-cube. Routing of messages in a k-ary n-cube network can be done in a similar way to that used in mesh networks. Figure 2.19 illustrates a possible path for a message sent from a source node (S) to a destination node (D). Notice that, depending on the directionality of links among nodes the possible route(s) will be decided. Another factor involved in the selection of route in a k-ary n-cube network is the minimality of the route, measured in terms of the number of hops (links) traversed by a message before reaching its destination. The length of the route between S and D in Figure 2.19b is 6. Notice that other routes exist between S and D but they are longer than the indicated route. The longest distance traveled between any two arbitrary nodes in a k-ary n-cube network is $O(n + k)$.

2.5 ANALYSIS AND PERFORMANCE METRICS

Having introduced the main architecture of multiprocessors, we now turn our attention to a discussion on the analysis and performance issues related to those architectures. We provide an introduction to the basic performance issues and performance metrics related to both static and dynamic interconnection networks. For dynamic networks, we discuss the performance issues related to *cost*, measured in terms of the number of cross points (switching elements), the *delay* (latency), the *blocking* characteristics, and the *fault tolerance*. For static networks, we discuss the performance issues related to *degree*, *diameter*, and *fault tolerance*. A more detailed discussion on assessing the performance of these networks will be given in Chapter 3.

2.5.1 Dynamic Networks

The Crossbar   The cost of the crossbar system can be measured in terms of the number of switching elements (cross points) required inside the crossbar. Recall that for an $N \times N$ crossbar, the network cost, measured in terms of the number of switching points, is N^2. This is because in an $N \times N$ crossbar a cross point is needed at the intersection of every two lines extended horizontally and vertically inside the switch. We, therefore, say that the crossbar possesses a quadratic rate of cost (complexity) given by $O(N^2)$. The delay (latency) within a crossbar switch, measured in terms of the amount of the input to output delay, is constant. This is because the delay from any input to any output is bounded. We, therefore, say that the crossbar possesses a constant rate of delay (latency) given by $O(1)$. It should be noted that the high cost (complexity) of the crossbar network pays off in the form of reduction in the time (latency). However, for a large multiprocessor system the cost (complexity) of the crossbar can become a dominant financial burden. The crossbar is however a *nonblocking* network; that is, it allows multiple output connection pattern (permutation) to be achieved (see Fig. 2.5). The nonblocking property of the crossbar is a highly desirable feature that allows concurrent (simultaneous) processor–memory accesses to take place.

A fault-tolerant system can be simply defined as a system that can still function even in the presence of faulty components inside the system. Fault tolerance is a desirable feature that allows a system to continue functioning despite the fact that it contains some faulty elements. The crossbar can be affected by a single-point failure. This is because a failure of a single cross point inside the switch can lead to the crossbar being unable to provide simultaneous connections among all its inputs and all its outputs. Consider, for example the cross-point failure shown in Figure 2.20. In this case, a number of simultaneous connections are possible to make within the switch. However, a connection between P_5 and M_4 cannot be made. Nevertheless, segmenting the crossbar and realizing each segment independently can reduce the effect of a single-point failure in a crossbar. It may also be possible to introduce routing algorithms such that more than one path exists for the establishment of a

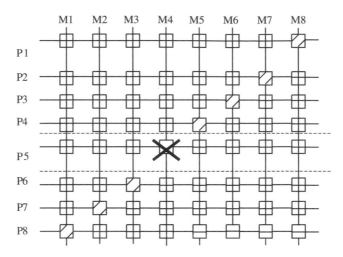

Figure 2.20   An 8 × 8 crossbar network with a single-point failure.

connection between any processor–memory pair. Therefore, the existence of a faulty cross point and/or link along one path will not cause the total elimination of a connection between the processor–memory pair.

Multiple Bus   In Section 2.2.2 we considered a number of different multiple bus arrangements. A general multiple bus arrangement is shown in Figure 2.21. It consists of M memory modules, N processors, and B buses. A given bus is dedicated

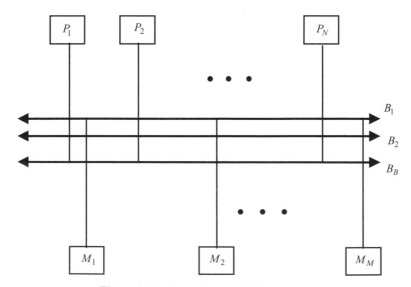

Figure 2.21   Example multiple bus system.

to a particular processor for the duration of a bus transaction. A processor–memory transfer can use any of the available buses. Given B buses in the system, then up to B requests for memory use can be served simultaneously. The cost of a multiple-bus system such as the ones shown in Figure 2.3 is measured in terms of the number of buses used, B. We therefore say that a multiple bus possesses an $O(B)$ rate of cost (complexity) growth. The delay (latency) of a multiple bus, measured in terms of the amount of the input to output delay, is proportional to $B \times N$. We therefore say that the multiple bus possesses an $O(B \times N)$ rate of delay (latency) growth.

Multiple bus multiprocessor organization offers the desirable feature of being highly reliable and fault-tolerant. This is because a single bus failure in a B bus system will leave $(B - 1)$ distinct fault-free paths between the processors and the memory modules. On the other hand, when the number of buses is less than the number of memory modules (or the number of processors), bus contention is expected to increase.

Multistage Interconnection Networks As mentioned before, the number of stages in an $N \times N$ MIN is $\log_2 N$. Each stage consists of $N/2$, 2×2 switching elements (SEs). The network cost (complexity), measured in terms of the total number of SEs, is $O(N \times \log_2 N)$. The number of SEs along a path from a given input to a given output is usually taken as a measure for the delay a message has to encounter as it finds its way from a source to a destination. The latency (time) complexity, measured by the number of SEs along the path from input to output, is $O(\log_2 N)$.

Simplicity of message routing inside a MIN is a desirable feature of such networks. There exists a unique path between a given input–output pair. However, this feature, while simplifying the routing mechanism, causes the MIN to be vulnerable to single-point failure. The failure of a component (a switch or a link) along a given path will render the corresponding path inoperable, thus causing the disconnection of the corresponding input–output pair. Therefore, MINs are characterized as being 0-fault tolerant; that is, a MIN cannot tolerate the failure of a single component. A number of solutions have been suggested in order to improve the fault-tolerance characteristics of MINs. One such solution has been to add an extra stage of SEs such that the number of stages becomes $(\log_2 N + 1)$. The addition of such a stage leads to the creation of two paths between an input–output pair and requires a minor modification in the routing strategy.

Based on the above discussion, Table 2.4 provides an overall performance comparison among different dynamic interconnection networks. Notice that in

TABLE 2.4 Performance Comparison of Dynamic Networks

Network	Delay (Latency)	Cost (Complexity)	Blocking	Degree of Fault Tolerance
Bus	$O(N)$	$O(1)$	Yes	0
Multiple bus	$O(mN)$	$O(m)$	Yes	$(m - 1)$
MINs	$O(\log N)$	$O(N \log N)$	Yes	0
Crossbar	$O(1)$	$O(N^2)$	No	0

this table N represent the number of inputs (outputs) while m represents the number of buses.

2.5.2 Static Networks

Before discussing performance issues related to static interconnection networks, we need to introduce a number of definitions and topological characteristics:

- *Degree* of a node, d, is defined as the number of channels incident on the node. The number of channels into the node is the *in-degree*, d_{in}. The number of channels out of a node is the *out-degree*, d_{out}. The total degree, d, is the sum, $d = d_{in} + d_{out}$.
- *Diameter*, D, of a network having N nodes is defined as the longest path, p, of the shortest paths between any two nodes $D = \max(\min_{p \in p_{ij}} length(p))$. In this equation, p_{ij} is the length of the path between nodes i and j and $length$ (p) is a procedure that returns the length of the path, p. For example, the diameter of a 4×4 Mesh $D = 6$.
- A network is said to be *symmetric* if it is isomorphic to itself with any node labeled as the origin; that is, the network looks the same from any node. Rings and Tori networks are symmetric while linear arrays and mesh networks are not.

Having introduced the above definitions, we now proceed to introduce the basic issues related to the performance of a number of static networks.

Completely Connected Networks (CCNs)   As mentioned before, in a completely connected network each node is connected to all other nodes in the network. Thus, the cost of a completely connected network having N nodes, measured in terms of the number of links in the network, is given by $N(N-1)/2$, that is, $O(N^2)$. The delay (latency) complexity of CCNs, measured in terms of the number of links traversed as messages are routed from any source to any destination, is constant, that is, $O(1)$. Notice also that the degree of a node in CCN is $N-1$, that is, $O(N)$, while the diameter is $O(1)$.

Linear Array Networks   In this network architecture, each node is connected to its two immediate neighboring nodes. Each of the two nodes at the extreme ends of the network is connected only to its single immediate neighbor. The network cost (complexity) measured in terms of the number of nodes of the linear array is $O(N)$. The delay (latency) complexity measured in terms of the average number of nodes that must be traversed to reach from a source node to a destination node is $N/2$, that is, $O(N)$. The node degree in the linear array is 2, that is, $O(1)$ and the diameter is $(N-1)$, that is, $O(N)$.

Tree Networks   In a tree-connected network, a given node is connected to both its parent node and to its children nodes. In a k-level complete binary tree network, the network cost (complexity) measured in terms of the number of nodes in the network is $O(2^k)$ and the delay (latency) complexity is $O(\log_2 N)$. The degree of a node in a binary tree is 3, that is, $O(1)$, while the diameter is $O(\log_2 N)$.

Cube-Connected Networks   An n-cube network has 2^n nodes where two nodes are connected if the binary representation of their addresses differs by one and only one bit. The cost (complexity) of an n-cube measured in terms of the number of nodes in the cube is $O(2^n)$ while the delay (latency) measured in terms of the number of nodes traversed while going from a source node to a destination node is $O(\log_2 N)$. The node degree in an n-cube is $O(\log_2 N)$ and the diameter of an n-cube is $O(\log_2 N)$.

Mesh-Connected Networks   A 2D mesh architecture connects $n \times n$ nodes in a 2D manner such that a node whose position is (i, j) is connected to its neighbors at positions $(i \pm 1, j \pm 1)$. The cost (complexity) of a 2D mesh measured in terms of the number of nodes is $O(n^2)$, while the delay (latency) measured in terms of the number of nodes traversed while going from a source to a destination is $O(n)$. The node degree in a 2D mesh is 4 and the diameter is $O(n)$.

The k-ary n-Cube Networks   The k-ary n-cube architecture is a radix k cube with n dimensions. The number of nodes in a k-ary n-cube is $N = k^n$. The cost (complexity) measured in terms of the number of nodes is $O(k^n)$ and the delay (latency) measured in terms of the number of nodes traversed while going from a source to a destination is $O(n + k)$. The node degree of a k-ary n-cube is $2n$ and the diameter is $O(n \times k)$. The relationship among the topological characteristics introduced above for a k-ary n-cube network is summarized below.

$$d_{in} = d_{\text{out}} = n$$
$$d = 2n$$
$$D = \frac{nk}{2}$$

Having briefly discussed the basic performance characteristics of a number of static interconnection networks, Table 2.5 summarizes those topological characteristics. In this table, N is the number of nodes and n is the number of dimensions.

2.6 CHAPTER SUMMARY

In this chapter, we have navigated through a number of system configurations for multiprocessors. We have discussed the different topologies used for interconnecting multiprocessors. Taxonomy for interconnection networks based on

TABLE 2.5   Performance Characteristics of Static Networks

Network	Degree (d)	Diameter (D)	Cost (No. of Links)	Symmetry	Worst Delay
CCNs	$N - 1$	1	$N(N - 1)/2$	Yes	1
Linear array	2	$N - 1$	$N - 1$	No	N
Binary tree	3	$2(\lceil \log_2 N \rceil - 1)$	$N - 1$	No	$\log_2 N$
n-cube	$\log_2 N$	$\log_2 N$	$nN/2$	Yes	$\log_2 N$
2D-mesh	4	$2(n - 1)$	$2(N - n)$	No	$\sqrt{N}$
k-ary n-cube	$2n$	$N \lfloor k/2 \rfloor$	$n \times N$	Yes	$k \times \log_2 N$

their topology is introduced. Dynamic and static interconnection schemes have been studied. In the dynamic interconnection scheme, three main mechanisms have been covered. These are the bus topology, the crossbar topology, and the multistage topology. In the static interconnection scheme, three main mechanisms have been covered. These are the hypercube topology, the mesh topology, and the k-ary n-cube topology. A number of basic performance aspects related to both dynamic and static interconnection networks have been introduced. These include the cost (complexity), delay (latency), diameter, node degree, and symmetry. Illustrative examples have been used throughout the chapter in introducing new concepts and system configurations. In Chapter 3, we will elaborate on the performance aspects of parallel architectures.

PROBLEMS

1. Design a nonblocking *Clos* network that connects 16 processors and 16 memory modules. Show clearly the number of crossbar switches needed, together with their interconnection pattern.

2. Consider the case of an 8×8 single-stage recirculating Shuffle–Exchange network. Determine all input–output combinations that require the maximum number of passes through the network.

3. Consider the case of an 8×8 Banyan multistage interconnection network similar to the one shown in Figure 2.8. Determine whether it is possible to connect input #I to output (i mod 8) for all I simultaneously. If it is possible show the routing in each case.

4. Consider a simple cost comparison between an $n \times n$ crossbar and an $n \times n$ Shuffle–Exchange MIN. While the crossbar uses cross points, the Shuffle network uses 2×2 switching elements (SEs). Assume that the cost of a $2 \times 2SE$ is four times that of a cross point. What is the relative cost of an $n \times n$ Shuffle–Exchange network with respect to that of a crossbar of the same size? Determine the smallest value of n for which the cost of the crossbar is four times that of the Shuffle–Exchange.

5. In computing the number of connections for different multiple-bus systems, it is noticed that all multiple-bus systems require at least BN connections. However, they differ in the number of additional connections required. For example, while the MBFBMC requires BM additional connections, the MBSBMC requires only M additional connections. You are required to compare the four multiple-bus systems in terms of the additional number of connections required for each. You may assume some numerical values for B, N, M, g, and k. Consider the case of connecting $N = 100$ processors to $M = 400$ memory modules using $B = 40$ buses. Determine the optimal values for g and k such that the MBCBMC system is always better that the MBPBMC in terms of the number of additional connections.

6. Consider the two MINs shown in Figures 2.10 and 2.11. At first glance one can notice the difference between these two networks. In particular, while the first one (the Shuffle–Exchange) uses straight connections between the input processors and the network inputs and straight connections between the output of the network and the output memory modules, the second network (the Banyan network) uses straight connections at the inputs but a shuffle connection at the output. If we generalize that principle such that at the input and the output we can have either straight or shuffle connections while keeping the connection among stages as shown, how many different types of networks will result? Characterize the resulting networks in terms of their ability to interconnect all inputs to all outputs simultaneously.

7. Repeat Problem 6 above for the cases whereby the interstage connection patterns can be either straight or shuffle.

8. Assume that we define a new operation, call it *inverse shuffle* (IS), which is defined as

$$IS(p_{m-1} p_{m-2} \cdots p_1 p_0) = p_0 p_{m-1} p_{m-2} \cdots p_1$$

Repeat Problems 7 and 8 above if the IS is used instead of the shuffle operation.

9. Determine the maximum speedup of a single-bus multiprocessor system having N processors if each processor uses the bus for a fraction f of every cycle.

10. Discuss in some details the fault-tolerance features of dynamic INs such as multiple-bus, MINs, and crossbar. In particular, discuss the effect of failure of nodes and/or links on the ability of routing in each network. Repeat the same for static networks such as hypercubes, meshes, and tree networks.

11. Determine the condition under which a binary tree of height h has a larger diameter and larger number of links than each of the followings: (a) an n-dimensional hypercube, (b) an $r \times r$ 2D mesh with $r = \sqrt{N}$, and (c) a k-ary n-cube.

12. What are the minimum and the maximum distances a message has to travel in an n-dimensional hypercube? Can you use such information to compute the average distance a message has to travel in such cube? Show how?

13. Repeat Problem 12 for the case of an $r \times r$ 2D mesh with $r = \sqrt{N}$.

14. Repeat Problem 12 for the case of a binary tree whose height is h and assuming that all possible source/destination pairs are equally likely.

15. Routing of messages between two nodes A and B in a binary tree has been described in general terms in Section 2.4 of this chapter. You are required to obtain a step-by-step algorithm for routing messages between any two nodes in a binary tree given the following information:

    (a) the root node is numbered as 1 and is considered at level 1;

    (b) the left and right nodes of a node whose number is x are respectively $2x$ and $2x + 1$;

    (c) the binary representation of the numbers of nodes at level i are i bits long; and

    (d) the left and right children of a node are having a 0 or a 1 appended to their parent's number, respectively.

    Show how to apply your algorithm to route messages between node number 8 and node number 13 in a 4 level binary tree.

REFERENCES

Abraham, S. and Padmanabhan, K. Performance of the direct binary n-cube network for multiprocessors. *IEEE Transactions on Computers*, 38 (7), 1000–1011 (1989).

Agrawal, P., Janakiram, V. and Pathak, G. Evaluating the performance of multicomputer configurations. *IEEE Transaction on Computers*, 19 (5), 23–27 (1986).

Almasi, G. and Gottlieb, A. *Highly Parallel Computing*, Benjamin Cummings, 1989.

Al-Tawil, K., Abd-El-Barr, M. and Ashraf, F. A survey and comparison of wormhole routing techniques in mesh networks. *IEEE Network*, March/April 1997, 38–45 (1997).

Bhuyan, L., Yang, Q. and Agrawal, D. Performance of multiprocessor interconnection networks. *IEEE Computer*, 25–37 (1989).

Chen, W.-T. and Sheu, J.-P. Performance analysis of multiple bus interconnection networks with hierarchical requesting model. *IEEE Transactions on Computers*, 40 (7), 834–842, (1991).

Dasgupta, S. *Computer Architecture: A Modern Synthesis, Vol. 2: Advanced Topics*, John Wiley, 1989.

Decegama, A. *The Technology of Parallel Processing: Parallel Processing Architectures and VLSI Hardware*, Vol. 1, Prentice-Hall, 1989.

Dongarra, J. *Experimental Parallel Computing Architectures*, North-Holland, 1987.

Goyal, A. and Agerwala, T. Performance analysis of future shared storage systems. *IBM Journal of Research and Development*, 28 (1), 95–107 (1984).

Juang, J.-Y. and Wah, B. A contention-based bus-control scheme for multiprocessor systems, *IEEE Transactions on Computers*, 40 (9), 1046–1053 (1991).

Linder, D. and Harden, J. An adaptive and fault tolerant wormhole routing strategy for k-ary n-cubes. *IEEE Transactions on Computers*, 40 (1), 2–12 (1991).

Ni, L. and McKinely, P. A survey of wormhole routing techniques in direct networks. *IEEE Computer*, February 1993, 62–76 (1993).

Patel, J. Performance of processor–memory interconnections for multiprocessor computer systems. *IEEE Transactions*, 28 (9), 296–304 (1981).

Reed, D. and Fujimoto, R. *Multicomputer Networks: Message-Based Parallel Processing*, MIT Press, 1987.

Sima, E., Fountain, T. and Kacsuk, P. *Advanced Computer Architectures: A Design Space Approach*, Addison-Wesley, 1996.

Stone, H. *High Performance Computer Architecture*, 3rd edition, Addison Wesley, 1993.

Wilkinson, B. *Computer Architecture: Design and Performance*, 2nd edition, Prentice-Hall, 1996.

Yang, Q. and Zaky, S. Communication performance in multiple-bus systems. *IEEE Transactions on Computers*, 37 (7), 848–853 (1988).

Youn, H. and Chen, C. A comprehensive performance evaluation of crossbar networks. *IEEE Transactions on Parallel and Distribute Systems*, 4 (5), 481–489 (1993).

Zargham, M. *Computer Architecture: Single and Parallel Systems*, Prentice-Hall, 1996.

CHAPTER 3

Performance Analysis of Multiprocessor Architecture

In the previous chapter, we introduced the fundamental concepts related to the design and analysis of multiple-processor systems. We have also touched upon some of the basic issues in the performance analysis of static and dynamic interconnection networks. In this Chapter, we will build on this foundation by providing an in-depth analysis of the performance measures of parallel architectures. Our coverage in this chapter starts by introducing the concept of computational models as related to multiprocessors. The emphasis here is on the computational aspects of the processing elements (processors). Two computational models are studied, namely the equal duration processes and the parallel computation with serial sections models. In studying these models, we discuss two measures. These are the speedup factor and the efficiency. The impact of the communication overhead on the overall speed performance of multiprocessors is emphasized in these models. Having introduced the computational models, we move on to present a number of arguments in support of parallel architectures. Following that, we study a number of performance measures (metrics) of interconnection networks. We define performance metrics such as the bandwidth, worst-case delay, utilization, average distance traveled by a message, cost, and interconnectivity. We will show how to compute those measures for sample dynamic and static networks. Our coverage continues with a discussion on the scalability of parallel systems. A discussion on the important topic of benchmark performance concludes our coverage in this chapter.

3.1 COMPUTATIONAL MODELS

In developing a computational model for multiprocessors, we assume that a given computation can be divided into concurrent tasks for execution on the multiprocessor. Two computational models, thus, arise. These are discussed below.

Advanced Computer Architecture and Parallel Processing, by H. El-Rewini and M. Abd-El-Barr
ISBN 0-471-46740-5 Copyright © 2005 John Wiley & Sons, Inc.

3.1.1 Equal Duration Model

In this model, it is assumed that a given task can be divided into n equal subtasks, each of which can be executed by one processor. If t_s is the execution time of the whole task using a single processor, then the time taken by each processor to execute its subtask is $t_m = t_s/n$. Since, according to this model, all processors are executing their subtasks simultaneously, then the time taken to execute the whole task is $t_m = t_s/n$. The speedup factor of a parallel system can be defined as the ratio between the time taken by a single processor to solve a given problem instance to the time taken by a parallel system consisting of n processors to solve the same problem instance.

$$S(n) = \text{speedup factor}$$

$$= \frac{t_s}{t_m} = \frac{t_s}{t_s/n} = n$$

The above equation indicates that, according to the equal duration model, the speedup factor resulting from using n processors is equal to the number of processors used, n.

One important factor has been overlooked in the above derivation. This factor is the communication overhead, which results from the time needed for processors to communicate and possibly exchange data while executing their subtasks. Assume that the time incurred due to the communication overhead is called t_c then the actual time taken by each processor to execute its subtask is given by $t_m = (t_s/n) + t_c$.

$$S(n) = \text{speedup factor with communication overhead}$$

$$= \frac{t_s}{t_m} = \frac{t_s}{\dfrac{t_s}{n} + t_c} = \frac{n}{1 + n \times \dfrac{t_c}{t_s}}$$

The above equation indicates that the relative values of t_s and t_c affect the achieved speedup factor. A number of cases can then be contemplated: (1) if $t_c \ll t_s$ then the potential speedup factor is approximately n; (2) if $t_c \gg t_s$ then the potential speedup factor is $t_s/t_c \ll 1$; (3) if $t_c = t_s$ then the potential speedup factor is $n/n + 1 \cong 1$, for $n \gg 1$.

In order to scale the speedup factor to a value between 0 and 1, we divide it by the number of processors, n. The resulting measure is called the *efficiency*, ξ. The efficiency is a measure of the speedup achieved per processor. According to the simple equal duration model, the efficiency ξ is equal to 1 if the communication overhead is ignored. However if the communication overhead is taken into consideration, the efficiency can be expressed as

$$\xi = \frac{1}{1 + n \times \dfrac{t_c}{t_s}}.$$

Although simple, the equal duration model is however unrealistic. This is because it is based on the assumption that a given task can be divided into a number of equal subtasks that can be executed by a number of processors in parallel. However, it is sufficient here to indicate that real algorithms contain some (serial) parts that cannot be divided among processors. These (serial) parts must be executed on a single processor. Consider, for example, the program segments given in Figure 3.1. In these program segments, we assume that we start with a value from each of the two arrays (vectors) a and b stored in a processor of the available n processors. The first program block (enclosed in a square) can be done in parallel; that is, each processor can compute an element from the array (vector) c. The elements of array c are now distributed among processors, and each processor has an element. The next program segment cannot be executed in parallel. This block will require that the elements of array c be communicated to one processor and are added up there. The last program segment can be done in parallel. Each processor can update its elements of a and b.

This illustrative example shows that a realistic computational model should assume the existence of (serial) parts in the given task (program) that cannot be divided. This is the basis for the following model.

3.1.2 Parallel Computation with Serial Sections Model

In this computational model, it is assumed that a fraction f of the given task (computation) is not dividable into concurrent subtasks. The remaining part $(1 - f)$ is assumed to be dividable into concurrent subtasks. Performing similar

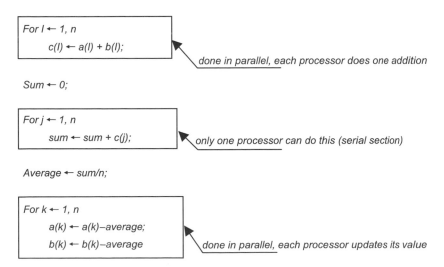

Figure 3.1 Example program segments.

derivations to those done in the case of the equal duration model will result in the following.

The time required to execute the task on n processors is $t_m = ft_s + (1 - f)(t_s/n)$. The speedup factor is therefore given by

$$S(n) = \frac{t_s}{ft_s + (1 - f)\dfrac{t_s}{n}} = \frac{n}{1 + (n - 1)f}$$

According to this equation, the potential speedup due to the use of n processors is determined primarily by the fraction of code that cannot be divided. If the task (program) is completely serial, that is, $f = 1$, then no speedup can be achieved regardless of the number of processors used. This principle is known as *Amdahl's law*. It is interesting to note that according to this law, the maximum speedup factor is given by $\lim_{n \to \infty} S(n) = 1/f$. Therefore, according to Amdahl's law the improvement in performance (speed) of a parallel algorithm over a sequential one is limited not by the number of processors employed but rather by the fraction of the algorithm that cannot be parallelized. A first glance at Amdahl's law indicates that regardless of the number of processors used, there exists an intrinsic limit on the potential usefulness of using parallel architectures. For some time and according to Amdahl's law, researchers were led to believe that a substantial increase in speedup factor would not be possible by using parallel architectures. We will discuss the validity of that and similar postulates in the next section. However, let us show the effect of the communication overhead on the speedup factor, given that a fraction, f, of the computation is not parallelizable. As stated earlier, the communication overhead should be included in the processing time. Considering the time incurred due to this communication overhead, the speedup factor is given by

$$S(n) = \frac{t_s}{ft_s + (1 - f)(t_s/n) + t_c} = \frac{n}{f(n - 1) + 1 + n(t_c/t_s)}$$

The maximum speedup factor under such conditions is given by

$$\lim_{n \to \infty} S(n) = \lim_{n \to \infty} \frac{n}{f(n - 1) + 1 + n(t_c/t_s)} = \frac{1}{f + (t_c/t_s)}$$

The above formula indicates that the maximum speedup factor is determined not by the number of parallel processors employed but by the fraction of the computation that is not parallelized and the communication overhead.

Having considered the speedup factor, we now touch on the efficiency measure. Recall that the efficiency is defined as the ratio between the speedup factor and the number of processors, n. The efficiency can be computed as:

$$\xi \text{ (no communication overhead)} = \frac{1}{1 + (n-1)f}$$

$$\xi \text{ (with communication overhead)} = \frac{1}{f(n-1) + 1 + n(t_c/t_s)}$$

As a last observation, one has to notice that in a parallel architecture, processors must maintain a certain level of efficiency. However, as the number of processors increases, it may become difficult to use those processors efficiently. In order to maintain a certain level of processor efficiency, there should exist a relationship between the fraction of serial computation, f, and the number of processor employed (see Problem 6).

After introducing the above two computational models, we now turn our attention to a discussion on some performance laws (postulates) that were hypothesized regarding the potential gain of parallel architectures. Among these are Grosch's, Amdahl's and Gustafson–Brasis's laws.

3.2 AN ARGUMENT FOR PARALLEL ARCHITECTURES

In this section, we introduce a number of postulates that were introduced by some well-known computer architects expressing skepticism about the usefulness of parallel architectures. We will also provide rebuttal to those concerns.

3.2.1 Grosch's Law

It was as early as the late 1940s that H. Grosch studied the relationship between the power of a computer system, P, and its cost, C. He postulated that $P = K \times C^s$, where s and K are positive constants. Grosch postulated further that the value of s would be close to 2. Simply stated, *Grosch's law* implies that the power of a computer system increases in proportion to the square of its cost. Alternatively, one can express the cost of a system as $C = \sqrt{(P/K)}$ assuming that $s = 2$. The relation between computing power and cost according to Grosch's law is shown in Figure 3.2.

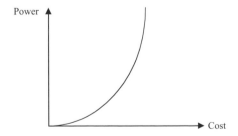

Figure 3.2 Power–cost relationship according to *Grosch's law*.

According to Grosch's law, in order to sell a computer for twice as much, it must be four times as fast. Alternatively, to do a computation twice as cheaply, one has to do it four times slower. With the advances in computing, it is easy to see that Grosch's law is repealed, and it is possible to build faster and less expensive computers over time.

3.2.2 Amdahl's Law

Recall that in Section 3.1.2 we defined the speedup factor of a parallel system as the ratio between the time taken by a single processor to solve a given problem instance to the time taken by a parallel system consisting of n processors to solve the same problem instance.

$$S(n) = \frac{t_s}{ft_s + (1-f)(t_s/n)} = \frac{n}{1 + (n-1)f}$$

$$\lim_{n \to \infty} S(n) = \frac{1}{f}$$

Similar to Grosch's law, *Amdahl's law* made it so pessimistic to build parallel computer systems due to the intrinsic limit set on the performance improvement (speed) regardless of the number of processors used. An interesting observation to make here is that according to Amdahl's law, f is fixed and does not scale with the problem size, n. However, it has been practically observed that some real parallel algorithms have a fraction that is a function of n. Let us assume that f is a function of n such that $\lim_{n \to \infty} f(n) = 0$. Hence,

$$\lim_{n \to \infty} S(n) = \lim_{n \to \infty} \frac{n}{1 + (n-1)f(n)} = n$$

This is clearly in contradiction to Amdahl's law. It is therefore possible to achieve a linear speedup factor for large-sized problems, given that $\lim_{n \to \infty} f(n) = 0$, a condition that has been practically observed. For example, researchers at the Sandia National Laboratories have shown that using a 1024-processor hypercube multiprocessor system for a number of engineering problems, a linear speedup factor can be achieved.

Consider, for example, the well-known engineering problem of multiplying a large square matrix $A(m \times m)$ by a vector $X(m)$ to obtain a vector, that is, $C(m) \leftarrow A(m \times m) * X(m)$. Assume further that the solution of such a problem is performed on a binary tree architecture consisting of n nodes (processors). Initially, the root node stores the vector $X(m)$ and the matrix $A(m \times m)$ is distributed row-wise among the n processors such that the maximum number of rows in any processor is $\lfloor \frac{m}{n} \rfloor + 1$. A simple algorithm to perform such computation consists of the following three steps:

1. The root node sends the vector $X(m)$ to all processors in $O(m \log n)$

2. All processors perform the product $c_i \leftarrow \sum_{j=1}^{m} a_{ij} * x_j$ in

$$O\left(m \times \left(\left\lfloor \frac{m}{n} \right\rfloor + 1\right)\right) = O(m) + O\left(\frac{m^2}{n}\right)$$

3. All processors send their c_i values to the root node in $O(m \log n)$.

According to the above algorithm, the amount of computation needed is

$$O(m \log n) + O(m) + O\left(\frac{m^2}{n}\right) + O(m \log n) = O(m^2)$$

The indivisible part of the computation (steps 1 and 3) is equal to $O(m) + O(m \log n)$. Therefore, the fraction of computation that is indivisible $f(m) = (O(m) + O(m \log n))/O(m^2) = O((1 + \log n)/m)$. Notice that $\lim_{m \to \infty} f(m) = 0$. Hence, contrary to Amdahl's law, a linear speedup can be achieved for such a large-sized problem.

It should be noted that in presenting the above scenario for solving the matrix vector multiplication problem, we have assumed that the memory size of each processor is large enough to store the maximum number of rows expected. This assumption amounts to us saying that with n processors, the memory is n times larger. Naturally, this argument is more applicable to message passing parallel architectures than it is to shared memory ones (shared memory and message passing parallel architectures are introduced in Chapters 4 and 5, respectively). The Gustafson–Barsis law makes use of this argument and is presented below.

3.2.3 Gustafson–Barsis's Law

In 1988, Gustafson and Barsis at Sandia Laboratories studied the paradox created by Amdahl's law and the fact that parallel architectures comprised of hundreds of processors were built with substantial improvement in performance. In introducing their law, Gustafson recognized that the fraction of indivisible tasks in a given algorithm might not be known *a priori*. They argued that in practice, the problem size scales with the number of processors, n. This contradicts the basis of Amdahl's law. Recall that Amdahl's law assumes that the amount of time spent on the parts of the program that can be done in parallel, $(1 - f)$, is independent of the number of processors, n. Gustafson and Brasis postulated that when using a more powerful processor, the problem tends to make use of the increased resources. They found that to a first approximation the parallel part of the program, not the serial part, scales up with the problem size. They postulated that if s and p represent respectively the serial and the parallel time spent on a parallel system, then $s + p \times n$ represents the time needed by a serial processor to perform the computation. They therefore, introduced a new factor, called the scaled speedup factor, $SS(n)$, which can be computed as:

$$SS(n) = \frac{s + p \times n}{s + p} = s + p \times n = s + (1 - s) \times n = n + (1 - n) \times s$$

This equation shows that the resulting function is a straight line with a slope $= (1 - n)$. This shows clearly that it is possible, even easier, to achieve efficient parallel performance than is implied by Amdahl's speedup formula. Speedup should be measured by scaling the problem to the number of processors, not by fixing the problem size.

Having considered computational models and rebutted some of the criticism set forth by a number of computer architects in the face of using parallel architectures, we now move to consider some performance issues in dynamic and static interconnection networks. The emphasis will be on the performance of the interconnection networks rather than the computational aspects of the processors (the latter was considered in Section 3.1).

3.3   INTERCONNECTION NETWORKS PERFORMANCE ISSUES

In this section, we introduce a number of metrics for assessing the performance of dynamic and static interconnection networks. In introducing the metrics, we will show how to compute them for sample networks chosen from those introduced in Chapter 2. The reader is reminded to review the definitions given in Chapter 2 before proceeding with this section. In particular, the reader should review the definitions given about the diameter D, the degree d, and the *symmetry* of a network. In addition to those definitions, we provide the following definition.

- *Channel bisection width* of a network, B, is defined as the minimum number of wires that, when cut, divide the network into equal halves with respect to the number of nodes. The wire bisection is defined as the number of wires crossing this cut of the network. For example, the bisection width of a 4-cube is $B = 8$.

  Table 3.1 provides some numerical values of the above topological characteristics for sample static networks. General expressions for the topological characteristics of a number of static interconnection networks are summarized in Table 3.2. It should be noted that in this table, N is the number of nodes and n is the number of dimensions. In presenting these expressions, we assume that the reader is familiar with their topologies as given in Chapter 2.

TABLE 3.1   Topological Characteristics of Static Networks

Network Configuration	Bisection Width (B)	Node Degree (d)	Diameter (D)
8-ary 1-cube	2	2	4
8-ary 2-cube	16	4	8
4-cube	8	4	4
$3 \times 3 \times 2$ Mesh	9	3	5

TABLE 3.2 Topological Characteristics of a Number of Static Networks

Network	Degree (d)	Diameter (D)	Bisection Width (B)	Symmetry
CCNs	$N-1$	1	$(N/2)^2$	Yes
Linear array	2	$N-1$	1	No
Binary tree	3	$2 \times (\lceil \log_2 N \rceil - 1)$	1	No
Binary cube	$\log_2 N$	$\log_2 N$	$N/2$	Yes
2D-mesh	4	$2(n-1)$	$\sqrt{N}$	No
k-ary n-cube	$2n$	$n\lfloor k/2 \rfloor$	$2 \times k^{n-1}$	Yes

- *Bandwidth* The bandwidth of a network can be defined as the data transfer rate of the network. In a more formal way, the bandwidth is defined as the asymptotic traffic load supported by the network as its utilization approaches unity.

3.3.1 Bandwidth of a Crossbar

We will define the bandwidth for the crossbar as the average number of requests that can be accepted by a crossbar in a given cycle. As processors make requests for memory modules in a crossbar, contention can take place when two or more processors request access to the same memory module. Consider, for example, the case of a crossbar consisting of three processors p_1, p_2, and p_3 and three memory modules M_1, M_2, and M_3. As processors make requests for accessing memory modules, the following cases may take place:

1. All three processors request access to the same memory module: In this case, only one request can be accepted. Since there are three memory modules, then there are three ways (three accepted requests) in which such a case can arise.
2. All three processors request access to two different memory modules: In this case two requests can be granted. There are 18 ways (36 accepted requests) in which such a case can arise.
3. All three processors request access to three different memory modules: In this case all three requests can be granted. There are six ways (18 accepted requests) in which such a case can arise.

From the above enumeration, it is clear that of the 27 combinations of 3 requests taken from 3 possible requests, there are 57 requests that can be accepted (causing no memory contention). Therefore, we say that the bandwidth of such a crossbar is $BW = 57/27 = 2.11$. It should be noted that in computing the bandwidth in this simple example, we made a simplified assumption that all processors make requests for memory module access in every cycle.

In general, for M memory modules and n processors, if a processor generates a request with probability ρ in a cycle directed to each memory with equal probability, then the expression for the bandwidth can be computed as follows. The probability that a processor requests a particular memory module is ρ/M. The probability that a processor does not request that memory module during a given cycle is $(1 - \rho/M)$. The probability that none of the P processors request that memory module during a cycle is $(1 - (\rho/M))^n$. The probability that at least one request is made to that memory module is $(1 - (1 - (\rho/M))^n)$. Therefore, the expected number of distinct memory modules with at least one request (the bandwidth) is $BW = M(1 - (1 - (\rho/M))^n)$.

Notice that in case there is equal probability that any module be requested by a processor, then the term ρ/M in the above equation will become $1/M$. Now, considering the case $M = 3$ and $n = 3$, the $BW = 19/9 = 2.11$, the same as before.

In deriving the above expression, we have assumed that all processors generate requests for memory modules during a given cycle. A similar expression can be derived for the case whereby only a fraction of processors generate requests during a given cycle (see the exercise at the end of the chapter).

3.3.2 Bandwidth of a Multiple Bus

We will develop an expression for the bandwidth of the general multiple bus arrangement shown in Figure 3.3. It consists of M memory modules, n processors, and B buses. A given bus is dedicated to a particular processor for the duration of a bus transaction. A processor–memory transfer can use any of the available buses. Given B buses in the system, then up to B requests for memory use can be served simultaneously. In order to resolve possible conflicts in accessing a given memory module out of the available M modules, M arbiters, one for each memory module, are used to arbitrate among the requests made for a given memory module. The set of M arbiters accepts only one request for each memory module at any given time. Let us assume that a processor generates a request with probability ρ in a cycle directed to each memory with equal probability. Therefore, out of all possible memory requests, only up to M memory requests can be accepted. The probability that a memory module has at least one request is given by (see the crossbar analysis) $\beta = 1 - (1 - (\rho/M))^n$. Owing to the availability of only B buses, then of all memory requests, only B request can be satisfied. The

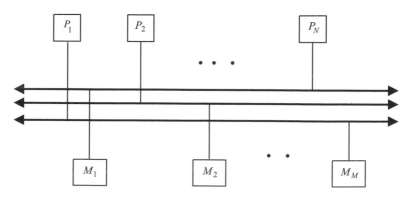

Figure 3.3 A multiple bus system.

probability that exactly k different memory modules are requested during a given cycle can be expressed as $\alpha = \begin{pmatrix} N \\ k \end{pmatrix} \times \beta^k \times (1 - \beta)^{N-k}$. Two cases have to be considered. These are the case where fewer than B different requests being made while fewer than B buses are being used and the case where B or more different requests are made while all B buses are in use. Given these two cases, the bandwidth of the B buses system can be expressed as

$$BW = \sum_{k=1}^{B} k \times \beta + \sum_{k=B+1}^{N} B \times \beta$$

3.3.3 Bandwidth of a Multistage Interconnection Network (MIN)

In this subsection, we compute the bandwidth of a MIN. A simplifying assumption that we make is that the MIN consists of stages of $a \times b$ crossbar switches. One such MIN is the *Delta* network. This assumption is made such that the results we obtained for the bandwidth of the crossbar network can be utilized.

Let us assume that the request rate at the input of the first stage is given by r_0. The number of requests accepted by the first stage and passed on to the next stage is $R_1 = (1 - (1 - (r_0/b))^a)$. The number of requests at any of the b output lines of the first stage is $r_1 = 1 - (1 - (r_0/b))^a$. Since these requests become the input to the next stage, then by analogy the number of requests at the output of the second stage is given by $r_2 = 1 - (1 - (r_1/b))^a$. This recursive relation can be extended to compute the number of requests at the output of stage j in terms of the rate of input requests passed on from stage $j - 1$ as follows: $r_j = 1 - (1 - (r_{j-1}/b))^a$ for $1 \leq j \leq n$ where n is the number of stages. Based on this, the bandwidth of the MIN is given by $BW = b^n \times r_n$.

- *Latency* is defined as the total time required to transmit a message from a source node to a destination node in a parallel architecture machine.

It should be noted that parallel machines attempt to minimize the communication latency by increasing the interconnectivity. In our discussion, we will show the latency caused by the time spent in switching elements. Latency caused by software overhead, routing delay, and connection delay are overlooked in this discussion.

The latency of a k-ary n-cube is $k \times \log_2 N$, that of binary hypercube is given by $(\log_2 N)$, while that of a 2D mesh is given by $\sqrt{N}$.

- *Average distance*, d_a, traveled by a message in a static network, is a measure of the typical number of links (hops) a message has to traverse as it makes its way from any source to any destination in the network. In a network consisting of N nodes, the average distance can be computed using the following relation:

$$d_a = \frac{\sum_{d=0}^{max} d \times N_d}{N - 1}$$

TABLE 3.3   Distance from Node 0000 to all Other Nodes

Path	Distance
$0000 \rightarrow 0001$	1
$0000 \rightarrow 0010$	1
$0000 \rightarrow 0011$	2
$0000 \rightarrow 0100$	1
$0000 \rightarrow 0101$	2
$0000 \rightarrow 0110$	2
$0000 \rightarrow 0111$	3
$0000 \rightarrow 1000$	1
$0000 \rightarrow 1001$	2
$0000 \rightarrow 1010$	2
$0000 \rightarrow 1011$	3
$0000 \rightarrow 1100$	2
$0000 \rightarrow 1101$	3
$0000 \rightarrow 1110$	3
$0000 \rightarrow 1111$	4
Total	32

In the above relation N_d is the number of nodes separated by d links and max is the maximum distance necessary to interconnect two nodes in the network. Consider, for example, a 4-cube network. The average distance between two nodes in such a network can be computed as follows. We compute the distance between node (0000) and all other 15 nodes in the cube. These are shown in Table 3.3. From these, therefore, the average distance for a 4-cube is $(32/15) \cong 2.13$.

- *Complexity (Cost)* of a static network can be measured in terms of the number of links needed to realize the topology of the network.

The cost of a k-ary n-cube measure in terms of the number of links is given by $n \times N$, that of a hypercube is given by $(n \times N)/2$, that of a 2D mesh (having N nodes) is given by $2(N - 2)$, and that of a binary tree is given by $(N - 1)$.

- *Interconnectivity of a network* is a measure of the existence of alternate paths between each source–destination pair. The importance of network connectivity is that it shows the resistance of the network to node and link failures. Network

TABLE 3.4   Performance Measure for a Number of Dynamic Networks

Network	Worst-Case Delay	Bandwidth	Complexity (Cost)
Bus	$O(N)$	$1/N$	$O(1)$
Multiple bus	$O(N/k)$	$BW = \sum_{k=1}^{B} k \times \beta + \sum_{k=B-1}^{N} B \times \beta$	$O(k)$
Multistage	$O(\log N)$	$BW = b^n \times r_n$	$O(N \log N)$
Crossbar	$O(1)$	$BW = M(1 - (1 - (\rho/M)^n)$	$O(N^2)$

TABLE 3.5 Performance Measure for a Number of Static Networks

Network	Worst-Case Delay	Cost (No. of Links)	Connectivity (Nodes and Links)
CCNs	1	$N(N-1)/2$	(1, 1)
Linear array	N	$N-1$	(1, 1)
Binary hybercube	$\log_2 N$	$N/2 \times \log_2 N$	($\log_2 N$, $\log_2 N$)
2D-mesh	$\sqrt{N}$	$2(N-n)$	(4, 4)
Binary tree	$\log N$	$N-1$	(1, 1)
k-ary n-cube	$k \times \log_2 N$	nN	($2k$, $2k$)

connectivity can be represented by the two components: node connectivity and link connectivity.

Consider, for example, the binary tree architecture. The failure of a node, for example, the root node, can lead to the partitioning of the network into two disjoint halves. Similarly, the failure of a link can lead to the partitioning of the network. We therefore say that the binary tree network has a node connectivity of 1 and a link connectivity of 1.

Based on the above discussion and the information provided in Chapter 2, the following two tables, Tables 3.4 and 3.5, provide overall performance comparison among different dynamic interconnection networks and different static networks, respectively. Having presented a number of performance measures for static and dynamic networks, we now turn our attention to the important issue of parallel architecture scalability.

3.4 SCALABILITY OF PARALLEL ARCHITECTURES

A parallel architecture is said to be scalable if it can be expanded (reduced) to a larger (smaller) system with a linear increase (decrease) in its performance (cost). This general definition indicates the desirability for providing equal chance for scaling up a system for improved performance and for scaling down a system for greater cost-effectiveness and/or affordability. Unless otherwise mentioned, our discussion in this section will assume the scaling up of systems. In this context, *scalability* is used as a measure of the system's ability to provide increased performance, for example, speed as its size is increased. In other words, scalability is a reflection of the system's ability to efficiently utilize the increased processing resources. In practice, the scalability of a system can be manifested in a number of forms. These forms include speed, efficiency, size, applications, generation, and heterogeneity.

In terms of speed, a scalable system is capable of increasing its speed in proportion to the increase in the number of processors. Consider, for example, the case of adding m numbers on a 4-cube ($n = 16$ processors) parallel system. Assume for simplicity that m is a multiple of n. Assume also that originally each processor has (m/n) numbers stored in its local memory. The addition can then proceed as follows. First, each processor can add its own numbers sequentially in (m/n) steps. The addition operation is performed simultaneously in all processors. Secondly, each pair of neighboring processors can communicate their results to one of them whereby the communicated result is added to the local result. The second step can be repeated ($\log_2 n$) times, until the final result of the addition process is stored in one of the processors. Assuming that each computation and the communication takes one unit time then the time needed to perform the addition of these m numbers is $T_p = (m/n) + 2 \times \log_2 n$. Recall that the time required to perform the same operation on a single processor is $T_s = m$. Therefore, the speedup is given by

$$S = \frac{m}{(m/n) + 2 \times \log_2 n}$$

Table 3.6 provides the speedup S for different values of m and n. It is interesting to notice from the table that for the same number of processors, n, a larger instance of the same problem, m, results in an increase in the speedup, S. This is a property of a scalable parallel system.

In terms of efficiency, a parallel system is said to be scalable if its efficiency can be kept fixed as the number of processors is increased, provided that the problem size is also increased. Consider, for example, the above problem of adding m numbers on an n-cube. The efficiency of such a system is defined as the ratio between the actual speedup, S, and the ideal speedup, n. Therefore, $\xi = (S/n) = m/(m + 2n \times \log_2 n)$. Table 3.7 shows the values of the efficiency, ξ, for different values of m and n. The values in the table indicate that for the same number of processors, n, higher efficiency is achieved as the size of the problem, m, is increased. However, as the number of processors, n, increases, the efficiency continues to decrease. Given these two observations, it should be possible to keep the efficiency fixed by increasing simultaneously both the size of the problem, m, and the number of processors, n. This is a property of a scalable parallel system.

It should be noted that the degree of scalability of a parallel system is determined by the rate at which the problem size must increase with respect to n in order to maintain a fixed efficiency as the number of processors increases. For example, in a highly scalable parallel system the size of the problem needs to grow linearly

TABLE 3.6   The Possible Speedup for Different m and n

m	$n = 2$	$n = 4$	$n = 8$	$n = 16$	$n = 32$
64	1.88	3.2	4.57	5.33	5.33
128	1.94	3.55	5.82	8.00	9.14
256	1.97	3.76	6.74	10.67	14.23
512	1.98	3.88	7.31	12.8	19.70
1024	1.99	3.94	7.64	14.23	24.38

TABLE 3.7 Efficiency for Different Values of m and n

m	$n = 2$	$n = 4$	$n = 8$	$n = 16$	$n = 32$
64	0.94	0.8	0.57	0.33	0.167
128	0.97	0.888	0.73	0.5	0.285
256	0.985	0.94	0.84	0.67	0.444
512	0.99	0.97	0.91	0.8	0.62
1024	0.995	0.985	0.955	0.89	0.76

with respect to n to maintain a fixed efficiency. However, in a poorly scalable system, the size of the problem needs to grow exponentially with respect to n to maintain a fixed efficiency.

Recall that the time spent by each processor in performing parallel execution in solving the problem of adding m numbers on an n-cube is given by $(m/n) + 2 \times \log_2 n$. Of this time, approximately (m/n) is spent performing the actual execution, while the remaining portion of the time, T_{oh}, is an overhead incurred in performing tasks such as interprocessor communication. The following relationship applies: $T_{oh} = n \times T_p - T_s$. For example, the overall overhead for the addition problem considered above is given by $T_{oh} = 2n \times \log_2 n$. It is interesting to note that a sequential algorithm running on a single processor does not suffer from such overhead. Now, we can rewrite the expression for the efficiency as $\xi = m/(m + T_{oh})$, which leads to the equation $m = \zeta/(1 - \zeta)T_{oh}$. Consider again the problem of adding m numbers using an n-cube. For this problem the problem size $m = 2 \times \zeta/(1 - \zeta) \times n \times \log_2 n = Kn \times \log_2 n = \Theta(n \times \log_2 n)$. The rate at which the problem size, m, is required to grow with respect to the number of processors, n, to keep the efficiency, ξ, fixed is called the isoefficiency of a parallel system and can be used as a measure of the scalability of the system. A highly scalable parallel system has a small isoefficiency, while a poor parallel system has a large isoefficiency. Theoretically speaking, a parallel system is considered scalable if its isoefficiency function exists; otherwise the system is considered not scalable. Recall that Gustafson has shown that by scaling up the problem size, m, it is possible to obtain near-linear speedup on as many as 1024 processors (see Section 3.2).

Having discussed the issues of speedup and efficiency of scalable parallel systems, we now conduct a discussion on their relationship. It is useful to indicate at the outset that typically an increase in the speedup of a parallel system (benefit), due to an increase in the number of processors, comes at the expense of a decrease in the efficiency (cost). In order to study the actual behavior of speedup and efficiency, we need first to introduce a new parameter, called the *average parallelism* (Q). It is defined as the average number of processors that are busy during the execution of given parallel software (program), provided that an unbounded number of processors are available. The average parallelism can equivalently be defined as the speedup achieved assuming the availability of an unbounded number of processors. A number of other equivalent definitions exist for the average parallelism. It has been shown that once Q is determined, then the following bounds are attainable for the speedup and the efficiency on an n-processor system:

$$S(n) \geq \frac{nQ}{n + Q - 1}, \qquad \lim_{Q \to \infty} S(n) = n, \qquad \text{and} \quad \lim_{n \to \infty} S(n) = Q$$

$$\zeta(n) \geq \frac{Q}{n + Q - 1}$$

The above two bounds show that the sum of the attained fraction of the maximum possible speedup, $S(n)/Q$, and attained efficiency, must always exceed 1. Notice also that, given a certain average parallelism, Q, the efficiency (cost) incurred to achieve a given speedup is given by $\zeta(n) \geq (Q - S(n))/(Q - 1)$. It is therefore fair to say that the average parallelism of a parallel system, Q, determines the associated speedup versus efficiency tradeoff.

In addition to the above scalability metrics, there has been a number of other unconventional metrics used by some researchers. A number of these are explained below.

Size scalability measures the maximum number of processors a system can accommodate. For example, the size scalability of the IBM SP2 is 512, while that of the symmetric multiprocessor (SMP) is 64.

Application scalability refers to the ability of running application software with improved performance on a scaled-up version of the system. Consider, for example, an n-processor system used as a database server, which can handle 10,000 transactions per second. This system is said to possess application scalability if the number of transactions can be increased to 20,000 using double the number of processors.

Generation scalability refers to the ability of a system to scale up by using next-generation (fast) components. The most obvious example for generation scalability is the IBM PCs. A user can upgrade his/her system (hardware or software) while being able to run their code generated on their existing system without change on the upgraded one.

Heterogeneous scalability refers to the ability of a system to scale up by using hardware and software components supplied by different vendors. For example, under the IBM Parallel Operating Environment (POE) a parallel program can run without change on any network of RS6000 nodes; each can be a low-end PowerPC or a high-end SP2 node.

In his vision on the scalability of parallel systems, Gordon Bell has indicated that in order for a parallel system to survive, it has to satisfy five requirements. These are size scalability, generation scalability, space scalability, compatibility, and competitiveness. As can be seen, three of these long-term survivability requirements have to do with different forms of scalability.

As can be seen from the above introduction, *scalability*, regardless of its form, is a desirable feature of any parallel system. This is because it guarantees that with sufficient parallelism in a program, the performance, for example, speedup, can be improved by including additional hardware resources without requiring program change. Owing to its importance, there has been an evolving design trend, called *design for scalability* (DFS), which promotes the use of scalability as a major design objective. Two different approaches have evolved as DFS. These are overdesign and backward compatibility. Using the first approach, systems are designed with additional features in anticipation for future system scale-up. An illustrative example for such approach is the design of modern processors with 64-bit address, that is, 2^{64} bytes address space. It should be noted that the current UNIX operating system supports only 32-bit address space. With memory space overdesign, future transition to 64-bit UNIX can be performed with minimum system changes. The other form of DFS is the backward compatibility. This approach considers the requirements for scaled-down systems. Backward compatibility allows scaled-up components (hardware or software) to be usable with both the original and the scaled-down systems. As an example, a new processor should be able to execute code generated by old processors. Similarly, a new version of an operating system should preserve all useful functionality of its predecessor such that application software that runs under the old version must be able to run on the new version.

Having introduced a number of scalability metrics for parallel systems, we now turn our attention to the important issue of benchmark performance measurement.

3.5 BENCHMARK PERFORMANCE

Benchmark performance refers to the use of a set of integer and floating-point programs (known collectively as a benchmark) that are designed to test different performance aspects of the computing system(s) under test. Benchmark programs should be designed to provide fair and effective comparisons among high-performance computing systems. For a benchmark to be meaningful, it should evaluate faithfully the performance for the intended use of the system. Whenever advertising for their new computer systems, companies usually quote the benchmark ratings of their systems as a trusted measure. These ratings are usually used for performance comparison purposes among different competing systems.

Among the first known examples of benchmarks are the Dhrystone and Whetstone benchmarks. These are synthetic (not real) benchmarks intended to measure performance of real machines. The Dhrystone benchmark addresses integer performance. It consists of 100 statements and does not use floating-point operations or data. The rate obtained from Dhrystone is used to compute the MIPS index as a performance measure. This makes the Dhrystone rather unreliable as a source for performance measure. The Whetstone, on the other hand, is a kernel program that addresses floating-point performance for arithmetic operations, array indexing, conditional branch, and subroutine calls. The execution speed obtained using Whetstone is used solely to determine the system performance. This leads to a single figure measure for performance, which makes it unreliable. Synthetic benchmarks were superseded by a number of application software segments that reflect real engineering and scientific applications. These include PERFECT (Performance Evaluation for Cost-Effective Transformations), TPC

TABLE 3.8   SPEC Integer Programs

Program	Description/Area
Compress	Adaptive compression
eqntott	Logic design
espresso	Functional minimization
gcc	GNU C compiler
sc	Spreadsheet
xlisp	Lisp interpreter

measure for database I/O performance and SPEC (Standard Performance Evaluation Corporation) measure.

The SPEC is a nonprofit corporation formed to "establish, maintain, and endorse a standardized set of relevant benchmarks that can be applied to the newest generation of high-performance computers"[1]. The first SPEC benchmark suite was released in 1989 (SPEC89). It consisted of ten engineering/scientific programs. Two measures were derived from SPEC89. The SPECmark measures the ten programs' execution rates and SPECthruput, which examines the system's throughput. Owing to its unsatisfactory results, SPEC89 was replaced by SPEC92 in 1992.

The SPEC92 consists of two suites: CINT92, which consists of six integer intensive *C* programs (see Table 3.8), and CFP92, which consists of 14 floating-point intensive C and Fortran programs (see Table 3.9).

In SPEC92, the measure SPECratio represents the ratio of the actual execution time to the predetermined reference[2] time for a given program. In addition, SPEC92 uses the measure SPECint92 as the geometric mean of the SPECratio for the programs in CINT92. Similarly, the measure SPECfp92 is the geometric mean of the SPECratio for the programs in CFP92. In using SPEC for performance measures, three major steps have to be taken: building the tools, preparing auxiliary files, and running the benchmark suites. The tools are used to compile, run, and evaluate the benchmarks. Compilation information such as the optimization flags and references to alternate source code is kept in what is called makefile wrappers and configuration files. The tools and the auxiliary files are then used to compile and execute the code and compute the SPEC metrics.

The use of the geometric mean to obtain the average time ratio for all programs in the SPEC92 has been subject to a number of criticisms. The premise for these criticisms is that the geometric mean is bound to cause distortion in the obtained results. For example, Table 3.10 shows the execution times (in seconds) obtained using the 14 floating-point programs in SPEC92 for two systems: Silicon Graphics' Challenger XL/Onyx and the Sun Sparc Center with eight CPUs.

As can be observed from Table 3.10 the SG XL/Onyx runs the SPEC92 benchmarks 13.8% (1772.1 − 1557.3/1557.3) faster than the Sun Sparc. However, the

---

[1]From SPEC's Bylaw, *Netnews* posting, October 1994.
[2]The predetermined reference time is usually taken as that of the VAX 11/780.

TABLE 3.9   SPEC Floating-Point Programs

Program	Description/Area
Alvinn	Neural networks/robotics
Doduce	Nuclear reactor sim/physics
Ear	Ear simulation/medicine
Fpppp	Electron integral/chemistry
Hydro2d	Jet computation/astrophysics
Mdljdp2	Motion equation/Chem (D. precis.)
Mdljsp2	Motion equation/Chem (S. precis.)
nasa7	Floating-point kernels
Ora	Ray tracing/optics
Spicc	Circuit simulator/circuit design
su2cor	Mass of particles/quantum physics
Swm256	Water equation solver/simulation
Tomcatv	Mesh-generation program
Wave5	Maxwell's equation solver

Sun Sparc is ranked as 12.5% (109.2 − 97.1/97.1) higher on the SPECrate using the geometric mean. It is such a drawback that causes skepticism among computer architects for the use of the geometric mean in SPEC92. This is because a large improvement of only one program can boost the geometric mean significantly. It was because of this observation that Giladi and Ahituv have suggested that the geometric mean be replaced by the harmonic mean.

TABLE 3.10   SPEC92 Execution Time (in Seconds) for Two Systems

	SG	XL/Onyx	Sun Sparc	Center 2000
Program	Time	Ratio	Time	Ratio
Alvinn	67.6	113.8	52.2	147.3
Doduce	22.4	83.0	38.2	48.7
Ear	120.3	212.0	329.9	77.3
Fpppp	111.4	82.6	130.9	70.3
hydro2d	116.0	118.1	58.4	234.6
mdljdp2	54.7	129.6	107.7	65.8
mdljsp2	50.3	66.6	103.6	32.3
nasa7	142.9	117.6	206.1	81.5
Ora	66.6	111.4	13.0	570.8
Spice	364.8	65.8	571.4	42.0
Su2cor	116.2	111.0	49.8	259.0
swm256	250.4	50.7	37.4	339.6
Tomcatv	25.0	106.0	17.0	155.9
wave5	48.7		56.5	65.5
Total time	1557.3		1772.1	
Geometric mean		97.1		109.2

Subsequently, there arose a concern about the sensitivity of SPEC metrics to compiler flags. For example, Mirghafori and others have computed the average improvement of SPECpeak with respect to PSECbase for CINT92 and CFP92 on a number of platforms. Recall that PSECpeaks are those ratings that are reported by vendors in their advertisement of new products. The SPECbase is a new measurement to the SPEC92, which has been designed to accurately reflect the typical usage of compiler technology (introduced by PSEC in 1994). The Mirghafori study revealed that compiler flag tunings have brought about 11% increase in the SPEC ratings. In addition, it has been reported that a number of tuning parameters are usually used by vendors in obtaining their reported SPECpeak and SPECbase ratings and that reproducibility of those ratings is sometimes impossible. To show the discrepancy between the reported SPECbase and SPECpeak performance by a number of vendors, Table 3.11 shows a sample of eight CFP92 results reported in the SPEC newsletter (the June and September 1994 issues). As can be seen from the table, while some machines show superior performance to other machines based on the reported SPECbase, they show inferior performance using the SPECpeak, and vice versa.

For the abovementioned observations, it became apparent to a number of computer architects that SPEC92 does not predict faithfully the performance of computers on random software for a typical user.

In October 1995, SPEC announced the release of the SPEC95 suite, which replaced the SPEC92 suite fully in September 1996. SPEC95 consists of two CPU-intensive applications: CINT95, a set of eight integer programs and CFP95, a set of 10 floating-point programs. According to SPEC, all SPEC95 performance results published consider the SUN SPARC station 10/40 as the reference machine. Performance results are therefore shown as ratios compared to that machine. Each metric used by SPEC95 is the aggregate overall benchmark of a given suite by taking the geometric mean of the ratios of the individual benchmarks. In presenting the performance results, SPEC takes the speed metrics to measure the ratios to execute a single copy of the benchmark, while the throughput metrics measure the ratios to execute multiple copies of the benchmark. For example, the SPEC95 performance results of a Digital AlphaStation 500, which uses a 500 MHz Alpha 21164 processor with 8 MB cache and 128 MB memory, are shown in the Table 3.12. In this table,

TABLE 3.11 Five Misleading Reported CFP92

Machine	Peak	Base	Machine	Peak	Base
IBM RISC/6000 66.67 MHz	255.7	211.7	Digital DEC 3000 225 MHz	230.6	213.3
SUN SuperSparc 60 MHz	127.1	111.0	HP 9000 80 MHz	120.9	114.0
Hitachi 3500 80 MHz	121.3	107.7	HP 9000 80 MHz	120.9	114.0
Hitachi 3500 50 MHz	81.9	72.8	SUN SPARC 50 MHz	78.8	73.2
IBM RISC/6000 66.67 MHz PowerPC	76.0	65.5	Intel Pentium 735/90	72.7	67.8

TABLE 3.12   **Sample SPEC95 Performance Results**

Metric	Speed		Throughput	
	95	_base95	_rate95	_rate_base95
SPECint	15	12.6	135	113
SPECfp	20.4	18.3	18.3	165

the SPECint_rate_base95 is obtained by taking the geometric mean of the rates of the eight benchmarks of the CIT95, where each benchmark is compiled with a low optimization. The rate of each benchmark is measured by running multiple copies of the benchmark for a week, and normalizing the execution time with respect to the SUN SPARCstation 10/40. Therefore, the number 113 means that the AlphaStation executes 112 times more copies of the CINT95 than the SUN in a week.

The SPECfp is obtained by taking the geometric mean of the ratios of the ten benchmarks of the CFP95, where each benchmark is compiled with aggressive optimization. The rate of each benchmark is measured by running a single copy of the benchmark for a week, and normalizing the execution time with respect to the SUN SPARCstation 10/40. Therefore, the number 20.4 means that the Alpha-Station is 19.4 times faster than the SUN in executing a single copy of the CFP95.

On June 30, 2000, SPEC retired the SPEC95 and replaced it with SPEC CPU2000. The new benchmark suite consists of 26 benchmarks in total (12 integer and 14 floating-point benchmarks). It has 19 applications that have never been in a SPEC CPU suite. The CPU2000 integer and floating-point benchmark suites are shown in Tables 3.13 and 3.14, respectively. Three subjective criteria are achieved

TABLE 3.13   **The CPU2000 Integer Benchmark Suite**

Benchmark	Language	Resident Size (Mbytes)	Virtual Size (Mbytes)	Description
SPECint2000				
164.gzip	C	181	200	Compression
175.vpr	C	50	55.2	FPGA application
176.gcc	C	155	158	C compiler
181.mcf	C	190	192	Combinatorial optimization
186.crafty	C	2.1	4.2	Chess game
197.parser	C	37	62.5	Word processing
252.eon	C++	0.7	3.3	Computer visualization
253.perlbmk	C	146	159	Perl programming
254.gap	C	193	196	Interpreter (group theory)
255.vortex	C	72	81	OOB database
256.bzip2	C	185	200	Compression
300.twolf	C	1.9	4.1	Place and route simulator

TABLE 3.14 The CPU2000 Floating-Point Benchmark Suite

Benchmark	Language	Resident Size (Mbytes)	Virtual Size (Mbytes)	Description
SPECfp2000				
168.wupwise	F77	176	177	Quantum chromo-dynamics
171.swin	F77	191	192	Shallow water modeling
172.mgrid	F77	56	56.7	3D potential filed
173.applu	F77	181	191	Partial differential equations
177.mesa	C	9.5	24.7	3D graphics library
178.galgel	F90	63	155	Computational fluid dynamics
179.art	C	3.7	5.9	Neural networks applications
183.equake	C	49	51.1	Seismic wave propagation simulation
187.facerec	F90	16	18.5	Image processing: Face recognition
188.ammp	C	26	30	Computational chemistry
189.lucas	F90	142	143	Number theory
191.fma3d	F90	103	105	Finite element simulation
200.sixtrack	F77	26	59.8	Nuclear physics applications
301.apsi	F77	191	192	Meteorology: Pollutant distribution

in the CPU2000. These are confidence in the benchmark maintainability, transparency, and vendor interest.

Performance results of the 26 CPU2000 benchmarks (both integer and floating-point) were reported for three different configured systems using the Alpha 21164 chip. These systems are the AlphaStation 500/500 (System #1), the Personal Workstation 500au (System #2), and the AlphaServer 4100 5/533 (System #3). The performance is stated relative to a reference machine, a 300 MHz Sun Ultra5_10, which gets a score of 100. It was reported that the performance of the 26 benchmarks on the 21164 systems ranges from 92.3 (for the 172.mgrid) to 331 (for the 179.art). It was also found that the 500 MHz Systems # and System #2 differ by more than 5% on 17 of the 26 benchmarks. The 533 MHz (system #3), with a 7% megahertz advantage, wins by more than 10% three times (176.gcc, 253.perlbmk, 199.art), by less than 3% three times (197.parser, 253.eon, 256.bzip2), and loses to the 500 MHz three times (181.mcf, 172.mgrid, 188.ammp).

3.6 CHAPTER SUMMARY

In this chapter, we have covered a number of important issues related to the performance of multiprocessor systems. Two computational models: equal duration and parallel computations with serial sections have been first introduced. In each case the speedup and efficiency have been computed with and without the **effect of the** communication overhead. A rebuttal to a number of critical views about the effectiveness of parallel architectures has been made. This includes Grosch's and Amdahl's laws. In addition, the Gustafson–Barsis law, which supports the use of multiprocessor architecture, has been introduced. A number of performance metrics for static and dynamic interconnection networks has then been provided. The metrics include the bandwidth, delay, and complexity. The scalability of parallel architectures in terms of speed and efficiency has been discussed, followed by the issue of isoefficiency. A number of unconventional metrics for scalability has also been discussed. Finally, the issue of benchmark performance measurement has been introduced. The main shortcomings and the advantages of the SPEC benchmark software have then been identified.

PROBLEMS

1. Consider the case of a multiple-bus system consisting of 50 processors, 50 memory modules, and 10 buses. Assume that a processor generates a memory request with probability ρ in a given cycle. Compute the bandwidth of such system for $\rho = 0.2$, 0.5, and 1.0. Show also the effect on the bandwidth if the number of buses is increased to $B = 20$, 30, and 40 for the same request probability values.

2. In deriving the expression for the bandwidth of a crossbar system, we have assumed that all processors generate requests for memory modules during a given cycle. Derive a similar expression for the case whereby only a fraction of processors, f, generate requests during a given cycle. Consider the two cases whereby a processor generates a memory request with probability ρ in a given cycle and whereby a processor can request any memory module.

3. Consider the recursive expression developed for the bandwidth of a *Delta MIN* network consisting of stages of $a \times b$ crossbar switches. Assuming that $a = 2$, $b = 4$, and $r_a = 0.5$, compute the bandwidth of such a network.

4. Consider the case of a binary n-cube having N nodes. Compute the bandwidth of such a cube given that ρ is the probability that a node receives an external request and v is the probability that a node generates a request (either internally or passes on an external request). Assume that a fraction f of the external requests received by a node is passed onwards to another node.

5. Consider the expressions obtained for efficiency under the two computational models presented in the chapter. Compute the expected efficiency values for different values of t_c and t_s.

6. Starting from the equation for the speedup factor given by

$$S(n) = \frac{1}{f + \dfrac{(1-f)}{n}},$$

show the inequality that relates the fraction of serial computation, f, and the number of processors employed, n, if a 50% efficiency is to be achieved.

7. Contrast the following two approaches for building a parallel system. In this first approach, a small number of powerful processors is used in which each processor is capable of performing serial computations at a given rate, Ψ. In the second approach, a large number of simple processors are used in which each processor is capable of performing serial computations at a lower rate, $\Phi < \Psi$. What is the condition under which the second system will execute a given computation more slowly than a single processor of the first system?

8. Consider a parallel architecture built using processors each capable of sustaining 0.5 megaflop. Consider a supercomputer capable of sustaining 100 megaflops. What is the condition (in terms of f) under which the parallel architecture can exceed the performance of the supercomputer?

9. Consider an algorithm in which $(1/\alpha)$ th of the time is spent executing computations that must be done in a serial fashion. What is the maximum speedup achievable by a parallel form of the algorithm?

10. Show that the lower bound on the isoefficiency function of a parallel system is given by $\Theta(n)$. Hint: If the problem size m grows at a rate slower than $\Theta(n)$ as the number of processors increases, then the number of processors can exceed the problem size m.

11. Compute the isoefficiency of a parallel system having an overhead $T_{\text{oh}} = n^{4/3} + m^{3/4} \times n^{3/2}$.

12. In addition to the two definitions offered in Section 3.4, one can also define the average parallelism, Q, as the intersection point of the hardware bound and the software bound on speedup. Show that the three definitions are equivalent.

REFERENCES

Abraham, S. and Padmanabhan, K. Performance of the direct binary n-cube network for multiprocessors. *IEEE Transactions on Computers*, 38 (7), 1000–1011 (1989).

Agrawal, P., Janakiram, V. and Pathak, G. Evaluating the performance of multicomputer configurations. *IEEE Transaction on Computers*, 19 (5), 23–27 (1986).

Al-Tawil, K., Abd-El-Barr, M. and Ashraf, F. A survey and comparison of wormhole routing techniques in mesh networks. *IEEE Network*, March/April 1997, 38–45 (1997).

Almasi, G. and Gottlieb, A. *Highly Parallel Computing*, Benjamin Cummings, 1989.

Bell, G. Why there won't be apps: The problem with MPPs. *IEEE Parallel and Distribute Technology*, Fall 1994, 5–6 (1994).

Bhuyan, L., Yang, Q. and Agrawal, D. Performance of multiprocessor interconnection networks. *IEEE Computer*, 25–37 (1989).

Chan, Y., Sudarsanam, A. and Wolf, A. The effect of compiler flag tuning on SPEC benchmark performance. *Computer Architecture News*, 22 (4), 60–70 (1994).

Chen, W.-T. and Sheu, J.-P. Performance analysis of multiple bus interconnection networks with hierarchical requesting model. *IEEE Transactions on Computers*, 40 (7), 834–842 (1991).

Cosnard, M., Robert, Y. and Toourancheau, B. Evaluating speedups on distributed memory architectures. *Parallel Computing*, 10, 247–253 (1989).

Cosnard, M. and Trystram, D. *Parallel Algorithms and Architectures*, International Thomson Computer Press, 1995.

Curnow, H. and Wichmann, B. A synthestic benchmark. *The Computer Journal*, 19 (1), 43–49 (1976).

Dasgupta, S. *Computer Architecture: A Modern Synthesis, Vol. 2: Advanced Topics*, John Wiley, 1989.

Decegama, A. *The Technology of Parallel Processing*: *Parallel Processing Architectures and VLSI Hardware*, Vol. 1, Prentice-Hall, 1989.

Dixit, K. and Reilly, J. SPEC developing new component benchmark suits. *SPEC Newsletter*, 3 (4), 14–17 (1991).

Dixit, K. The SPEC benchmarks. *Parallel Computing*, 17, 1195–1209 (1991).

Dongarra, J. *Experimental Parallel Computing Architectures*, North-Holland, 1987.

Eager, D., Zahorjan, J. and Lazowska, E. Speedup versus efficiency in parallel systems. *IEEE Transactions on Computers*, 38 (3), 408–423 (1989).

Ein-Dor, P. Grosch's law revisited: CPU power and the cost of computation. *Communications of the ACM*, 28 (2), 142–151 (1985).

Gee, J., Hill, M., Pnevmatikatos, D. and Smith, A. Cache performance of the SPEC92 benchmark suite. *IEEE Micro*, 15 (4), 17–27 (1993).

Giladi, R. and Ahituv, N. SPEC as a performance evaluation measure. *Computer* 28 (8), 33–42 (1995).

Goyal, A. and Agerwala, T. Performance analysis of future shared storage systems. *IBM Journal of Research and Development*, 28 (1), 95–107 (1984).

Grama, A., Gupta, A. and Kumar, V. Isoefficiency: Measuring the scalability of parallel algorithms and architectures. *IEEE Parallel & Distribute Technology*, 12–21 (1993).

Gupta, A. and Kumar, V. Performance properties of large scale parallel systems. *Journal of Parallel and Distribute Computing*, 19, 234–244 (1993).

Gustafson, J. Reevaluating Amdahl's law. *Communications of the ACM*, 31 (5), 532–533 (1988).

Henning, J. L. SPEC CPU2000: Measuring CPU performance in the new millennium. *IEEE Computer*, July 2000, 28–34 (2000).

Hill, M. What is scalability? *Computer Architecture News*, 18 (4), 18–21 (1990).

Juang, J.-Y. and Wah, B. A contention-based bus-control scheme for multiprocessor systems. *IEEE Transactions on Computers*, 40 (9), 1046–1053 (1991).

Kumar, V. and Gupta, A. Analyzing scalability of parallel algorithms and architectures. *Journal of Parallel and Distributed Computing*, 22, 379–391 (1994).

Linder, D. and Harden, J. An adaptive and fault tolerant wormhole routing strategy for *k*-ary *n*-cubes. *IEEE Transactions on Computers*, 40 (1), 2–12 (1991).

Lubeck, O., Moore, J. and Mendez, R. A benchmark comparison of three supercomputers. *Computer*, 18 (12), 10–24 (1985).

Mirghafori, N., Jacoby, M. and Patterson, D. Truth in SPEC benchmarks. *Computer Architecture News*, 23 (5), 34–42 (1995).

Ni, L. and McKinely, P. A survey of wormhole routing techniques in direct networks. *IEEE Computer*, 62–76 (1993).

Patel, J. Performance of processor–memory interconnections for multiprocessor computer systems. *IEEE Transactions*, 28 (9), 296–304 (1981).

Reed, D. and Fujimoto, R. *Multicomputer Networks: Message-Based Parallel Processing*, MIT Press, 1987.

Sima, E., Fountain, T. and Kacsuk, P. *Advanced Computer Architectures: A Design Space Approach*, Addison Wesley, 1996.

Smith, J. Characterizing computer performance with a single number. *Communications of the ACM*, 31 (10), 1202–1206 (1988).

SPEC Newsletters, 1–10, 1989–1998.

Stone, H. *High Performance Computer Architecture*, 3rd edition, Addison Wesley, 1993.

Wilkinson, B. *Computer Architecture: Design and Performance*, 2nd edition, Prentice-Hall, 1996.

Yang, Q. and Zaky, S. Communication performance in multiple-bus systems. *IEEE Transactions on Computers*, 37 (7), 848–853 (1988).

Youn, H. and Chen, C. A comprehensive performance evaluation of crossbar networks. *IEEE Transactions on Parallel and Distribute Systems*, 4 (5), 481–489 (1993).

Zargham, M. *Computer Architecture: Single and Parallel Systems*, Prentice-Hall, 1996.

CHAPTER 4

Shared Memory Architecture

Shared memory systems form a major category of multiprocessors. In this category, all processors share a global memory. Communication between tasks running on different processors is performed through writing to and reading from the global memory. All interprocessor coordination and synchronization is also accomplished via the global memory. A shared memory computer system consists of a set of independent processors, a set of memory modules, and an interconnection network as shown in Figure 4.1.

Two main problems need to be addressed when designing a shared memory system: performance degradation due to contention, and coherence problems. Performance degradation might happen when multiple processors are trying to access the shared memory simultaneously. A typical design might use caches to solve the contention problem. However, having multiple copies of data, spread throughout the caches, might lead to a coherence problem. The copies in the caches are coherent if they are all equal to the same value. However, if one of the processors writes over the value of one of the copies, then the copy becomes inconsistent because it no longer equals the value of the other copies. In this chapter we study a variety of shared memory systems and their solutions of the cache coherence problem.

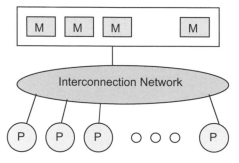

Figure 4.1 Shared memory systems.

Advanced Computer Architecture and Parallel Processing, by H. El-Rewini and M. Abd-El-Barr
ISBN 0-471-46740-5   Copyright © 2005 John Wiley & Sons, Inc.

4.1 CLASSIFICATION OF SHARED MEMORY SYSTEMS

The simplest shared memory system consists of one memory module (M) that can be accessed from two processors (P_1 and P_2); see Figure 4.2. Requests arrive at the memory module through its two ports. An arbitration unit within the memory module passes requests through to a memory controller. If the memory module is not busy and a single request arrives, then the arbitration unit passes that request to the memory controller and the request is satisfied. The module is placed in the busy state while a request is being serviced. If a new request arrives while the memory is busy servicing a previous request, the memory module sends a wait signal, through the memory controller, to the processor making the new request. In response, the requesting processor may hold its request on the line until the memory becomes free or it may repeat its request some time later. If the arbitration unit receives two requests, it selects one of them and passes it to the memory controller. Again, the denied request can be either held to be served next or it may be repeated some time later. Based on the interconnection network used, shared memory systems can be categorized in the following categories.

4.1.1 Uniform Memory Access (UMA)

In the UMA system a shared memory is accessible by all processors through an interconnection network in the same way a single processor accesses its memory. All processors have equal access time to any memory location. The interconnection network used in the UMA can be a single bus, multiple buses, or a crossbar switch. Because access to shared memory is balanced, these systems are also called SMP (symmetric multiprocessor) systems. Each processor has equal opportunity to read/write to memory, including equal access speed. Commercial examples of SMPs are Sun Microsystems multiprocessor servers and Silicon Graphics Inc. multiprocessor servers. A typical bus-structured SMP computer, as shown in Figure 4.3, attempts to reduce contention for the bus by fetching instructions and data directly from each individual cache, as much as possible. In the extreme, the bus contention might be reduced to zero after the cache memories are loaded from the global memory, because it is possible for all instructions and data to be completely contained within the cache. This memory organization is the most popular among

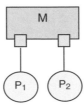

Figure 4.2 Shared memory via two ports.

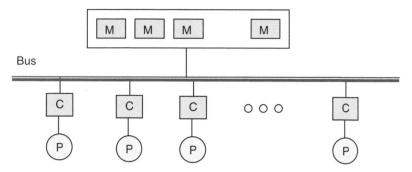

Figure 4.3 Bus-based UMA (SMP) shared memory system.

shared memory systems. Examples of this architecture are Sun Starfire servers, HP V series, and Compaq AlphaServer GS.

4.1.2 Nonuniform Memory Access (NUMA)

In the NUMA system, each processor has part of the shared memory attached. The memory has a single address space. Therefore, any processor could access any memory location directly using its real address. However, the access time to modules depends on the distance to the processor. This results in a nonuniform memory access time. A number of architectures are used to interconnect processors to memory modules in a NUMA. Among these are the tree and the hierarchical bus networks. Examples of NUMA architecture are BBN TC-2000, SGI Origin 3000, and Cray T3E. Figure 4.4 shows the NUMA system organization.

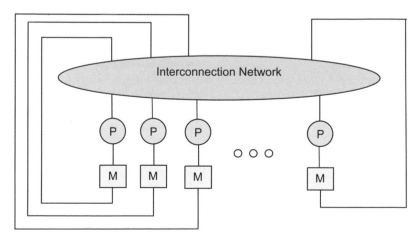

Figure 4.4 NUMA shared memory system.

4.1.3   Cache-Only Memory Architecture (COMA)

Similar to the NUMA, each processor has part of the shared memory in the COMA. However, in this case the shared memory consists of cache memory. A COMA system requires that data be migrated to the processor requesting it. There is no memory hierarchy and the address space is made of all the caches. There is a cache directory (D) that helps in remote cache access. The Kendall Square Research's KSR-1 machine is an example of such architecture. Figure 4.5 shows the organization of COMA.

4.2   BUS-BASED SYMMETRIC MULTIPROCESSORS

Shared memory systems can be designed using bus-based or switch-based interconnection networks. The simplest network for shared memory systems is the bus. The bus/cache architecture alleviates the need for expensive multiported memories and interface circuitry as well as the need to adopt a message-passing paradigm when developing application software. However, the bus may get saturated if multiple processors are trying to access the shared memory (via the bus) simultaneously. A typical bus-based design uses caches to solve the bus contention problem. High-speed caches connected to each processor on one side and the bus on the other side mean that local copies of instructions and data can be supplied at the highest possible rate. If the local processor finds all of its instructions and data in the local cache, we say the hit rate is 100%. The miss rate of a cache is the fraction of the references that cannot be satisfied by the cache, and so must be copied from the global memory, across the bus, into the cache, and then passed on to the local processor. One of the goals of the cache is to maintain a high hit rate, or low miss rate under high processor loads. A high hit rate means the processors are not using the bus as much. Hit rates are determined by a number of factors, ranging from the application programs being run to the manner in which cache hardware is implemented.

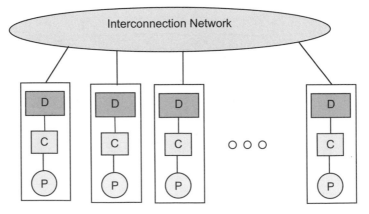

Figure 4.5   COMA shared memory system.

A processor goes through a duty cycle, where it executes instructions a certain number of times per clock cycle. Typically, individual processors execute less than one instruction per cycle, thus reducing the number of times it needs to access memory. Subscalar processors execute less than one instruction per cycle, and superscalar processors execute more than one instruction per cycle. In any case, we want to minimize the number of times each local processor tries to use the central bus. Otherwise, processor speed will be limited by bus bandwidth.

We define the variables for hit rate, number of processors, processor speed, bus speed, and processor duty cycle rates as follows:

- N = number of processors;
- h = hit rate of each cache, assumed to be the same for all caches;
- $(1 - h)$ = miss rate of all caches;
- B = bandwidth of the bus, measured in cycles/second;
- I = processor duty cycle, assumed to be identical for all processors, in fetches/ cycle; and
- V = peak processor speed, in fetches/second.

The effective bandwidth of the bus is BI fetches/second. If each processor is running at a speed of V, then misses are being generated at a rate of $V(1 - h)$. For an N-processor system, misses are simultaneously being generated at a rate of $N(1 - h)V$. This leads to saturation of the bus when N processors simultaneously try to access the bus. That is, $N(1 - h)V \leq BI$. The maximum number of processors with cache memories that the bus can support is given by the relation,

$$N \leq \frac{BI}{(1 - h)V}$$

Example 1 Suppose a shared memory system is constructed from processors that can execute $V = 107$ instructions/s and the processor duty cycle $I = 1$. The caches are designed to support a hit rate of 97%, and the bus supports a peak bandwidth of $B = 106$ cycles/s. Then, $(1 - h) = 0.03$, and the maximum number of processors N is $N \leq 106/(0.03 * 107) = 3.33$. Thus, the system we have in mind can support only three processors!

We might ask what hit rate is needed to support a 30-processor system. In this case, $h = 1 - BI/NV = 1 - (106(1))/((30)(107)) = 1 - 1/300$, so for the system we have in mind, $h = 0.9967$. Increasing h by 2.8% results in supporting a factor of ten more processors.

4.3 BASIC CACHE COHERENCY METHODS

Multiple copies of data, spread throughout the caches, lead to a coherence problem among the caches. The copies in the caches are coherent if they all equal the same value. However, if one of the processors writes over the value of one of the copies, then the copy becomes inconsistent because it no longer equals the value of the other copies. If data are allowed to become inconsistent (incoherent), incorrect results will be propagated through the system, leading to incorrect final results. Cache coherence algorithms are needed to maintain a level of consistency throughout the parallel system.

4.3.1 Cache–Memory Coherence

In a single cache system, coherence between memory and the cache is maintained using one of two policies: (1) write-through, and (2) write-back. When a task running on a processor P requests the data in memory location X, for example, the contents of X are copied to the cache, where it is passed on to P. When P updates the value of X in the cache, the other copy in memory also needs to be updated in order to maintain consistency. In write-through, the memory is updated every time the cache is updated, while in write-back, the memory is updated only when the block in the cache is being replaced. Table 4.1 shows the write-through versus write-back policies.

4.3.2 Cache–Cache Coherence

In multiprocessing system, when a task running on processor P requests the data in global memory location X, for example, the contents of X are copied to processor P's local cache, where it is passed on to P. Now, suppose processor Q also accesses X. What happens if Q wants to write a new value over the old value of X?

There are two fundamental cache coherence policies: (1) write-invalidate, and (2) write-update. Write-invalidate maintains consistency by reading from local caches until a write occurs. When any processor updates the value of X through a write, posting a dirty bit for X invalidates all other copies. For example, processor Q invalidates all other copies of X when it writes a new value into its cache. This sets the dirty bit for X. Q can continue to change X without further notifications to other caches because Q has the only valid copy of X. However, when processor P wants to read X, it must wait until X is updated and the dirty bit is cleared. Write-update maintains consistency by immediately updating all copies in all caches. All dirty bits are set during each write operation. After all copies have been updated, all

TABLE 4.1 Write-Through vs. Write-Back

Serial	Event	Write-Through		Write-Back	
		Memory	Cache	Memory	Cache
1		X		X	
2	P reads X	X	X	X	X
3	P updates X	X′	X′	X	X′

TABLE 4.2   **Write-Update vs. Write-Invalidate**

Serial	Event	Write-Update		Write-Invalidate	
		P's Cache	Q's Cache	P's Cache	Q's Cache
1	P reads X	X		X	
2	Q reads X	X	X	X	X
3	Q updates X	X'	X'	INV	X'
4	Q updates X'	X''	X''	INV	X''

dirty bits are cleared. Table 4.2 shows the write-update versus write-invalidate policies.

4.3.3 Shared Memory System Coherence

The four combinations to maintain coherence among all caches and global memory are:

- Write-update and write-through;
- Write-update and write-back;
- Write-invalidate and write-through; and
- Write-invalidate and write-back.

If we permit a write-update and write-through directly on global memory location X, the bus would start to get busy and ultimately all processors would be idle while waiting for writes to complete. In write-update and write-back, only copies in all caches are updated. On the contrary, if the write is limited to the copy of X in cache Q, the caches become inconsistent on X. Setting the dirty bit prevents the spread of inconsistent values of X, but at some point, the inconsistent copies must be updated.

4.4 SNOOPING PROTOCOLS

Snooping protocols are based on watching bus activities and carry out the appropriate coherency commands when necessary. Global memory is moved in blocks, and each block has a state associated with it, which determines what happens to the entire contents of the block. The state of a block might change as a result of the operations Read-Miss, Read-Hit, Write-Miss, and Write-Hit. A cache miss means that the requested block is not in the cache or it is in the cache but has been invalidated. Snooping protocols differ in whether they update or invalidate shared copies in remote caches in case of a write operation. They also differ as to where to obtain the new data in the case of a cache miss. In what follows we go over some examples of snooping protocols that maintain cache coherence.

TABLE 4.3 Write-Invalidate Write-Through Protocol

State	Description
Valid [VALID]	The copy is consistent with global memory.
Invalid [INV]	The copy is inconsistent.

Event	Actions
Read-Hit	Use the local copy from the cache.
Read-Miss	Fetch a copy from global memory. Set the state of this copy to Valid.
Write-Hit	Perform the write locally. Broadcast an Invalid command to all caches. Update the global memory.
Write-Miss	Get a copy from global memory. Broadcast an invalid command to all caches. Update the global memory. Update the local copy and set its state to Valid.
Block replacement	Since memory is always consistent, no write-back is needed when a block is replaced.

4.4.1 Write-Invalidate and Write-Through

In this simple protocol the memory is always consistent with the most recently updated cache copy. Multiple processors can read block copies from main memory safely until one processor updates its copy. At this time, all cache copies are invalidated and the memory is updated to remain consistent. The block states and protocol are summarized in Table 4.3.

Example 2 Consider a bus-based shared memory with two processors P and Q as shown in Figure 4.6. Let us see how the cache coherence is maintained using Write-Invalidate Write-Through protocol. Assume that that X in memory was originally set to 5 and the following operations were performed in the order given: (1) P reads X; (2) Q reads X; (3) Q updates X; (4) Q reads X; (5) Q updates X; (6) P updates X; (7) Q reads X. Table 4.4 shows the contents of memory and the

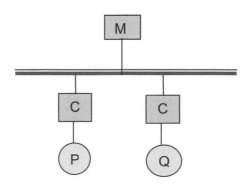

Figure 4.6 A bus-based shared memory system with two processors P and Q.

TABLE 4.4   Example 2 (Write-Invalidate Write-Through)

Serial	Event	Memory Location X	P's Cache Location X	State	Q's Cache Location X	State
0	Original value	5				
1	P reads X (Read-Miss)	5	5	VALID		
2	Q reads X (Read-Miss)	5	5	VALID	5	VALID
3	Q updates X (Write-Hit)	10	5	INV	10	VALID
4	Q reads X (Read-Hit)	10	5	INV	10	VALID
5	Q updates X (Write-Hit)	15	5	INV	15	VALID
6	P updates X (Write-Miss)	20	20	VALID	15	INV
7	Q reads X (Read-Miss)	20	20	VALID	20	VALID

two caches after the execution of each operation when Write-Invalidate Write-Through was used for cache coherence. The table also shows the state of the block containing X in P's cache and Q's cache.

4.4.2   Write-Invalidate and Write-Back (Ownership Protocol)

In this protocol a valid block can be owned by memory and shared in multiple caches that can contain only the shared copies of the block. Multiple processors can safely read these blocks from their caches until one processor updates its copy. At this time, the writer becomes the only owner of the valid block and all other copies are invalidated. The block states and protocol are summarized in Table 4.5.

Example 3   Consider the shared memory system of Figure 4.6 and the following operations: (1) P reads X; (2) Q reads X; (3) Q updates X; (4) Q reads X; (5) Q updates X; (6) P updates X; (7) Q reads X. Table 4.6 shows the contents of memory and the two caches after the execution of each operation when Write-Invalidate Write-Back was used for cache coherence. The table also shows the state of the block containing X in P's cache and Q's cache.

4.4.3   Write-Once

This write-invalidate protocol, which was proposed by Goodman in 1983, uses a combination of write-through and write-back. Write-through is used the very first

TABLE 4.5 **Write-Invalidate Write-Back Protocol**

State	Description
Shared (Read-Only) [RO]	Data is valid and can be read safely. Multiple copies can be in this state.
Exclusive (Read-Write) [RW]	Only one valid cache copy exists and can be read from and written to safely. Copies in other caches are invalid.
Invalid [INV]	The copy is inconsistent.

Event	Action
Read-Hit	Use the local copy from the cache.
Read-Miss	If no Exclusive (Read-Write) copy exists, then supply a copy from global memory. Set the state of this copy to Shared (Read-Only). If an Exclusive (Read-Write) copy exists, make a copy from the cache that set the state to Exclusive (Read-Write), update global memory and local cache with the copy. Set the state to Shared (Read-Only) in both caches.
Write-Hit	If the copy is Exclusive (Read-Write), perform the write locally. If the state is Shared (Read-Only), then broadcast an Invalid to all caches. Set the state to Exclusive (Read-Write).
Write-Miss	Get a copy from either a cache with an Exclusive (Read-Write) copy, or from global memory itself. Broadcast an Invalid command to all caches. Update the local copy and set its state to Exclusive (Read-Write).
Block replacement	If a copy is in an Exclusive (Read-Write) state, it has to be written back to main memory if the block is being replaced. If the copy is in Invalid or Shared (Read-Only) states, no write-back is needed when a block is replaced.

time a block is written. Subsequent writes are performed using write-back. The block states and protocol are summarized in Table 4.7.

Example 4   Consider the shared memory system of Figure 4.6 and the following operations: (1) P reads X; (2) Q reads X; (3) Q updates X; (4) Q reads X; (5) Q updates X; (6) P updates X; (7) Q reads X. Table 4.8 shows the contents of memory and the two caches after the execution of each operation when Write-Once was used for cache coherence. The table also shows the state of the block containing X in P's cache and Q's cache.

4.4.4 Write-Update and Partial Write-Through

In this protocol an update to one cache is written to memory at the same time it is broadcast to other caches sharing the updated block. These caches snoop on the bus

TABLE 4.6   Example 3 (Write-Invalidate Write-Back)

		Memory	P's Cache		Q's Cache	
Serial	Event	Location X	Location X	State	Location X	State
0	Original value	5				
1	P reads X (Read-Miss)	5	5	RO		
2	Q reads X (Read-Miss)	5	5	RO	5	RO
3	Q updates X (Write-Hit)	5	5	INV	10	RW
4	Q reads X (Read-Hit)	5	5	INV	10	RW
5	Q updates X (Write-Hit)	5	5	INV	15	RW
6	P updates X (Writc-Miss)	5	20	RW	15	INV
7	Q reads X (Read-Miss)	20	20	RO	20	RO

and perform updates to their local copies. There is also a special bus line, which is asserted to indicate that at least one other cache is sharing the block. The block states and protocol are summarized in Table 4.9.

Example 5   Consider the shared memory system of Figure 4.6 and the following operations: (1) P reads X; (2) P updates X; (3) Q reads X; (4) Q updates X; (5) Q reads X; (6) Block X is replaced in P's cachc; (7) Q updates X; (8) P updates X. Table 4.10 shows the contents of memory and the two caches after the execution of each operation when Write-Update Partial Write-Through was used for cache coherence. The table also shows the state of the block containing X in P's cache and Q's cache.

4.4.5   Write-Update and Write-Back

This protocol is similar to the previous one except that instead of writing through to the memory whenever a shared block is updated, memory updates are done only when the block is being replaced. The block states and protocol are summarized in Table 4.11.

Example 6   Consider the shared memory system of Figure 4.6 and the following operations: (1) P reads X; (2) P updates X; (3) Q reads X; (4) Q updates X; (5) Q reads X; (6) Block X is replaced in Q's cache; (7) P updates X; (8) Q updates X. Table 4.12 shows the contents of memory and the two caches after the execution

TABLE 4.7   Write-Once Protocol

State	Description
Invalid [INV]	The copy is inconsistent.
Valid [VALID]	The copy is consistent with global memory.
Reserved [RES]	Data have been written exactly once and the copy is consistent with global memory. There is only one copy of the global memory block in one local cache.
Dirty [DIRTY]	Data have been updated more than once and there is only one copy in one local cache. When a copy is dirty, it must be written back to global memory.

Event	Actions
Read-Hit	Use the local copy from the cache.
Read-Miss	If no Dirty copy exists, then supply a copy from global memory. Set the state of this copy to Valid. If a dirty copy exists, make a copy from the cache that set the state to Dirty, update global memory and local cache with the copy. Set the state to VALID in both caches.
Write-Hit	If the copy is Dirty or Reserved, perform the write locally, and set the state to Dirty. If the state is Valid, then broadcast an Invalid command to all caches. Update the global memory and set the state to Reserved.
Write-Miss	Get a copy from either a cache with a Dirty copy or from global memory itself. Broadcast an Invalid command to all caches. Update the local copy and set its state to Dirty.
Block replacement	If a copy is in a Dirty state, it has to be written back to main memory if the block is being replaced. If the copy is in Valid, Reserved, or Invalid states, no write-back is needed when a block is replaced.

TABLE 4.8   Example 4 (Write-Once Protocol)

Serial	Event	Memory Location X	P's Cache Location X	State	Q's Cache Location X	State
0	Original value	5				
1	P reads X (Read-Miss)	5	5	VALID		
2	Q reads X (Read-Miss)	5	5	VALID	5	VALID
3	Q updates X (Write-Hit)	10	5	INV	10	RES
4	Q reads X (Read-Hit)	10	5	INV	10	RES
5	Q updates X (Write-Hit)	10	5	INV	15	DIRTY
6	P updates X (Write-Miss)	10	20	DIRTY	15	INV
7	Q reads X (Read-Miss)	20	20	VALID	20	VALID

TABLE 4.9   Write-Update Partial Write-Through Protocol

State	Description
Valid Exclusive [VAL-X]	This is the only cache copy and is consistent with global memory.
Shared [SHARE]	There are multiple cache copies shared. All copies are consistent with memory.
Dirty [DIRTY]	This copy is not shared by other caches and has been updated. It is not consistent with global memory. (Copy ownership.)

Event	Action
Read-Hit	Use the local copy from the cache. State does not change.
Read-Miss	If no other cache copy exists, then supply a copy from global memory. Set the state of this copy to Valid Exclusive. If a cache copy exists, make a copy from the cache. Set the state to Shared in both caches. If the cache copy was in a Dirty state, the value must also be written to memory.
Write-Hit	Perform the write locally and set the state to Dirty. If the state is Shared, then broadcast data to memory and to all caches and set the state to Shared. If other caches no longer share the block, the state changes from Shared to Valid Exclusive.
Write-Miss	The block copy comes from either another cache or from global memory. If the block comes from another cache, perform the update and update all other caches that share the block and global memory. Set the state to Shared. If the copy comes from memory, perform the write and set the state to Dirty.
Block replacement	If a copy is in a Dirty state, it has to be written back to main memory if the block is being replaced. If the copy is in Valid Exclusive or Shared states, no write-back is needed when a block is replaced.

of each operation when Write-Update Write-Back was used for cache coherence. The table also shows the state of the block containing X in P's cache and Q's cache.

4.5   DIRECTORY BASED PROTOCOLS

Owing to the nature of some interconnection networks and the size of the shared memory system, updating or invalidating caches using snoopy protocols might become unpractical. For example, when a multistage network is used to build a large shared memory system, the broadcasting techniques used in the snoopy protocols becomes very expensive. In such situations, coherence commands need to be sent to only those caches that might be affected by an update. This is the idea behind directory-based protocols. Cache coherence protocols that somehow store information on where copies of blocks reside are called directory schemes. A directory is a data structure that maintains information on the processors that share a memory block and on its state. The information maintained in the directory could

TABLE 4.10   Example 5 (Write-Update Partial Write-Through)

Serial	Event	Memory Location X	P's Cache Location X	P's Cache State	Q's Cache Location X	Q's Cache State
0	Original value	5				
1	P reads X (Read-Miss)	5	5	VAL-X		
2	P updates X (Write-Hit)	5	10	DIRTY		
3	Q reads X (Read-Miss)	10	10	SHARE	10	SHARE
4	Q updates X (Write-Hit)	15	15	SHARE	15	SHARE
5	Q reads X (Read-Hit)	15	15	SHARE	15	SHARE
6	Block X is replaced in P's cache (Replace)	15	–	–	15	VAL-X
7	Q updates X (Write-Hit)	15	–	–	20	DIRTY
8	P updates X (Write-Miss)	25	25	SHARE	25	SHARE

be either centralized or distributed. A Central directory maintains information about all blocks in a central data structure. While Central directory includes everything in one location, it becomes a bottleneck and suffers from large search time. To alleviate this problem, the same information can be handled in a distributed fashion by allowing each memory module to maintain a separate directory. In a distributed directory, the entry associated with a memory block has only one pointer one of the cache that requested the block.

4.5.1   Protocol Categorization

A directory entry for each block of data should contain a number of pointers to specify the locations of copies of the block. Each entry might also contain a dirty bit to specify whether or not a unique cache has permission to write this memory block. Most directory-based protocols can be categorized under three categories: *full-map* directories, *limited* directories, and *chained* directories.

Full-Map Directories   In a full-map setting, each directory entry contains N pointers, where N is the number of processors. Therefore, there could be N cached copies of a particular block shared by all processors. For every memory block, an N-bit vector is maintained, where N equals the number of processors in

TABLE 4.11   Write-Update Write-Back Protocol

State	Description
Valid Exclusive [VAL-X]	This is the only cache copy and is consistent with global memory.
Shared Clean [SH-CLN]	There are multiple cache copies shared.
Shared Dirty [SH-DRT]	There are multiple shared cache copies. This is the last one being updated. (Ownership.)
Dirty [DIRTY]	This copy is not shared by other caches and has been updated. It is not consistent with global memory. (Ownership.)

Event	Action
Read-Hit	Use the local copy from the cache. State does not change.
Read-Miss	If no other cache copy exists, then supply a copy from global memory. Set the state of this copy to Valid Exclusive. If a cache copy exists, make a copy from the cache. Set the state to Shared Clean. If the supplying cache copy was in a Valid Exclusion or Shared Clean, its new state becomes Shared Clean. If the supplying cache copy was in a Dirty or Shared Dirty state, its new state becomes Shared Dirty.
Write-Hit	If the sate was Valid Exclusive or Dirty, perform the write locally and set the state to Dirty. If the state is Shared Clean or Shared Dirty, perform update and change state to Shared Dirty. Broadcast the updated block to all other caches. These caches snoop the bus and update their copies and set their state to Shared Clean.
Write-Miss	The block copy comes from either another cache or from global memory. If the block comes from another cache, perform the update, set the state to Shared Dirty, and broadcast the updated block to all other caches. Other caches snoop the bus, update their copies, and change their state to Shared Clean. If the copy comes from memory, perform the write and set the state to Dirty.
Block replacement	If a copy is in a Dirty or Shared Dirty state, it has to be written back to main memory if the block is being replaced. If the copy is in Valid Exclusive, no write back is needed when a block is replaced.

the shared memory system. Each bit in the vector corresponds to one processor. If the ith bit is set to one, it means that processor i has a copy of this block in its cache. Figure 4.7 illustrates the fully mapped scheme. In the figure the vector associated with block X in memory indicates that X is in Cache C0 and Cache C2. Clearly the space is not utilized efficiently in this scheme, in particular if not many processors share the same block.

Limited Directories   Limited directories have a fixed number of pointers per directory entry regardless of the number of processors. Restricting the number of

TABLE 4.12   Example 6 (Write-Update Write-Back)

Serial	Event	Memory Location X	P's Cache Location X	P's Cache State	Q's Cache Location X	Q's Cache State
0	Original value	5				
1	P reads X (Read-Miss)	5	5	VAL-X		
2	P updates X (Write-Hit)	5	10	DIRTY		
3	Q reads X (Read-Miss)	5	10	SH-DRT	10	SH-CLN
4	Q updates X (Write-Hit)	5	15	SH-CLN	15	SH-DRT
5	Q reads X (Read-Hit)	5	15	SH-CLN	15	SH-DRT
6	Block X is replaced in Q's cache (Replace)	15	15	VAL-X	–	–
7	P updates X (Write-Hit)	15	20	DIRTY	–	–
8	Q updates X (Write-Miss)	15	25	SH-CLN	25	SH-DRT

simultaneously cached copies of any block should solve the directory size problem that might exist in full-map directories. Figure 4.8 illustrates the limited directory scheme. In this example, the number of copies that can be shared is restricted to two. This is why the vector associated with block X in memory has only two locations. The vector indicates that X is in Cache C0 and Cache C2.

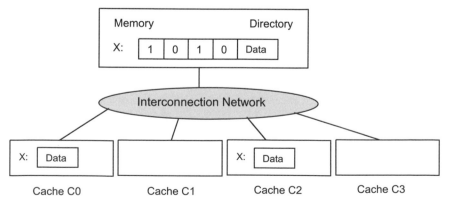

Figure 4.7   Fully mapped directory.

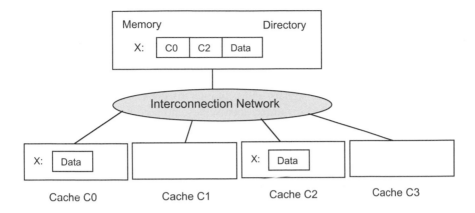

Figure 4.8 Limited directory (maximum sharing = 2).

Chained Directories Chained directories emulate full-map by distributing the directory among the caches. They are designed to solve the directory size problem without restricting the number of shared block copies. Chained directories keep track of shared copies of a particular block by maintaining a chain of directory pointers. Figure 4.9 shows that the directory entry associated with X has a pointer to Cache C2, which in turn has a pointer to Cache C0. That is, block X exists in the two Caches C0 and Cache C2. The pointer from Cache C0 is pointing to terminator (CT), indicating the end of the list.

4.5.2 Invalidate Protocols

Centralized Directory Invalidate When a write request is issued, the central directory is used to determine which processors have a copy of the block.

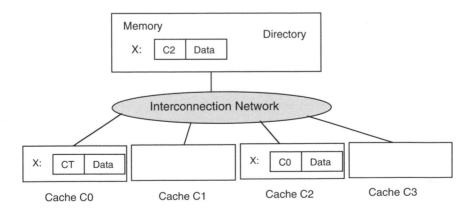

Figure 4.9 Chained directory.

Invalidating signals and a pointer to the requesting processor are forwarded to all processors that have a copy of the block. Each invalidated cache sends an acknowledgment to the requesting processor. After the invalidation is complete, only the writing processor will have a cache with a copy of the block. Figure 4.10 shows a write-miss request from Cache C3. Upon receiving the request, the memory sends invalidating signals and a pointer to the Cache C3 to Cache C0 and Cache C2. These caches invalidate themselves and send invalidation acknowledgment to Cache C3. After the invalidation is done, Cache C3 will have exclusive read-write access to X.

Scalable Coherent Interface (SCI) The scalable coherent interface (SCI) protocols are based on a doubly linked list of distributed directories. Each cached block is entered into a list of processors sharing that block. For every block address, the memory and cache entries have additional tag bits. Part of the memory tag identifies the first processor in the sharing list (the head). Part of each cache tag identifies the previous and following sharing list entries. Without counting the number of bits needed in the local caches for the pointers, the directory size in memory equals the number of memory blocks times $\log_2$ (number of caches).

Initially memory is in the uncached state and cached copies are invalid. A read request is directed from a processor to the memory controller. The requested data is returned to the requester's cache and its entry state is changed from invalid to the head state. This changes the memory state from uncached to cached. When a new requester directs its read request to memory, the memory returns a pointer to the head. A cache-to-cache read request (called Prepend) is sent from the requester to the head cache. On receiving the request, the head cache sets its backward pointer to point to the requester's cache. The requested data is returned to the requester's cache and its entry state is changed to the head state. The head of the list has the authority to purge other entries in the list to obtain an exclusive (read-write) entry. The initial transaction to the second sharing list entry purges that entry and

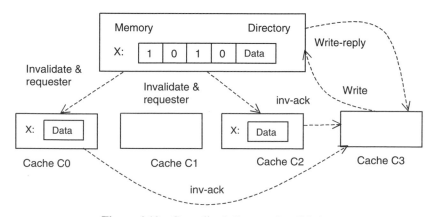

Figure 4.10 Centralized directory invalidation.

returns its forward pointer. The forward pointer is used to purge the next entry and so on. Entries can also delete themselves from the list when they are needed to cache other block addresses. Figure 4.11 shows the sharing list addition and removal operations in SCI.

Stanford Distributed Directory (SDD) The Stanford distributed directory (SDD) protocol is based on a singly linked list of distributed directories. Similar to the SCI protocol, memory points to the head of the sharing list. Each processor points only to its predecessor. The sharing list additions and removals are handled differently from the SCI protocol.

On a read-miss, a new requester sends a read-miss message to memory. The memory updates its head pointers to point to the requester and send a read-miss-forward signal to the old head. On receiving the request, the old head returns the requested data along with its address as a read-miss-reply. When the reply is received, at the requester's cache, the data is copied and the pointer is made to point to the old head.

On a write-miss, a requester sends a write-miss message to memory. The memory updates its head pointers to point to the requester and sends a write-miss-forward signal to the old head. The old head invalidates itself, returns the requested data

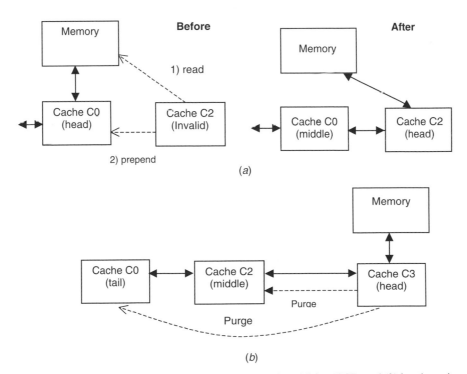

Figure 4.11 Scalable coherent interface (*a*) sharing list addition (SCI); and (*b*) head purging other entries (SCI).

as a write-miss-reply-data signal, and send a write-miss-forward to the next cache in the list. When the next cache receives the write-miss-forward signal, it invalidates itself and sends a write-miss-forward to the next cache in the list. When the write-miss-forward signal is received by the tail or by a cache that no longer has a copy of the block, a write-miss-reply is sent to the requester. The write is complete when the requester receives both write-miss-reply-data and write-miss-reply. Figure 4.12 shows the sharing list addition and removal operations in SDD.

4.6 SHARED MEMORY PROGRAMMING

Shared memory parallel programming is perhaps the easiest model to understand because of its similarity with operating systems programming and general multiprogramming. Shared memory programming is done through some extensions to existing programming languages, operating systems, and code libraries. In a shared memory parallel program, there must exist three main programming constructs: (1) task creation, (2) communication, and (3) synchronization.

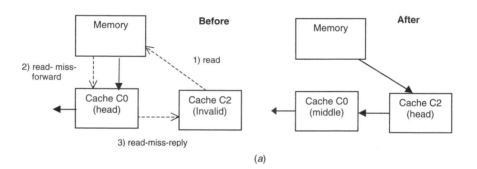

(a)

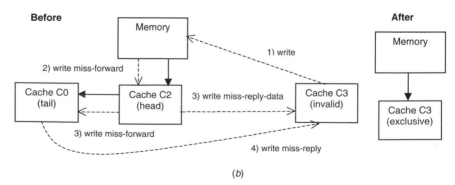

(b)

Figure 4.12 Stanford distributed directory (*a*) sharing list addition (SDD); and (*b*) write miss sharing list removal (SDD).

4.6.1 Task Creation

At the large-grained level, a shared memory system can provide traditional time-sharing. Each time a new process is initiated, idle processors are supplied to run the new process. If the system is loaded, the processor with least amount of work is assigned the new process. These large-grained processes are often called heavy weight tasks because of their high overhead. A heavy weight task in a multitasking system like UNIX consists of page tables, memory, and file description in addition to program code and data. These tasks are created in UNIX by invocation of fork, exec, and other related UNIX commands. This level is best suited for heterogeneous tasks.

At the fine-grained level, lightweight processes makes parallelism within a single application practical, where it is best suited for homogeneous tasks. At this level, an application is a series of fork-join constructs. This pattern of task creation is called the supervisor–workers model, as shown in Figure 4.13.

4.6.2 Communication

In general, the address space on an executing process has three segments called the text, data, and stack. The text is where the binary code to be executed is stored; the data segment is where the program's data are stored; and the stack is where activation records and dynamic data are stored. The data and stack segments expand and contract as the program executes. Therefore, a gap is purposely left in between the data and stack segments. Serial processes are assumed to be mutually independent and do not share addresses. The code of each serial process is allowed to access data in its own data and stack segments only. A parallel process is similar to the serial process plus an additional shared data segment. This shared area is allowed to grow and is placed in the gap between private data and stack segments. Figure 4.14 shows the difference between a serial process and a parallel process.

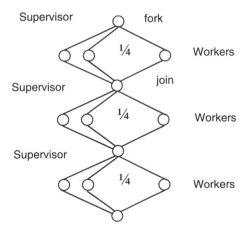

Figure 4.13 Supervisor–workers model used in most parallel applications on shared memory systems.

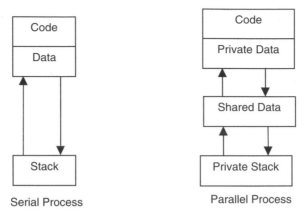

Figure 4.14 Serial process vs. parallel process.

Communication among parallel processes can be performed by writing to and reading from shared variables in the shared data segments as shown in Figure 4.15.

4.6.3 Synchronization

Synchronization is needed to protect shared variables by ensuring that they are accessed by only one process at a given time (mutual exclusion). They can also be used to coordinate the execution of parallel processes and synchronize at certain points in execution. There are two main synchronization constructs in shared memory systems: (1) locks and (2) barriers. Figure 4.16a shows three parallel processes using locks to ensure mutual exclusion. Process P2 has to wait until P1 unlocks the critical section; similarly P3 has to wait until P2 issues the unlock statement. In Figure 4.16b, P3 and P1 reach their barrier statement before P2, and

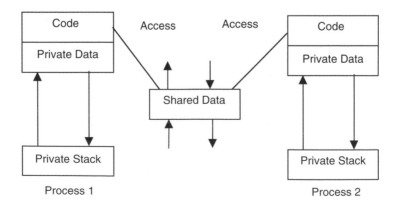

Figure 4.15 Two parallel processes communicate using the shared data segment.

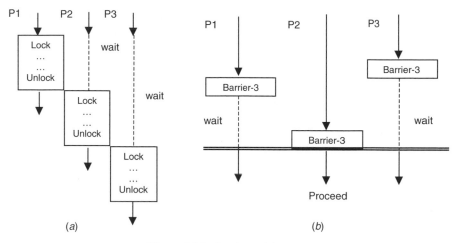

Figure 4.16 Locks and barriers.

they have to wait until P2 reaches its barrier. When all three reach the barrier statement, they all can proceed.

4.7 CHAPTER SUMMARY

A shared memory system is made of multiple processors and memory modules that are connected via some interconnection network. Shared memory multiprocessors are usually bus-based or switch-based. In all cases, each processor has equal access to the global memory shared by all processors. Communication among processors is achieved by writing to and reading from memory. Synchronization among processors is achieved using locks and barriers. The main challenges of shared memory systems are performance degradation due to contention and cache coherence problems. The performance of a shared memory system becomes an issue when the interconnection network connecting the processors to global memory becomes a bottleneck. Local caches are typically used to alleviate the bottleneck problem. However, scalability remains the main drawback of a shared memory system. The introduction of caches has created a consistency problem among caches and between memory and caches. Cache coherence schemes can be categorized into two main categories: snooping protocols and directory-based protocols. Snooping protocols are based on watching bus activities and carry out the appropriate coherency commands when necessary. In cases when the broadcasting techniques used in snooping protocols are unpractical, coherence commands need to be sent to only those caches that might be affected by an update. This is the idea behind directory-based protocols. Cache coherence protocols that somehow store information on where copies of blocks reside are called directory schemes.

The programming model in shared memory systems has proven to be easier to program compared to message passing systems. Therefore distributed-shared memory architecture began to appear in systems like the SGI Origin2000, and others. In such systems, memory is physically distributed; for example, the hardware architecture follows the message passing school of design (see Chapter 5), but the programming model follows the shared memory school of thought. In effect, software covers up the hardware. As far as a programmer is concerned, the architecture looks and behaves like a shared memory machine, but a message passing architecture lives underneath the software.

PROBLEMS

1. Explain mutual exclusion and its relation to the cache coherence problem.
2. Discuss the advantages and disadvantages of using the following interconnection networks in the design of a shared memory system.
   (a) Bus;
   (b) Crossbar switch;
   (c) Multistage network.
3. Some machines provide special hardware instructions that allows one to swap the contents of two words in one memory cycle. Show how the swap instruction can be used to implement mutual exclusion.
4. Consider a bus-based shared memory multiprocessor system. It is constructed using processors with speed of 10^6 instructions/s, and a bus with a peak bandwidth of 10^5 fetches/s. The caches are designed to support a hit rate of 90%.
   (a) What is the maximum number of processors that can be supported by this system?
   (b) What hit rate is needed to support a 20-processor system?
5. Determine the maximum speedup of a single-bus multiprocessor system having N processors if each processor uses the bus for a fraction f of every cycle.
6. Consider the two tasks T_0 and T_1 that are executed in parallel on processors P_1 and P_2, respectively, in a shared memory system. Assume that the print statement is uninterruptible, and A, B, C, D are initialized to 0.

T_0	T_1
A = 1;	C = 3;
B = 2;	D = 4;
Print A, D;	Print B, C;

Show four different possible outputs of the parallel execution of these two tasks.

7. Consider a bus-based shared memory system consisting of three processors. The shared memory is divided into four blocks x, y, z, w. Each processor has a cache that can fit only one block at any given time. Each block can be in one of two states: *valid* (*V*) or *invalid* (*I*). Assume that caches are initially flushed (empty) and that the contents of the memory are as follows:

Memory block	x	y	z	w
Contents	10	30	80	20

Consider, the following sequence of memory access events *given in order*:

```
1) P1:   Read(x),    2) P2:   Read(x),   3) P3:   Read(x),
4) P1:   x = x + 25, 5) P1:   Read(z),   6) P2:   Read(x),
7) P3: x = 15, 8) P1: z = z + 1
```

Show the contents of the caches and memory and the state of cache blocks after each of the above operations in the following cases: (1) write-through and write-invalidate and (2) write-back and write-invalidate.

8. Repeat Problem 7 assuming the following:

   (a) Each processor has a cache that has four block frames labeled 0, 1, 2, 3. The shared memory is divided into eight blocks 0, 1, ... , 7. Assume that the contents of the shared memory are as follows:

Block number	0	1	2	3	4	5	6	7
Contents	10	30	80	20	70	60	50	40

   (b) To maintain cache coherence, the system uses the *write-once protocol*.

   (c) Memory access events are as follows:

   ```
   1) P1: Read(0), 2) P2: Read(0), 3) P3: Read(0),
   4) P2: Read(2), 5) P1: Write(15 in 0),
   6) P3: Read(2), 7) P1: Write(25 in 0), 8) P1: Read(2),
   9) P3: Write(85 in 2), 10) P2: Read(7),
   11) P3: Read(7), 12) P1: Read(7)
   ```

   (Note that Write(x in i) means the value x is written in block i.)

REFERENCES

Bhuyan, L. N. (ed.) Interconnection networks for parallel and distributed processing. *Computer* (Special issue), 20 (6), 9–75 (1987).

Bhuyan, L. N., Yang, Q. and Agrawal, D. P. Performance of multiprocessor interconnection networks. *Computer*, 22 (2), 25–37 (1989).

Dubois, M. and Thakkar, S. Cache architectures in tightly coupled multiprocessors. *Computer*, 23 (6), 9–85 (1990).

Duncan, R. A survey of parallel computer architectures. *Computer*, 23 (2), 5–16 (1990).

El-Rewini, H. and Lewis, T. G. *Distributed and Parallel Computing*, Manning and Prentice Hall, 1998.

Flynn, M. *Computer Architecture: Pipelined and Parallel Processor Design*, Jones and Bartlett, 1995.

Goodman, J. R. Using cache memory to reduce processor–memory traffic. *Proceedings 10th Annual Symposium on Computer Architecture*, June 1983, pp. 124–131.

Hennessy, J. and Patterson, D. *Computer Architecture: A Quantitative Approach*, Morgan Kaufmann, 1990.

Hwang, K. and Briggs, F. A. *Computer Architecture and Parallel Processing*, McGraw-Hill, 1984.

Ibbett, R. N. and Topham, N. P. *Architecture of High Performance Computers II*, Springer-Verlag, 1989.

Lewis, T. G. and El-Rewini, H. *Introduction To Parallel Computing*, Prentice-Hall, 1992.

Stone, H. *High-Performance Computer Architecture*, 3rd edition, Addison-Wesley, 1993.

CHAPTER 5

Message Passing Architecture

Message passing systems provide alternative methods for communication and movement of data among multiprocessors (compared to shared memory multiprocessor systems). A *message passing system* typically combines local memory and the processor at each node of the interconnection network. There is no global memory so it is necessary to move data from one local memory to another by means of message passing. This is typically done by send/receive pairs of commands, which must be written into the application software by a programmer. Figure 5.1 shows a high-level description of a message passing system. Each processor has access to its own local memory and can communicate with other processors using the interconnection network. These systems eventually gave way to Internet-connected systems where the processor/memory nodes are cluster nodes, servers, clients, or nodes in a greater grid, as will be discussed in Chapter 7. In this chapter, we discuss different aspects of message passing systems including a programming model, message routing, network switching, processor support for message passing, and examples of message passing systems.

5.1 INTRODUCTION TO MESSAGE PASSING

A message passing architecture is used to communicate data among a set of processors without the need for a global memory. The basis for the scheme is that each processor has its own local memory and communicates with other processors using messages. The elimination of the need for a large global memory together with its synchronization requirement, gives message passing schemes an edge over shared memory schemes.

Figure 5.1 shows the main components of a message passing multiprocessor architecture. There are n nodes in the figure numbered N_1 to N_n. A node N_i consists of a processor P_i and a local memory M_i. Each processor has its own address space. Nodes communicate with each other by links (called *external channels*) and via an interconnection network, normally a static-type network. In particular, hypercubes and the nearest-neighbor two-dimensional and three-dimensional mesh interconnection

Advanced Computer Architecture and Parallel Processing, by H. El-Rewini and M. Abd-El-Barr
ISBN 0-471-46740-5   Copyright © 2005 John Wiley & Sons, Inc.

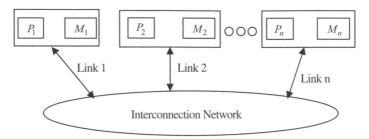

Figure 5.1 Message passing systems.

networks have received considerable attention over the years. As shown in Chapter 2, two important factors must be considered in designing message passing interconnection networks: *link bandwidth* and the *network latency*. The link bandwidth is defined as the number of bits that can be transmitted per unit of time (bits/s). Network latency is defined as the time to complete a message transfer through the network.

In executing a given application program, the program is divided into concurrent processes; each is executed on a separate processor. If the number of processes is larger than the number of processors, then more than one process will have to be executed on a processor in a time-shared fashion. Processes running on a given processor use what is called *internal channels* to exchange messages among themselves. Processes running on different processors use the external channels to exchange messages. Data exchanged among processors cannot be shared; it is rather copied (using send/receive messages). An important advantage of this form of data exchange is the elimination of the need for synchronization constructs, such as semaphores, which results in performance improvement. In addition, a message passing scheme offers flexibility in accommodating a large number of processors in addition to being readily scalable. It should be noted that a given node can execute more than one process, each at a given time.

Figure 5.2 shows an example message passing system consisting of four processes. In this figure, a horizontal line represents the execution of each process and lines extended among processes represent messages exchanged among these processes. A *message* is defined as a logical unit for internode communication; it is considered as a collection of related information that travels together as an entity. A message can be an instruction, data, synchronization, or interrupt signals. A message passing system interacts with the outside world by receiving input message(s) and/or outputting message(s). It is essential that the outside world perceives a consistent behavior of a given message passing system.

Process Granularity The size of a process in a message passing system can be described by a parameter called *process granularity*. This is defined as follows.

$$Process\ Granularity = \frac{computation\ time}{communication\ time}$$

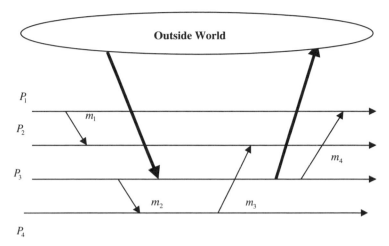

Figure 5.2   An example of a message passing system.

Three types of granularity can be distinguished. These are:

1. Coarse granularity: Each process holds a large number of sequential instructions and takes a substantial amount of time to execute.
2. Medium granularity: Since the process communication overhead increases as the granularity decreases, medium granularity describes a middle ground where communication overhead is reduced.
3. Fine granularity: Each process contains a few sequential instructions (as few as just one instruction).

Message passing multiprocessors uses mostly medium or coarse granularity.

5.2   ROUTING IN MESSAGE PASSING NETWORKS

Routing is defined as the techniques used for a message to select a path over the network channels. Formally speaking, routing involves the identification of a set of permissible paths that may be used by a message to reach its destination, and a function, η, that selects one path from the set of permissible paths.

A routing technique is said to be *adaptive* if, for a given source and destination pair, the path taken by the message depends on network conditions, such as network congestion. Contrary to adaptive routing, a *deterministic* routing technique, also called *oblivious*, determines the path using only the source and destination, regardless of the network conditions. Although simple, oblivious routing techniques make inefficient use of the bandwidth available between the source and destination.

Routing techniques can also be classified based on the method used to make the routing decision as *centralized* (*self*) or *distributed* routing. In centralized routing, the routing decisions regarding the entire path are made before sending the message. In distributed routing, each node decides by itself which channel should be used to forward the incoming message. Centralized routing requires complete knowledge of the status of the rest of the nodes in the network. Distributed routing requires knowledge of only the status of the neighboring nodes.

Examples of the deterministic routing algorithms include the *e-cube* or dimension order routing used in the mesh and torus multicomputer networks and the XOR routing in the hypercube. The following example illustrates the use of a deterministic routing technique in a hypercube network.

Example 1   Assume that $S = S_5 S_4 \ldots S_1 S_0$ to be the source node address, and that $D = D_5 D_4 \ldots D_1 D_0$ is the destination node address in a six-dimensional hypercube message passing system. Let $R = S \oplus D$ be the exclusive OR function executed bitwise for each node in the path. The results of the XOR-ing operation indicate the dimension in which the message should be sent in order to reach the destination. Consider the case whereby $S = 10(001010)$ and $D = 39(100111)$. Then $R = (101101)$; that is, the message has to be sent along dimensions 0, 2, 3, and 5 in order to reach the destination. The order in which these dimensions are traversed is not important. Let us assume that the message will follow the route by traversing the following dimensions 5, 3, 2, and 0. Then the route is totally determined as: $10(001010) \rightarrow 42(101010) \rightarrow 34(100010) \rightarrow 38(100110) \rightarrow 39(100111)$.

5.2.1 Routing for Broadcasting and Multicasting

There are two types of communication operations in message passing systems, that is, one-to-one (point-to-point or *unicast*) and *collective* communications. In unicast a node is allowed to communicate a message to only a single destination, which may be its immediate neighbors. A number of routing operations are defined under collective communication. Among these, *broadcast* and *multicast* are the most widely used. In broadcast, also known as the one-to-all operation, one node sends the same message to all other nodes. In multicast, also known as the one-to-many operation, one node sends its messages to k distinct destinations.

Broadcast is mainly used to distribute data from one node to others during computation of a distributed memory program. Multicast has several uses in large-scale multiprocessors, including parallel search algorithms and single program multiple data (SPMD) computation. Practical broadcast and multicast routing algorithms must be deadlock-free (see below) and should transmit the message to each destination node in as little time and using as short a path as possible. One technique to achieve this is to deliver the message along a common path to as many destinations as possible and then replicate the message and forward each copy on a different channel band for a unique set of destination nodes. The path followed by each copy may further branch in this manner until the message is delivered to every destination node. In such a *tree-based* communication model, the destination set is partitioned at the source and separate copies are sent on one or more outgoing links. A message may be replicated at intermediate nodes and forwarded along multiple outgoing links towards disjoint subsets of destinations. Another method to implement a multicast operation uses *separate addressing*. In this case, a separate copy of the message is sent directly from the source to every destination. Clearly, this is an inefficient technique. A hypercube broadcast tree-based nearest-neighbor communication is shown in Figure 5.3.

5.2.2 Routing Potential Problems

A number of possible problems can result from the use of certain routing mechanisms in message passing systems. These include *deadlock*, *livelock*, and *starvation*, which are explained below.

Deadlock   When two messages each hold the resources required by the other in order to move, both messages will be blocked. This is called a *deadlock*. It is a phenomenon that occurs whenever there exists cyclic dependency for resources. Management of resources in a network is the responsibility of the *flow control* mechanism used. Resources must be allocated in a manner that avoids deadlock. A straightforward, but inefficient, way to solve the deadlock problem is to allow rerouting (maybe discarding) of the messages participating in a deadlock situation. Rerouting of messages gives rise to nonminimal routing, while discarding messages requires that messages be recovered at the source and retransmitted. This preemptive technique leads to long latency and, therefore, is not used by most message passing networks.

   A more common technique is to avoid the occurrence of deadlock. This can be achieved by ordering network resources and requiring that messages request use of these resources in a strict monotonic order. This restricted way for using network resources prevents the occurrence of *circular wait*, and hence prevents the occurrence of deadlock. The *channel dependency graph* (CDG) is a technique used to develop a deadlock-free routing algorithm. A CDG is a directed graph $D = G(C, E)$, where the vertex set C consists of all the unidirectional channels in the network and the set of edges E includes all the pairs of connected channels,

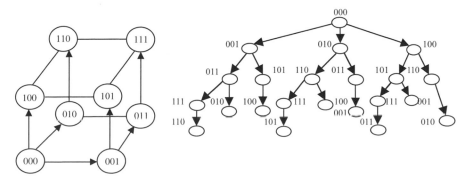

Figure 5.3   Hypercube broadcast tree-based communication.

as defined by the routing algorithm. In other words, if $(c_i, c_j) \in E$, then c_i and c_j are, respectively, an input channel and an output channel of a node and the routing algorithm may only route messages from c_i to c_j. A routing algorithm is deadlock-free if there are no cycles in its CDG. Consider, for example, the 4-node network shown in Figure 5.4a. The CDG of the network is shown in Figure 5.4b. There are two cycles in the CDG and therefore this network is subject to deadlock. Figure 5.4c shows one possible way to avoid the occurrence of deadlock, that is, disallowing messages to be forwarded from channel c_1 to c_2 and from c_7 to c_8.

Livelock *Livelock* describes a situation in which a message keeps going around the network and never reaches its destination. It is a phenomenon that results from using adaptive routing algorithms where messages are rerouted in the hope to find another path to their destinations. When nodes need to communicate, they inject their messages into the network. A *static injection* model results when all nodes inject their messages at the same moment, with the network clear of messages. This is to be compared to *dynamic injection*, according to which nodes can inject their messages at arbitrary times. Livelock can take place if dynamic injection is used. It cannot occur if static injection is used. A number of routing policies can

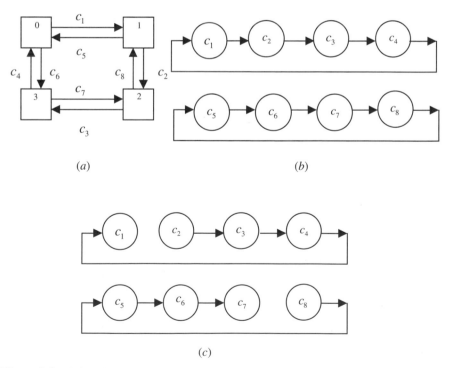

(a)   (b)

(c)

Figure 5.4 A 4-node network and its CDGs (a) a 4-node network; (b) channel dependency graph; and (c) CDG for a deadlock-free version of the network.

be used to avoid livelock. They are based on the following. Let S be a set of priorities that is totally ordered. Whenever a message is injected into the network, some priority is assigned to it. In order to avoid livelock, the following must hold.

1. Messages are routed according to their priorities;
2. Once a message has been injected, only a finite number of messages will be injected with higher or equal priority.

Starvation A node is said to suffer from *starvation* if it has a message to inject into the network but is never allowed to do so. Starvation cannot arise if static injection is used. A number of routing policies can be used in order to avoid starvation taking place. The simplest among them is to allow each node to have its injection queue, where it stores the messages it wants to inject into the network. This queue is considered in the same way as the queues of the incoming links to that node and it competes with them. As long as a fair queue management policy is used, this method prevents starvation from happening. The main disadvantage is that a node with a high message injection rate can slow down all the other nodes in the network.

5.3 SWITCHING MECHANISMS IN MESSAGE PASSING

Switching mechanisms refer to the mechanisms used to remove data from an input channel and place it on an output channel. Network latency is highly dependent on the switching mechanism used. A number of switching mechanisms have been in use. These are the *store-and-forward, circuit-switching, virtual cut-through, wormhole,* and *pipelined circuit-switching.* In this section, we study some of these techniques.

In *circuit-switching* networks, the path between the source and destination is first determined, all links along that path are reserved, and no buffers are needed in each node. After data transfer, reserved links are released for use by other messages. An important characteristic of the circuit-switching technique is that the source and destination are guaranteed a certain bandwidth and maximum latency when communication is established between them. This static bandwidth allocation regardless of the actual use is the main drawback of the circuit-switching approach. However, static bandwidth allocation leads to a simple buffering strategy. In addition, circuit-switching networks are characterized by having the smallest amount of delay. This is because message routing overhead is only needed when the circuit is set up; subsequent messages suffer no, or minimal, additional delay. Therefore, circuit-switching networks can be advantageously used in the case of a large number of message transfers.

The store-and-forward switching mechanism provides an alternate data transfer scheme. The main idea is to offer dynamic bandwidth allocation to messages as they flow through the network, thus avoiding the main drawback of the circuit-switching mechanism. Two main types of store-and-forward networks are common. These are *packet-switched* and *virtual cut-through* networks. In packet-switched networks, each message is divided into smaller fixed size parts, called *packets*, before being transmitted. Each node must contain enough buffers to hold received packets before transmitting them. A complete path from source to destination may not be available at the start of transmission. As links become available, packets are moved from node to node until they reach the destination node. Since packets are routed separately through the network, they may follow different paths to the destination node. This may lead to packets arriving out of order at the destination. Therefore, an end-to-end message assembly scheme is needed, incurring additional overhead. Packet-switched networks suffer also from the need for routing overhead for each packet, rather than message, sent into the network. In addition to dynamically allocating bandwidth, packet-switched networks have the advantage of reduced buffer requirements in each node.

In virtual cut-through, a packet is stored at an intermediate node only if the next required channel is busy. Virtual cut-through is similar to the packet-switching technique, with the following difference. In contrast to packet switching, when a packet arrives at an intermediate node and its selected outgoing channel is free, the packet is sent out to the adjacent node towards its destination before it is completely received. Therefore, the delay due to unnecessary buffering in front of an idle channel is avoided.

In order to reduce the size of the required buffers and decrease the incurred network latency, a technique called *wormhole routing* has been introduced. Here, a packet is divided into smaller units called *flits* (flow control bits). These *flits* move in a pipeline fashion with a header *flit* leading the way to the destination node. When the header flit is blocked due to network congestion, the remaining flits are also blocked. Only a buffer that can store a flit is required for a successful operation of the *wormhole routing* technique. The technique is known to produce a latency that is independent of the path length and it requires less storage at all nodes compared to the store-and-forward packet-switching technique.

Figures 5.5 and 5.6 illustrate the difference in performance between the store-and-forward (SF) and wormhole (WH) routing in terms of communication latency.

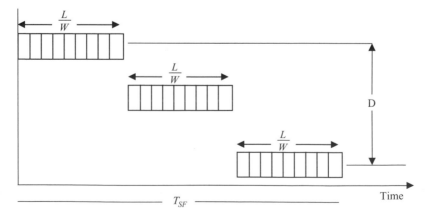

Figure 5.5 Communication latency in the store-and-forward (SF) technique.

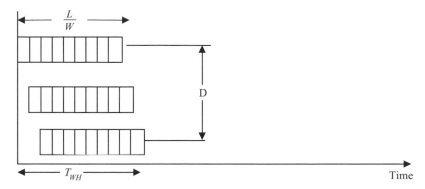

Figure 5.6 Communication latency in the wormhole (WH) technique.

In these figures, L represents the packet length in bits, W represents the channel bandwidth in bits/cycle, D is the number of channels, and T_c is the cycle time. As can be seen from the figures, the latency of the SF and that of the WH are given respectively by

$$T_{SF} = T_c\left(\frac{L}{W} \times D\right) \quad \text{and} \quad T_{WH} = T_c\left(\frac{L}{W} + D\right)$$

Table 5.1 shows an overall comparison of a number of switching mechanisms.

TABLE 5.1 Comparison Among a Number of Switching Techniques

Switching Mechanism	Advantages	Disadvantages
Circuit switching	1. Suitable for long messages 2. Deadlock-free	Wasting of bandwidth
Store-and-forward	1. Simple 2. Suitable for interactive traffic 3. Bandwidth on demand	1. Buffer for every packet 2. Potential long latency 3. Potential deadlock
Virtual cut-through	1. Good for long messages 2. Possible deadlock avoidance 3. Elimination of data-link protocol	1. Need for multiple message buffers 2. Wasting of bandwidth 3. Mainly used with profitable routing
Wormhole	1. Good for long messages 2. Reduced need for buffering 3. Reduced effect of path length	1. Possibility for deadlock 2. Inability to support backtracking

5.3.1 Wormhole Routing in Mesh Networks

An n-dimensional mesh is defined as the interconnection structure that has $K_0 \times K_1 \times \cdots \times K_{n-1}$ nodes, where n is the number of dimensions of the network and K_i is the radix of dimension i. Each node is identified by an *n-coordinate* vector $(x_0, x_1, \ldots, x_{n-1})$, where $0 \leq x_i \leq K_i - 1$. A number of routing techniques have been used for mesh networks. These include *dimension-ordered, dimension reversal, turn model*, and *message flow model*. In the following, we introduce the dimension-ordered of *X-Y* routing.

Dimension-Ordered (X-Y) Routing A channel numbering scheme often used in n-dimensional meshes is based on the dimension of channels. In dimension-ordered routing, each packet is routed in one dimension at a time, arriving at the proper coordinate in each dimension before proceeding to the next dimension. By enforcing a strict monotonic order on the dimensions traversed, deadlock-free routing is guaranteed. In a two-dimensional mesh, each node is represented by its position (x, y); the packets are first sent along the x-dimension and then along the y-dimension, hence the name *X-Y* routing.

In *X-Y* routing, messages are first sent along the *X*-dimension and then along the *Y*-dimension. In other words, at most one turn is allowed and that turn must be from the *X*-dimension to the *Y*-dimension. Let (s_x, s_y) and (d_x, d_y) denote the addresses of a source and destination node, respectively. Assume also that $(g_x, g_y) = (d_x - s_x, d_y - s_y)$. The *X-Y* routing can be implemented by placing g_x and g_y in the first two flits, respectively, of the message. When the first flit arrives at a node, it is decremented or incremented, depending on whether it is greater than 0 or less than 0. If the result is not equal to 0, the message is forwarded in the same direction in which it arrived. If the result equals 0 and the message arrived on the *Y*-dimension, the message is delivered to the local node. If the result equals 0 and the message arrived on the *X*-dimension, the flit is discarded and the next flit is examined on arrival. If that flit is 0, the packet is delivered to the local node; otherwise, the packet is forwarded in the *Y*-dimension. Figure 5.7 shows an example of the *X-Y* routing between a source node and a destination node in an 8×8 mesh network.

5.3.2 Virtual Channels

The principle of virtual channel was introduced in order to allow the design of deadlock-free routing algorithms. Virtual channels provide an inexpensive method to increase the number of logical channels without adding more wires. A number of adaptive routing algorithms are based on the use of virtual channels.

A network without virtual channels is composed of single lane streets. Adding virtual channels to an interconnection network is analogous to adding lanes to a street network, thus allowing blocked messages to be passed. In addition to increasing throughput, virtual channels provide an additional degree of freedom

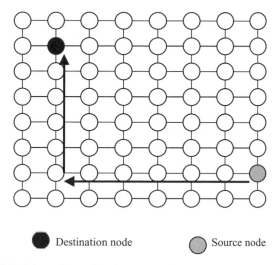

Destination node   Source node

Figure 5.7   Dimension-ordered (*X-Y*) routing in an 8 × 8 mesh network.

in allocating resources to messages in a network. Consider the simple network shown in Figure 5.8.

In this case, two paths X-A-B-Z and Y-A-B-W share the common link AB. It is, therefore, required to multiplex link AB between the two paths (two lanes). A provision is also needed such that data sent over the first path (lane) is sent from X to Z and not to W and similarly data sent over the second path (lane) is sent from Y to W and not to Z. This can be achieved if we assume that each physical link is actually divided into a number of unidirectional *virtual channels*. Each channel can carry data for one virtual circuit (one path). A circuit (path) from one node to another consists of a sequence of channels on the links along the path between the two nodes. When data is sent from node A to node B, then node B will have to determine the circuit associated with the data such that it can decide whether is should route the data to node Z or to node W. One way that can be used to provide such information is to divide the AB link into a fixed number of time slots and statically assign each time slot to a channel. This way, the time slot on which the data arrives

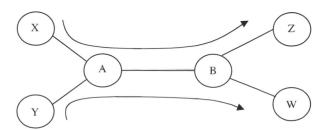

Figure 5.8   Path multiplexing through the same link.

identifies the sending channel and therefore can be used to direct the data to the appropriate destination.

One of the advantages of the virtual channel concept is deadlock avoidance. This can be done by assigning a few flits per node of buffering. When a packet arrives at a virtual channel, it is put in the buffer and sent along the appropriate time slot.

5.4 MESSAGE PASSING PROGRAMMING MODELS

A message passing architecture uses a set of primitives that allows processes to communicate with each other. These include the *send*, *receive*, *broadcast*, and *barrier* primitives. The *send* primitive takes a memory buffer and sends it to a destination node. The *receive* primitive accepts a message from a source node and stores it in a specified memory buffer. The basic programming model used in message passing architectures is based on the idea of matching a *send* request on one processor with a *receive* request on another. In such scheme, *send* and *receive* are blocking; that is, send blocks until the corresponding receive is executed before data can be transferred.

Implementation of the send/receive among processes requires a three-way protocol as shown in Figure 5.9. In this case, the sending process issues a request-to-send message to the receiver process. The latter stores the request and sends a reply message back. When the corresponding receive is executed, the sender process receives the reply and finally transfers the data. The blocking send/receive is simple; it requires no buffering at the source or the destination. However, the three-way hand-shaking used in blocking send/receive requires that both the sender and the receiver be blocked for at least a full round-trip time. During this time the processors are idle, thus leading to an increase in the network communication latency. In addition, with blocking send/receive, it is impossible to overlap communication with computation and thus the network bandwidth cannot be fully utilized.

The use of nonblocking operation is utilized by most message passing implementations in order to avoid the drawbacks of the three-phase protocol. In this case, *send* appears immediately to the user program. However, the message is buffered by the message layer until the network port is available. Only then, would the message be transmitted to the recipient. In there, the message is again buffered until a matching *receive* is executed.

Table 5.2 shows the performance of the send/receive on a number of message passing machines. In this table, T_s represents the message start-up cost, T_b represents the per-byte cost, and T_{fp} is the average cost of a floating-point operation. It should be noted that the *CM-5* is blocking and uses a three-phase protocol. The *iPSC* long

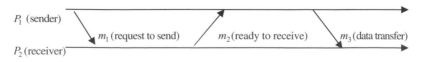

Figure 5.9   Blocking send/receive handshaking protocol.

TABLE 5.2   Performance of Send/Receive on a Number of Message Passing Machines

Machine	T_s (μs/mesg)	T_b (μs/mesg)	T_{fp} (μs/mesg)
iPSC	4100	2.8	25
nCUBE/10	400	2.6	8.3
iPSC/2	700	0.36	3.4
nCUBE/2	160	0.45	0.50
iPSC/860	160	0.36	0.033
CM-5	86	0.12	0.33

messages also use a three-phase protocol in order to guarantee that enough buffer space is available at the receiving node.

Example 2   Let us try to compute $y = (a + b) * (c + d)$ on a single processor and on a message architecture consisting of two processors. In presenting illustrative solutions to this problem, we will use simple and self-explanatory notations.

(a)   Using Single Processor

Time step
1 Load   1000 ; load a
2 Add   2000 ; add b to a
3 Store   1000 ; store a+b in 1000
4 Load   3000 ; load c
5 Add   4000 ; add d to c
6 Mult   1000 ; multiply (a + b)*(c + d)
7 Write   999   ; store the result in 999
8 Halt   ; done

999	
1000	a
2000	b
3000	c
4000	d

Number of time steps (polynomial complexity) = 8
Asymptotic complexity $T(n) = O(1)$

(b)   Message Passing With Two Processors P_1 and P_2

Assume that the operands are distributed between the two processors as shown.

P_1 ———— P_2

999		999		
1000	a	1000	c	
2000	b	2000	d	

Time step	P_1	Operations in P_1	P_2	Operations in P_2
1	Load 1000	; load a	Load 1000	; load c
2	Add 2000	; add b to a	Add 2000	; add d to c
3	Send 2000!	; send a+b to P_2	Store 1000	; store c+d in 1000
4	Halt	; done	Receive 2000?	; receive a+b from P_1
5			Mult 1000	; multiply $(a+b)^*(c+d)$
6			Write 999	; store result in 999 in P_2
7			Halt	; done

Number of time steps (polynomial complexity) $T(n, 2) = 7$

Asymptotic complexity $T(n, 2) = O(1)$

Speedup $SP(n, 2) = 8/7 = 1.19$

Example 3 It is required to sum all components of a vector A, having n components (for simplicity assume that n is a power of 2) using p processors, assuming that the vector components are distributed among the p processors.

- Initialization step: Each processor performs the partial sum of the vector components it has.
- *Repeat* using *index* $k = 1$ to $n/2$ in powers of 2.
- Processor j and processor $j + k$ **send** and **receive** data in pairwise fashion and perform the summation.

Figure 5.10 shows how the process can be performed in $\log_2 n$ steps.

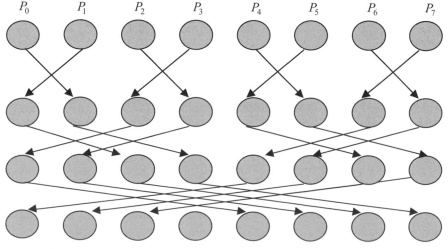

Figure 5.10 Summation in $\log_2 n$ steps using a message passing system.

5.5 PROCESSOR SUPPORT FOR MESSAGE PASSING

Processors that support message passing are those processors that contain the special instructions needed to support interprocess message communications. In order to support interprocess communications, a number of features are required. Among these, the following features are needed:

1. A port is a communication channel. It is a reference object for tasks and threads. Two main operations can be performed on ports: *send* and *receive*.
2. Messages are used as communication among objects. A message is divided into a header and a body. The size of the body is variable while that of the header is fixed. A message holds information exchanged between processes.
3. Port sets: A task can hold multiple access rights (send and receive) on ports. Multiple tasks can hold send access to a single port. On the other hand, one task can hold receive access at a given time. In port set, a task can have either all or none of the access rights to a group of ports. Ports must be mutually exclusive in the sense that a port cannot be in two different sets at a given time.

The Intel iPAX 432 uses message passing communications and supports them directly. It also uses port objects that work as a competitor to the path of the message. The processor contains a message queue. A message communication can be arranged depending on the following:

1. Time of arrival (such as the "first-in-first-out", FIFO);
2. Priority;
3. Deadline within priority.

The iPAX 432 produces a nonblocking message passing by using specific process that has conditional SEND and RECEIVE operations. The operand of these conditional operations is a specific Boolean flag. Thus, if the unconditional operation corresponding to the conditional one was blocking, the conditional operation result will be false and if it is nonblocking then the conditional operation will be true. In this case of the conditional operations, to support message passing, a correct communication and interaction between and within each process must be satisfied. This must be because the processor will continue executing a specific operation in case it cannot complete the communication operation. Therefore, a good program must be able to decide whether to retry the operation by testing the returned flag. There are also other kinds of message passing operations that are not blocking, such as the SURROGATE-SEND and SURROGATE-RECEIVE. These operations hold the operation in a waiting queue and are sufficient for use with high-level language interprocess communication. The operand of these operations is an event called DONE. These operations do the send and receive operations and put the message in the port's queue. The end or the completion of these operations has DONE (event) when the SURROGATE received the desired service. The original process is responsible for checking the completion of the operation by searching for the DONE event.

The IBM AS/400 supports message passing by having an event object type that contains a field supporting the contents of the message. This field is called the event-data field. AS/400 processor operations are *send* and *receive*. The send operation is used to send the interprocess message by a processor operation called SIGNAL-EVENT (PROC, EV, DATA). This processor operation has three parameters. The first two are essential to exist such that the event EV will be signaled within the processor PROC. The third parameter is unessential for that event. To receive the interprocess message, the WAIT-ON-EVENT, TEST-EVENT, MONITOR-EVENT, and RETRIEVE-EVENT-DATA are used. Note that an exactly blocking receive operation does not exist because the value of the timeout should be determined with every operation that might block the execution of a process.

5.6   EXAMPLE MESSAGE PASSING ARCHITECTURES

Examples of message passing machines include *Caltech Hypercube*, the *Inmos Transputer* systems, *Meiko CS-2*, *Cosmic Cube*, *nCUBE/2*, *iPSC/2*, *iPSC/860*, *CM-5*. Other recent systems include the IBM Scalable Power Series (*IBM POWERparallel 3*, *SP 3*).

The Caltech Hypercube (the Cosmic Cube) was an *n*-dimensional hypercube system with a single host, known as the Intermediate Host (IH), for global control. The original system was based on the simple store-and-forward routing mechanism. The system started with a set of routine libraries known as the crystalline operating system (CrOS), which supported C and FORTRAN. The system supported only collective operations (broadcast) to/from the IH. Two years later, the Caltech project team introduced a hardware wormhole routing chip. The Cosmic Cube is managed using a host runtime system called the Cosmic environment (CE). The processes of a given computation are called the process group. The system can be used by more than one user. Users have to specify the cube size needed using a CE routine. Allocation will be granted based on the available hypercube nodes. In this system, C programming is supported by the help of a dynamic process structure with active process scheduling.

The Cosmic Cube is considered the first working hypercube multicomputer message passing system. The Cosmic cube system has been constructed using 64 node for the Intel iPSC. Each node has 128 KB of dynamic RAM that has parity checking for error detection but no correction. In addition, each node has 8 KB of ROM in order to store the initialization and bootstrap programs. The basic packet size is 64 bits with queues in each node. In this system, messages are communicated via transmissions (send/receive). When a message request is made, the calls will return. In case the message request is not finished (pending), the calls will not return and the program will continue. Each node in this system has a kernel that requires about 9 KB of code and 4 KB of tables. This kernel, called the Reactive Kernel, is divided in two: an inner kernel, which is responsible for performing messages such as *send*, *receive*, *queue*, and *handling* messages, and an outer kernel, which includes processes to *create*, *copy*, and *stop* the processes.

The Meiko Computing Surface CS-1 was the first Inmos Transputer T800-based system. The Transputer was a 32-bit microprocessor with fast task-switching capability through hardware intercommunication. The system was programmed using a communication sequential processes (CSP) language called *Occam*. The language used abstract links known as channels and supported synchronous blocking send and receive primitives.

T9000 represented another version of the Inmos Transputer processor T800. T9000 has the ability to perform both integer and floating-point operations. Although T9000 is a RISC processor, it uses microprogramming. Instructions take one or more processor cycles to execute. Its internal memory capacity is at least 64 KB. It also has 16 KB instruction and data cache. The memory interface circuitry can generate a variety of signals to match the external memory chips. With the T9000, data transfers are synchronized using a *two-way hand-shaking* mechanism. According to this technique, synchronization is achieved using two different packets. The first one, called the *data packet*, is sent from the source to the destination transputer process. The other packet, called the *acknowledge packet*, is sent from the destination to the source transputer. When the destination transputer is ready to get the data from the data packet, it should send an acknowledge signal represented by the acknowledge packet telling the source transputer to send the data packet.

The Intel iPSC is a commercial message passing hypercube developed after the Cosmic Cube. The iPSC/1 used Intel 286 processors with a 287 floating-point coprocessor. Each node consists of a single board computer having two buses, a process bus and I/O bus. Nodes are controlled by the Cube manager. Each node has seven communication channels (links) to communicate with other nodes and a separate channel for communication with the Cube Manager. FORTRAN message passing routines are supported. The software environment used in iPSC1 was called NX1, and has a more distributed processes environment than those included in the Caltech CrOS. The NX1 was based on the Caltech Reactive Kernel. It provided the typical set of features needed in a message passing environment. These include communication topology hiding, multiple processes per node, any-to-any message passing, asynchronous messaging, and nonblocking communication primitives. Later, Intel machines implemented an improved version of NX, called NX2. In the case of the Paragon, NX2 was implemented upon an OSF/1 Unix microkernel.

The *nCUBE/2* has up to a few thousand nodes connected in a binary hypercube network. Each node consists of a CPU-chip and DRAM chips on a small double sided printed circuit board. The CPU chip contains a 64 bit integer unit, an IEEE floating-point unit, a DRAM memory interface, a network interface with 28 DMA channels, and routers that support cut-through routing across a 13-dimensional hypercube. The processor runs at 20 MHz and delivers roughly 5 MIPS or 1.5 MFLOPS.

The Thinking Machine CM-5 had up to a few thousand nodes interconnected in a hypertree (incomplete fat tree). Each node consists of a 33 MHz SPARC RISC processor chip-set, local DRAM memory, and a network interface to the hypertree and broadcast/scan/prefix control networks. Compared to its predecessors, CM-5 represented a true distributed memory message passing system. It featured two interconnection networks, and Sparc-based processing nodes. Each node has four vector units for pipeline arithmetic operations. The CM-5 programming environment consisted of the CMOST operating system, the CMMD message passing library, and various array-style compilers. The latter includes CMF, supporting a F90-like SIMD programming style. The CMMD message passing system offered users access to routines from the lowest level, the Active Message Layer (AML), a point-to-point library, channels, and a cooperative functions library.

Having briefly reviewed a number of the early introduced message passing systems, we now discuss in some detail the features of a recent message passing system, the IBM Scalable POWERparallel 3 system.

5.6.1 The IBM Scalable POWERparallel 3

The IBM POWER3 (SP 3) is the most recent IBM supercomputer series (1999/2000). The SP 3 consists of 2 to 512 POWER3 Architecture RISC System/6000 processor nodes. Each node has its own private memory and its own copy of the AIX operating system. The POWER3 processor is an eight-stage pipeline processor. Two instructions can be executed per clock-cycle except for the multiply and divide. A multiply instruction takes two clock cycles while a divide instruction takes 13 to 17 cycles. The FPU contains two execution units using double precision (64 bit). Both execution units are identical and conform to the IEEE 754 binary floating-point standard. Figure 5.11 shows a block diagram of a typical SP 3 node.

Nodes are connected by a high-performance scalable packet-switched network in a distributed memory and message passing. The network's building block is a two-staged 16×16 switch board, made up of 4×4 bidirectional crossbar switching elements (SEs). Each link is bidirectional and has a 40 MB/s bandwidth in each direction. The switch uses buffered cut-through wormhole routing. This interconnection arrangement allows all processors to send messages simultaneously. For full connectivity, at least one extra stage is provided. This stage guarantees that there are at least four different paths between every pair of nodes. This form of path redundancy helps in reducing network congestion as well as recovery in the presence of failures.

The communication protocol supports end-to-end packet acknowledgment. For every packet sent by a source node, there is a returned acknowledgment after the packet has reached the destination node. This allows source nodes to discover packet loss. Automatic retransmission of a packet is made if the acknowledgment is not received within a preset time interval.

A message passing programming style is the preferred style for performance on the SP 3. Several message passing libraries used by FORTRAN and C are supported

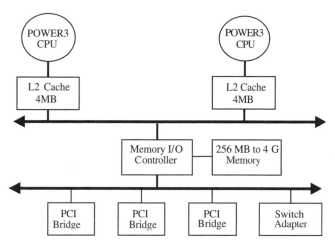

Figure 5.11 Typical SP 3 node.

on the SP 3. The SP 3 also supports the data parallel programming model with high-performance FORTRAN.

The message passing model in SP assumes that any task can send a message to any other task using message passing communication mechanism. The main message passing operations are the *send* and *receive* operations. The send operation can be either *synchronous* (returns only when a matching receive is called) or *asynchronous* (returns immediately without waiting for a matching receive call) and *blocking* (returns as soon as the send buffer has been cleared) or *nonblocking* (returns without waiting for clearing the send buffer). The receive operation can be either *blocking* (returns only after the data has been received) or *nonblocking* (returns immediately a flag that the data either are not available or are in the receive buffer). Particular implementation of the different message passing libraries in SP 3 is presented below.

The IBM SP 3 programming environment offers three message passing libraries: PVM, MPL, and MPI. The native library in the IBM SP-2 Parallel Operating Environment is MPL. It is implemented on top of HPS and IP protocols. The MPI implementation MPICH is implemented on top of MPL. The MPL is designed for SP-2 and, therefore, there is no special software initialization and messages are passed directly to hardware. Single-step asynchronous blocking subroutines are called mpc_bsend( ) and mpc_brecv( ). There are also dual asynchronous blocking subroutines mpc_bvsend( ) and mpc_bvrecv( ) for exchanging noncontiguous pieces of data. The MPI subroutine design for SP-2 is very similar to MPL; only the subroutine names and parameters differ. No encoding is needed and all messages are passed directly to hardware through MPL subroutines. Single step asynchronous blocking subroutines are called MPI_Send( ) and MPI_Recv( ).

The PVM is aimed at heterogeneous parallel systems. The asynchronous blocking send subroutine is pvm_send( ). Sending a message requires three steps. First, the PVM sending buffer has to be initialized by pvm_initsend( ). There are three defined input parameters, which determine a mechanism of data coding and packing:

PvmDataDefault, the data is packed into PVM buffer and encoded according to the XDR format; PvmDataRaw, the data is packed into the PVM buffer with no encoding; PvmDataInPlace, the data is not copied to the PVM buffer, but it is fetched from user space memory during execution pvm_send( ). Then the message is packed into the PVM buffer by using any combination of pvm_pack*( ) routines. Finally, the pvm_send( ) subroutine is called. The matching subroutine to pvm_send( ) is blocking pvm_recv( ). Receiving a message requires two steps. The incoming message has to be accepted by pvm_recv( ) and then it has to be unpacked into user data space using pvm_unpack*( ) functions.

The PVM and MPI message passing libraries are covered in more details in Chapters 8 and 9, respectively.

5.7 MESSAGE PASSING VERSUS SHARED MEMORY ARCHITECTURES

As indicated in Chapter 4, shared memory enjoys the desirable feature that all communications are done using implicit loads and stores to a global address space. Another fundamental feature of shared memory is that synchronization and communication are distinct. Special synchronization operations (mechanisms), in addition to the loads and stores operations, need to be employed in order to detect when data have been produced and/or consumed. On the other hand, message passing employs an explicit communication model. Explicit messages are exchanged among processors. Synchronization and communication are unified in message passing. The generation of remote, asynchronous events is an integral part of the message passing communication model. It is important, however, to indicate that shared memory and message passing communication models are universal; that is, it is possible to employ one to simulate the other. However, it is observed that it is easier to simulate shared memory using message passing than the converse. This is basically because of the asynchronous event semantics of message passing as compared to the polling semantics of the shared memory.

A number of desirable features characterize shared memory architectures (see Chapter 4). The shared memory communication model allows the programmer to concentrate on the issues related to parallelism by relieving him/her of the details of the interprocessor communication. In that sense, the shared memory communication model represents a straightforward extension of the uniprocessor programming paradigm. In addition, shared memory semantics are independent of the physical location and therefore they are open to the dynamic optimization offered by the underlying operating system. On the other hand, the shared memory communication model is in essence a polling interface. This is a drawback as far as synchronization is concerned. This fact has been recognized by a number of multiprocessor architects and their response has always been to augment the basic shared memory communication model with additional synchronization mechanisms. An additional drawback of shared memory is that in order for data to cross the network, a complete round trip has to be made. One-way communication of data is not possible.

Message passing can be characterized as employing an interrupt-driven communication model. In message passing, messages include both data and synchronization in a single unit. As such, the message passing communication model lends itself to those operating system activities in which communication patterns are explicitly known in advance, for example, I/O, interprocessor interrupts, and task and data migration. The message passing communication model lends itself also to applications that have large synchronization components, for example, solution of systems of sparse matrices and event-driven simulation. In addition, message passing communication models are natural client–server style decomposition. On the other hand, message passing suffers from the need for *marshaling cost*, that is, the cost of assembling and disassembling of the message.

One natural conclusion arising from the above discussion is that shared memory and message passing communication models each lend themselves naturally to certain application domains. Shared memory manifests itself to application writers while message passing manifests itself to operating systems designers. It is therefore natural to consider combining both shared memory and message passing in general-purpose multiprocessor systems. This has been the main driving force behind systems such as the Stanford FLexible Architecture for SHared memory (FLASH) system (see Problems). It is a multiprocessor system that efficiently integrates support for shared memory and message passing while minimizing both hardware and software overhead.

5.8 CHAPTER SUMMARY

Shared memory systems may be easier to program, but are difficult to scale up to a large number of processors. If scalability to larger and larger systems (as measured by the number of processing units) was to continue, systems had to use message passing techniques. It is apparent that message passing systems are the only way to efficiently increase the number of processors managed by a multiprocessor system. There are, however, a number of problems associated with message passing systems. These include communication overhead and difficulty of programming. In this chapter, we discussed the architecture and the network models of message passing systems. We shed some light on routing and network switching techniques. We concluded with a contrast between shared memory and message passing systems.

PROBLEMS

1. Contemplate the advantages and disadvantages of message passing architectures and compare them with those found in shared memory architectures.
2. Based on your finding in Problem 1, you may conclude that an architecture that combines the best of two worlds should be preferred over either of the two systems. Discuss the advantages and disadvantages of a combined shared memory message passing architecture.

3. In connection with Problem 2 above, an architecture that combines shared memory and message passing has been introduced by Stanford University. It is called the FLASH system. Write a complete report on that architecture, discussing its hardware and software features as well as its programming model. Support your report with illustrations, tables, and examples, whenever possible.

4. Discuss the conditions that lead to the occurrence of the deadlock problems in multicomputer message passing systems. Suggest ways to avoid the occurrence of such a problem. Provide some examples to support your suggestions.

5. Repeat Problem 4 considering the livelock problem instead.

6. Repeat Problem 4 considering the starvation problem instead.

7. Show how to perform the matrix-vector multiplication problem using collective communications in message passing systems. Compare the time complexity and the speedup resulting from using a multicomputer message passing as compared to using a single processor. Provide an illustrative example.

8. Repeat Problem 7 above for the problem of finding the min $(A(1), A(2), \ldots, A(n))$ in an n-element vector A.

9. Repeat Problem 7 considering execution of the following simple loop on a single processor compared with $k < n$ processors in a message passing arrangement.

$$\text{for } i = 1, n$$
$$C[i] = A[i] + B[i],$$

10. Design a message passing routing algorithm for an n-dimensional hypercube network that broadcasts a host message to all nodes in the hypercube at the greatest speed. Show how this algorithm can be implemented with message passing routines.

11. Repeat Problem 10 for the case where a node in the n-dimensional hypercube can broadcast a message to all other nodes. Show how this algorithm can be implemented with message passing routines.

12. Repeat Problem 10 for the case of an n-dimensional mesh network.

13. Repeat Problem 11 for the case of an n-dimensional mesh network.

REFERENCES

Al-Tawil, K., Abd-El-Barr, M. and Ashraf, F. A survey and comparison of wormhole routing techniques in mesh networks. *IEEE Network*, 38–45 (1997).

Almasi/Gottlieb. *Highly Parallel Computing*, 1989.

Ashraf, F. *Routing in Multicomputer Networks: A Classification and Comparison*, MS thesis, Department of Information and Computer Science, College of Computer Science and Engineering, King Fahd University of Petroleum and Minerals (KFUPM), June 1996.

Dally, W. and Seitz, C. Deadlock-free message routing in multiprocessor interconnection networks. *IEEE Transactions on Computers*, C-36 (5), 547–553 (1987).

Dikaiakos, M. D., Steiglits, K. and Rogers, A. *A Comparison of Techniques Used for Mapping Parallel Algorithms to Message-Passing Multiprocessors*, Department of Aston, Washington University, Seattle, WA, USA, 1994, pp. 434–442.

Eicken, T., Culler, D., Goldstein, S. and Schauser, K. *Active Messages: A Mechanism for Integrated Communication and Computation*, Proceedings 19th International Symposium on Computer Architecture, ACM Press, May 1992, Gold Coast, Australia.

Elnozahy, M., Alvisi, L., Wang, Y.-M. and Johnson, D., *A Survey of Rollback-Recovery Protocols in Message Massing Systems*.

Hsu, J.-M. and Banerjee, P. *A Message Passing Coprocessor for Distributed Memory Multicomputers*, Coordinated Scientific Lab., Illinois Univ., Urbana, IL, USA, 1990, pp. 720–729.

Johnson, S. and Ho, C.-T. High performance communications in processor networks. *Proceedings of the 16th ACM Annual International Symposium on Computer Architecture*, 150–157 (1989).

Klaiber, A. C. and Levy, H. M. *Comparison of Message Passing and Shared Memory Architecture for Data Parallel Program*, Department of Computer Science and Engineering, Washington University, Seattle, WA, USA, 1994, pp. 94–105.

Morin, S. *Implementing the Message Passing Interface Standard in Java*, MSc thesis, Electrical and Computing Engineering Department, University of Massachusetts, September 2000.

Ni, L. and McKinley. A survey of wormhole routing techniques in direct networks. *IEEE Computer Magazine*, 26 (2), 62–76 (1993).

PACT. *Message Passing Fundamentals*, PACT Training Group, NCSA 2001, University of Illinois, 2001.

Panda, D. Issues in designing efficient and practical algorithms for collective communication on wormhole-routed systems, *Proceedings of the 1995 ICCP Workshop on Challenges for Parallel Processing*, Vol. I, 8–15 (1995).

Pierce, P. The NX message passing interface. *Parallel Computing*, 20 (4), 463–480 (1994).

Richard, Y. *KAIN, Advanced Computer Architecture, A System Design Approach*, Prentice-Hall, 1995.

Stone. *High-Performance Computer Architecture*, 3rd edition, Addison-Wesley, 1993.

Suanya, R. and Birtwistle, G. (editors) *VLSI and Parallel Computation*, Morgan Kaufmann Publishing Co., 1990.

Wrllkinsen, B. *Computer Architecture: Design and Performance*, Prentice-Hall, 1996.

Websites

http://www.lysator.liu.se/ ~ oscar/sp2

http://www.npac.syr.edu/nse/hpccsurvey/orgs/ibm/ibm.html

http://cs.felk.cvut.cz/pcg/html/supeur96

http://citeseer.ist.psu.edu/dongarra99chapter.html

http://www-flash.stanford.edu/architecture/papers

CHAPTER 6

Abstract Models

In previous chapters, we learned that parallel architecture could be categorized into *shared memory* and *message passing* systems. In a shared memory system, processing elements communicate with each other via shared variables in the global memory, while in message passing systems, each processing element has its own local memory and communication is performed via message passing. In this chapter, we study abstract models for both shared memory and message passing systems. We will study several parallel and distributed algorithms and evaluate their complexities using these models.

At first glance, abstract models may appear to be inappropriate in real-world situations due to their idealistic nature. However, abstract machines have been very useful in studying parallel and distributed algorithms and evaluating their anticipated performance independent of real machines. Clearly, if the performance of an algorithm is not satisfactory on an abstract system, it is meaningless to implement it on a real system. Although abstract models do not consider some practical considerations in real parallel and distributed systems, they focus on the computational aspects of the algorithmic complexity, which makes it less difficult to find performance bounds and complexity estimates.

We begin by discussing a model of shared memory systems called *PRAM (Parallel Random Access Machine)*. We will study the PRAM model and the relationships between its different variations. We will also present a computational model for synchronous message passing systems. We will discuss complexity analysis of algorithms described in terms of both PRAM and message passing models. A number of algorithms for both models will be presented and evaluated.

6.1 THE PRAM MODEL AND ITS VARIATIONS

The purpose of the theoretical models for parallel computation is to give frameworks by which we can describe and analyze algorithms. These ideal models are used to obtain performance bounds and complexity estimates. One of the models that has been used extensively is the parallel random access machine (PRAM) model. The PRAM model was introduced by Fortune and Wyllie in 1978 for modeling idealized

Advanced Computer Architecture and Parallel Processing, by H. El-Rewini and M. Abd-El-Barr
ISBN 0-471-46740-5 Copyright © 2005 John Wiley & Sons, Inc.

parallel computers in which communication cost and synchronization overhead are negligible.

A PRAM consists of a control unit, a global memory shared by p processors, each of which has a unique index as follows: $P_1, P_2, \ldots, P_p$. In addition to the global memory via which the processors can communicate, each processor has its own private memory. Figure 6.1 shows a diagram illustrating the components in the PRAM model.

The p processors operate on a synchronized read, compute, and write cycle. During a computational step, an active processor may read a data value from a memory location, perform a single operation, and finally write back the result into a memory location. Active processors must execute the same instruction, generally, on different data. Hence, this model is sometimes called the shared memory, single instruction, multiple data (SM SIMD) machine. Algorithms are assumed to run without interference as long as only one memory access is permitted at a time. We say that PRAM guarantees atomic access to data located in shared memory. An operation is considered to be atomic if it is completed in its entirety or it is not performed at all (all or nothing).

There are different modes for read and write operations in a PRAM. These different modes are summarized as follows:

- Exclusive read (ER): Only one processor can read from any memory location at a time.
- Exclusive write (EW): Only one processor can write to any memory location at a time.
- Concurrent read (CR): Multiple processors can read from the same memory location simultaneously.

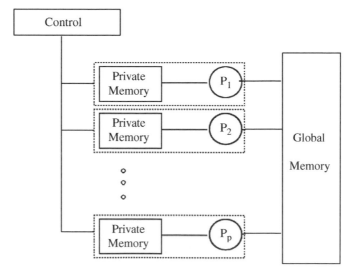

Figure 6.1   PRAM model for parallel computations.

- Concurrent write (CW): Multiple processors can write to the same memory location simultaneously. Write conflicts must be resolved using a well-defined policy such as:

    Common: All concurrent writes store the same value.

    Arbitrary: Only one value selected arbitrarily is stored. The other values are ignored.

    Minimum: The value written by the processor with the smallest index is stored. The other values are ignored.

    Reduction: All the values are reduced to only one value using some reduction function such as sum, minimum, maximum, and so on.

Based on the different modes described above, the PRAM can be further divided into the following subclasses:

- EREW PRAM: Access to any memory cell is exclusive. This is the most restrictive PRAM model.
- ERCW PRAM: This allows concurrent writes to the same memory location by multiple processors, but read accesses remain exclusive.
- CREW PRAM: Concurrent read accesses are allowed, but write accesses are exclusive.
- CRCW PRAM: Both concurrent read and write accesses are allowed.

6.2 SIMULATING MULTIPLE ACCESSES ON AN EREW PRAM

The EREW PRAM model is considered the most restrictive among the four subclasses discussed in the previous section. Only one processor can read from or write to a given memory location at any time. An algorithm designed for such a model must not rely on having multiple processors access the same memory location simultaneously in order to improve its performance. Obviously, an algorithm designed for an EREW PRAM can run on a CRCW PRAM. The algorithm simply will not use the concurrent access features in the CRCW PRAM. However, the contrary is not true, an algorithm designed for CRCW cannot run on an EREW PRAM.

Is it possible to simulate concurrent access in the EREW model? The answer is yes. In general, any algorithm designed to run on a given model can be simulated on a more restrictive model at the price of more time and/or memory requirements (Cosnard and Trystram, 1996). Clearly, the EREW PRAM model is the most restrictive among the four PRAM subclasses. Hence, it is possible to simulate the concurrent read and write operations on an EREW PRAM. In what follows, we show that this simulation can be done at the price of $O(\log p)$ time and $O(p)$ memory, where p is the number of processors, using a *broadcasting* procedure.

Suppose that a memory location x is needed by all processors at a given time in a PRAM. Concurrent read by all processors can be performed in the CREW and CRCW cases in constant time. In the EREW case, the following broadcasting mechanism can be followed (Akl, 1997; Kronsjo, 1996):

1. P_1 reads x and makes it known to P_2.
2. P_1 and P_2 make x known to P_3 and P_4, respectively, in parallel.
3. P_1, P_2, P_3, and P_4 make x known to P_5, P_6, P_7, and P_8, respectively, in parallel.
4. These eight processors will make x known to another eight processors, and so on.

In order to represent this algorithm in PRAM, an array L of size p is used as a working space in the shared memory to distribute the contents of x to all processors. Initially P_1 will read x in its private memory and writes it into $L[1]$. Processor P_2, will read x from $L[1]$ into its private memory and write it into $L[2]$. Simultaneously, P_3 and P_4 read x from $L[1]$ and $L[2]$, respectively, then write them into $L[3]$ and $L[4]$, respectively. Processors P_5, P_6, P_7, and P_8 will then simultaneously read $L[1]$, $L[2]$, $L[3]$, and $L[4]$, respectively, in parallel and write them into $L[5]$, $L[6]$, $L[7]$, and $L[8]$, respectively. This process will continue until eventually all the processors have read x. Figure 6.2 illustrates the idea of *Algorithm Broadcast_EREW*, when $p = 8$.

Algorithm Broadcast_EREW
Processor P_1
```
y (in P₁'s private memory) ← x
L[1] ← y
for i=0 to log p - 1 do
   forall Pⱼ, where 2ⁱ + 1 ≤ j ≤ 2ⁱ⁺¹ do in parallel
      y (in Pⱼ's private memory) ← L[j - 2ⁱ]
      L[j] ← y
   endfor
endfor
```

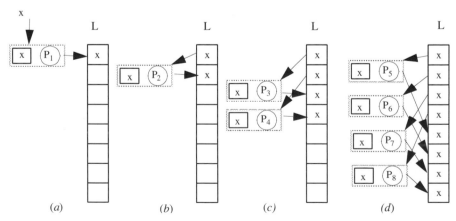

(a) (b) (c) (d)

Figure 6.2 Simulating concurrent read on EREW PRAM with eight processors using algorithm broadcast_EREW.

Since the number of processors having read x doubles in each iteration, the procedure terminates in $O(\log p)$ time. The array L is the price paid in terms of memory, which is $O(p)$.

6.3   ANALYSIS OF PARALLEL ALGORITHMS

The complexity of a sequential algorithm is generally determined by its time and space complexity. The time complexity of an algorithm refers to its execution time as a function of the problem's size. Similarly, the space complexity refers to the amount of memory required by the algorithm as a function of the size of the problem. The time complexity has been known to be the most important measure of the performance of algorithms. An algorithm whose time complexity is bounded by a polynomial is called a polynomial–time algorithm. An algorithm is considered to be efficient if it runs in polynomial time. Inefficient algorithms are those that require a search of the whole enumerated space and have an exponential time complexity.

For parallel algorithms, the time complexity remains an important measure of performance. Additionally, the number of processors plays a major role in determining the complexity of a parallel algorithm. In general, we say that the performance of a parallel algorithm is expressed in terms of how fast it is, and how many resources it uses when it runs. These criteria can be measured quantitatively as follows:

1. Run time, which is defined as the time spent during the execution of the algorithm.
2. Number of processors the algorithm uses to solve a problem.
3. The cost of the parallel algorithm, which is the product of the run time and the number of processors.

The run time of a parallel algorithm is the length of the time period between the time the first processor to begin execution starts and the time the last processor to finish execution terminates. However, since the analysis of algorithms is normally conducted before the algorithm is even implemented on an actual computer, the run time is usually obtained by counting the number of steps in the algorithm.

The cost of a parallel algorithm is basically the total number of steps executed collectively by all processors. If the cost of an algorithm is C, the algorithm can be converted into a sequential one that runs in $O(C)$ time on one processor. A parallel algorithm is said to be *cost optimal* if its cost matches the lower bound on the number of sequential operations to solve a given problem within a constant factor. It follows that a parallel algorithm is not cost optimal if there exists a sequential algorithm whose run time is smaller than the cost of the parallel algorithm.

It may be possible to speed up the execution of a cost-optimal PRAM algorithm by increasing the number of processors. However, we should be careful because using more processors may increase the cost of the parallel algorithm. Similarly, a PRAM algorithm may use fewer processors in order to reduce the cost. In this case the execution may be slowed down and offset the decrease in the number of processors. Therefore, using fewer processors requires that we make them work more efficiently. Further details on the relationship between the run time, number of processors, and optimal cost can be found in Brent (1974).

In order to design efficient parallel algorithms, one must consider the following general rules. The number of processors must be bounded by the size of the problem. The parallel run time must be significantly smaller than the execution time of the best sequential algorithm. The cost of the algorithm is optimal.

6.3.1 The NC-Class and P-Completeness

In the theory of sequential algorithms, we distinguish between tractable and intractable problems by categorizing them into different classes. For those who are not familiar with these classes, we define them in simple terms. A problem belongs to class P if a solution of the problem can be obtained by a polynomial–time algorithm. A problem belongs to class NP if the correctness of a solution for the problem can be verified by a polynomial–time algorithm. Clearly, every problem in P will also be in NP, or $P \subseteq NP$. It remain an open problem whether $P \subset NP$ or $P = NP$. However, it is not likely that $P = NP$ since this would imply that solving a problem is as easy as verifying whether a given solution to the problem is correct. A problem is in the class NP-hard if it is as hard as any problem in NP. In other words, every NP problem is polynomial–time reducible to any NP-hard problem. The existence of a polynomial–time algorithm for an NP-hard problem implies the existence of polynomial solutions for every problem in NP. Finally, NP-complete problems are the NP-hard problems that are also in NP.

The NP-complete problems are the problems that are strongly suspected to be computationally intractable. There is a host of important problems that are roughly equivalent in complexity and form the class of NP-complete problems. This class includes many classical problems in combinatorics, graph theory, and computer science such as the traveling salesman problem, the Hamilton circuit problem, and integer programming. The best known algorithms for these problems could take exponential time on some inputs. The exact complexity of these NP-complete problems has yet to be determined and it remains the foremost open problem in theoretical computer science. Either all these problems have polynomial–time solutions, or none of them does.

Similarly, in the world of parallel computation, we should be able to classify problems according to their use of the resources: time and processors. Let us define the class of the well-parallelizable problems, called NC, as the class of problem that have efficient parallel solutions. It is the class of problems that are solvable in time bounded by a polynomial in the log of the input size using a number of processors bounded by a polynomial in the input size. The time bound is sometimes referred to as *polylogarithmic* because it is polynomial in the log of the input size. In other words, the problems that can be solved by parallel algorithms that take polylogarithmic time using a polynomial number of processors, are said to belong to the class NC. The problems in the class NC are regarded as having efficient parallel solutions. The question now is: what is the relation between NC and P? It remain an open question whether $NC \subset P$ or $NC = P$. It appears that some problems

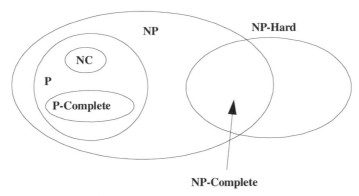

Figure 6.3 The relationships among P, NP, NP-complete, NP-hard, NC, and P-complete (if P ⊂ NP and NC ⊂ P).

in P cannot be solved in polylogarithmic time using a polynomial number of processors. Thus, it is not likely that NC = P.

We finally discuss the P-complete problems. A problem is in the class P-complete if it is as hard to parallelize as any problem in P. In other words, every P problem is polylogarithmic–time reducible to any P-complete problem using a polynomial number of processors. Also, the existence of a polylogarithmic–time algorithm for a P-complete problem implies the existence of polylogarithmic solutions for every problem in P using a polynomial number of processors. In other words, a P-complete problem is the problem that is solvable sequentially in polynomial time, but does not lie in the class NC unless every problem solvable in sequential polynomial time lies in NC. Among examples of P-complete problems are a depth-first search of an arbitrary graph, the maximum-flow problem, and the circuit value problem. The relationships between all these classes are illustrated in Figure 6.3, if we assume that P ⊂ NP and NC ⊂ P.

6.4 COMPUTING SUM AND ALL SUMS

In this section, we design a PRAM algorithm to compute all partial sums of an array of numbers. Given n numbers, stored in array $A\,[1\,.\,.\,n]$, we want to compute the partial sums $A[1], A[1] + A[2], A[1] + A[2] + A[3], \ldots, A[1] + A[2] + \cdots + A[n]$. At first glance, one might think that accumulating sums is an inherently serial process, because one must add up the first k elements before adding in element $k + 1$. We will show that parallelism can be exploited in solving this problem.

To make it easy for the reader to understand the algorithm, we start by developing a similar algorithm for the simpler problem of computing the simple sum of an array of n values. Then we extend the algorithm to compute all partial sums using what is learned from the simple summation problem. In all cases we provide description of the algorithm, complexity analysis, and an example that illustrates how the algorithm works.

6.4.1 Sum of an Array of Numbers on the EREW Model

In this section, we discuss an algorithm to compute the sum of n numbers. Summation can be done in time $O(\log n)$ by organizing the numbers at the leaves of a binary tree and performing the sums at each level of the tree in parallel.

We present this algorithm on an EREW PRAM with $n/2$ processors because we will not need to perform any multiple read or write operations on the same memory location. Recall that in an EREW PRAM, read and write conflicts are not allowed. We assume that the array $A[1 . . n]$ is stored in the global memory. The summation will end up in the last location $A[n]$. For simplicity, we assume that n is an integral power of 2. The algorithm will complete the work in $\log n$ iterations as follows. In the first iteration, all the processors are active. In the second iteration, only half of the processors will be active, and so on. The details are described in *Algorithm Sum_EREW* given below.

```
Algorithm Sum_EREW
for i=1 to log n do
  forall Pⱼ, where 1 ≤ j ≤ n/2 do in parallel
    if (2j modulo 2ⁱ) =0 then
      A[2j] ← A[2j] + A[2j − 2^{i-1}]
    endif
  endfor
endfor
```

Complexity Analysis The for loop is executed $\log n$ times, and each iteration has constant time complexity. Hence the run time of the algorithm is $O(\log n)$. Since the number of processors used is $n/2$, the cost is obviously $O(n \log n)$. The complexity measures of *Algorithm Sum_EREW* are summarized as follows:

1. Run time, $T(n) = O(\log n)$.
2. Number of processors, $P(n) = n/2$.
3. Cost, $C(n) = O(n \log n)$.

Since a good sequential algorithm can sum the list of n elements in $O(n)$, this algorithm is not cost optimal.

Example 1 Figure 6.4 illustrates the algorithm on an array of eight elements: 5, 2, 10, 1, 8, 12, 7, 3. In order to sum eight elements, three iterations are needed as follows. In the first iteration, processors P_1, P_2, P_3, and P_4 add the values stored at locations 1, 3, 5, and 7 to the numbers stored at locations 2, 4, 6, and 8, respectively. In the second iteration, processors P_2 and P_4 add the values stored at locations 2 and 6 to the numbers stored at locations 4 and 8, respectively. Finally, in the third iteration processor P_4 adds the value stored at location 4 to the value stored at location 8. Thus, location 8 will eventually contain the sum of all numbers in the array.

6.4.2 All Partial Sums of an Array

Take a closer look at *Algorithm Sum_EREW* and notice that most of the processors are idle most of the time. However, by exploiting the idle processors, we should be

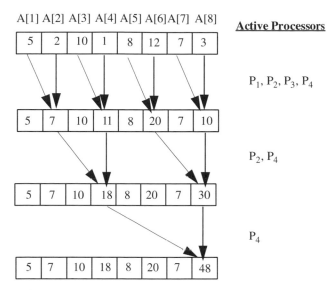

Figure 6.4 Example of *Algorithm Sum-EREW* when $n = 8$.

able to compute all partial sums of the array in the same amount of time it takes to compute the single sum. We present *Algorithm AllSums_EREW* to calculate all partial sums of an array on an EREW PRAM with $n-1$ processors $(P_2, P_3, \ldots, P_n)$. Again the elements of the array $A[1 .. n]$ are assumed to be in the global shared memory. The partial sum algorithm replaces each $A[k]$ by the sum of all elements preceding and including $A[k]$.

In *Algorithm Sum_EREW* presented earlier, during iteration i, only $n/2^i$ processors are active, while in the algorithm we present here, nearly all processors are in use. The details of the algorithm are shown in *Algorithm AllSums_EREW*:

Algorithm AllSums_EREW
for i=1 **to** log n **do**
  forall P$_j$, **where** $2^{i-1} + 1 \leq j \leq n$ **do in parallel**
  A[j] ← A [j] + A[j − 2^{i-1}]
  endfor
endfor

The picture given in Figure 6.5 illustrates the three iterations of the algorithm on an array of eight elements named $A[1]$ through $A[8]$.

Complexity Analysis The complexity measures of *Algorithm AllSums_EREW* are summarized as follows:

1. Run time, $T(n) = O(\log n)$.
2. Number of processors, $P(n) = n - 1$.
3. Cost, $C(n) = O(n \log n)$.

Is *Algorithm AllSums-EREW* cost optimal? (See Problem 5.)

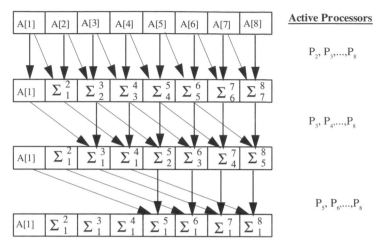

Figure 6.5   Computing partial sums of an array of eight elements.

6.5   MATRIX MULTIPLICATION

In this section, we study matrix multiplication in parallel. We present an algorithm for multiplying two $n \times n$ matrices. For clarity, we assume that n is a power of 2. We use the CREW PRAM model to allow multiple read operations from the same memory locations. Recall that in a CREW PRAM, multiple read operations can be conducted concurrently, but multiple write operations are performed exclusively. We start by presenting the algorithm on a CREW PRAM with n^3 processors. We will then show how to reduce the cost by using fewer processors. We assume that the two input matrices are stored in the shared memory in the arrays $A[1 .. n, 1 .. n]$, $B[1 .. n, 1 .. n]$.

6.5.1   Using n^3 Processors

We consider the n^3 processors as being arranged into a three-dimensional array. Processor $P_{i,j,k}$ is the one with index (i, j, k). A three-dimensional array $C[i, j, k]$, where $1 \le i, j, k \le n$, in the shared memory will be used as working space. The resulting matrix will be stored in locations $C[i, j, n]$, where $1 \le i, j \le n$.

The algorithm consists of two steps. In the first step, all n^3 processors operate in parallel to compute n^3 multiplications. For each of the n^2 cells in the output matrix, n products are computed. In the second step, the n products computed for each cell in the output matrix are summed to produce the final value of this cell. This summation can be performed in parallel in $O(\log n)$ time as shown in *Algorithm Sum_EREW* discussed earlier. The two steps of the algorithm are given as:

1. Each processor $P_{i,j,k}$ computes the product of $A[i, k] * B[k, j]$ and stores it in $C[i, j, k]$.
2. The idea of *Algorithm Sum_EREW* is applied along the k dimension n^2 times in parallel to compute $C[i, j, n]$, where $1 \le i, j \le n$.

The details of these two steps are presented in *Algorithm MatMult_CREW*:

```
Algorithm MatMult_CREW
/* Step 1 */
forall P_{i,j,k}, where 1 ≤ i, j, k ≤ n do in parallel
  C[i,j,k] ← A[i,k]*B[k,j]
endfor

/* Step 2 */
for l=1 to log n do
  forall P_{i,j,k}, where 1 ≤ i, j ≤ n & 1 ≤ k ≤ n/2 do in parallel
    if (2k modulo 2^l) =0 then
      C[i,j,2k] ← C[i,j,2k] + C[i,j, 2k − 2^{l-1}]
    endif
  endfor
  /* The output matrix is stored in locations
    C[i,j,n], where 1 ≤ i,j ≤ n     */
endfor
```

Figure 6.6 shows the activities of the active processors after each of the two steps of *Algorithm MatMult_CREW* when used to multiply two 2×2 matrices.

Complexity Analysis In the first step, the products are conducted in parallel in constant time, that is, $O(1)$. These products are summed in $O(\log n)$ time during the second step. Therefore, the run time is $O(\log n)$. Since the number of processors used is n^3, the cost is $O(n^3 \log n)$. The complexity measures of the matrix multiplication on CREW PRAM with n^3 processors are summarized as:

1. Run time, $T(n) = O(\log n)$.
2. Number of processors, $P(n) = n^3$.
3. Cost, $C(n) = O(n^3 \log n)$.

Since an $n \times n$ matrix multiplication can be done sequentially in less than $O(n^3 \log n)$, this algorithm is not cost optimal. In order to reduce the cost of this parallel algorithm, we should try to reduce the number of processors.

6.5.2 Reducing the Number of Processors

In the above algorithm, although all the processors were busy during the first step, not all of them performed addition operations during the second step. As you can see, the second step consists of $\log n$ iterations. During the first iteration, only $n^3/2$ processors performed addition operations, only $n^3/4$ performed addition operations in the second iteration, and so on. With this understanding, we may be able to use a smaller machine with only $n^3/\log n$ processors. But how can this be done? The

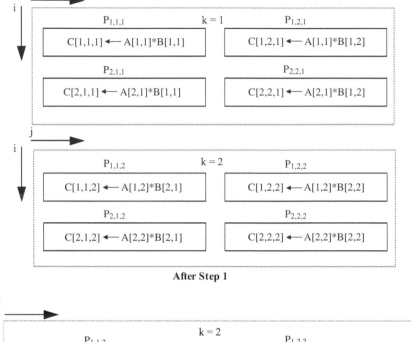

Figure 6.6   Multiplying two 2×2 matrices using *Algorithm MatMult_CREW*.

idea is to arrange the processors in $n \times n \times n/\log n$ three-dimensional array. The two steps of the *Algorithm MatMult_CREW* can be modified as:

1. Each processor $P_{i,j,k}$, where $1 \leq k \leq n/\log n$, computes the sum of $\log n$ products. This step will produce $(n^3/\log n)$ partial sums.
2. The sum of products produced in step 1 are added to produce the resulting matrix as discussed before.

Complexity Analysis   Since each processor is responsible for computing $\log n$ product terms and obtaining their sum in step 1, each processor performs $\log n$ multiplications and $\log n - 1$ additions during this step. These products are summed in $\log(n/\log n)$ time during step 2. Therefore, the execution time of step 1 and step 2 of the algorithm is $2 \log n - 1 + \log(n/\log n)$, which can be approximated as $O(\log n)$ for large values of n. The complexity measures of the matrix multiplication on CREW PRAM with $n^3/\log n$ processors are summarized as:

1. Run time, $T(n) = O(\log n)$.
2. Number of processors, $P(n) = n^3/\log n$.
3. Cost, $C(n) = O(n^3)$.

Is *Algorithm MatMult_CREW* after modification cost optimal? (See Problem 5.)

6.6 SORTING

The sorting algorithm we present here is based on the *enumeration* idea. Given an unsorted list of n elements $a_1, a_2, \ldots, a_i, \ldots, a_n$, an enumeration sort determines the position of each element a_i in the sorted list by computing the number of elements smaller than it. If c_i elements are smaller than a_i, then it is the $(c_i + 1)^{\text{th}}$ element in the sorted list. If two or more elements have the same value, the element with the largest index in the unsorted list will be considered as the largest in the sorted list. For example, suppose that $a_i = a_j$, then a_i will be considered the larger of the two if $i > j$, otherwise a_j is the larger.

We present this simple algorithm on a CRCW PRAM with n^2 processors. Recall that in a CRCW PRAM multiple read operations can be conducted concurrently; so are multiple write operations. However, write conflicts must be resolved according to a certain policy. In this algorithm, we assume that when multiple processors try to write different values into the same address, the sum of these values will be stored in that address.

Consider the n^2 processors as being arranged into n rows of n elements each. The processors are numbered as follows: $P_{i,j}$ is the processor located in row i and column j in the grid of processors. We assume that the sorted list is stored in the global memory in an array $A[1..n]$. Another array $C[1..n]$ will be used to store the number of elements smaller than every element in A.

The algorithm consists of two steps:

1. Each row of processors i computes $C[i]$, the number of elements smaller than $A[i]$. Each processor $P_{i,j}$ compares $A[i]$ and $A[j]$, then updates $C[i]$ appropriately.
2. The first processor in each row $P_{i,1}$ places $A[i]$ in its proper position in the sorted list ($C[i] + 1$).

The details of these two steps are presented in *Algorithm Sort_CRCW*:

Algorithm Sort_CRCW

```
/* Step 1 */
forall P_i,j, where 1 ≤ i, j ≤ n do in parallel
```

```
if A[i] > A[j] or (A[i]=A[j] and i > j) then
  C[i] ← 1
else
  C[i] ← 0
endif
endfor

/* Step 2 */
forall P_{i,1}, where 1 ≤ i ≤ n do in parallel
  A[C[i] + 1] ← A[i]
endfor
```

Complexity Analysis   The complexity measures of the enumerating sort on CRCW PRAM are summarized as:

1. Run time, $T(n) = O(1)$.
2. Number of processors, $P(n) = n^2$.
3. Cost, $C(n) = O(n^2)$.

The run time of this algorithm is constant because each of the two steps of the algorithm consumes a constant amount of time. Since the number of processors used is n^2, the cost is obviously $O(n^2)$. Since a good sequential algorithm can sort a list of n elements in $O(n \log n)$, this algorithm is not cost optimal. Although the above algorithm sorts n elements in constant time, it has no practical value because it uses a very large number of processors in addition to its reliance on a very powerful PRAM model (CRCW). How can you reduce the cost? (See Problem 7.)

Example 2   Let us sort the array $A = [6, 1, 3]$. As shown in Figure 6.7, we need nine processors to perform the sort. The figure shows the contents of the shared memory and the elements that each processor compares.

6.7   MESSAGE PASSING MODEL

An algorithm designed for a message passing system consists of a collection of local programs running concurrently on the different processing units in a distributed system. Each local program performs a sequence of computation and message passing operations. Message passing in distributed systems can be modeled using a communication graph. The nodes of the graph represent the processors (or the processes running on them) and the edges represent communication links between processors. Throughout this chapter, we will not distinguish between a processor and its process. Each node representing a process has a set of neighbors with which it can communicate. The communication graph may be directed or undirected. A directed edge indicates unidirectional communication, while an undirected edge implies bidirectional communication. The two graphs of Figure 6.8 are examples of unidirectional and bidirectional communication. For example, it can be seen in Figure 6.8a that the outgoing neighbors of P_3 are P_1 and P_5, while its

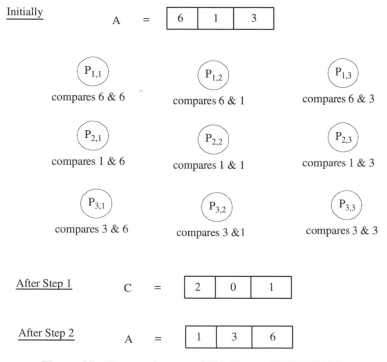

Figure 6.7 Enumeration sort of [6,1,3] on a CRCW PRAM.

incoming neighbors are P_2 and P_4. In Figure 6.8*b*, processes P_1, P_2, P_4, and P_5 are incoming as well as outgoing neighbors of P_3.

A message passing distributed system may operate in synchronous, asynchronous, or partially synchronous modes. In the synchronous extreme, the execution is completely lock–step and local programs proceed in synchronous rounds. For example, in one round each local program sends messages to its outgoing neighbors, waits for the arrival of messages from its incoming neighbors, and performs some computation upon the receipt of the messages. In the other extreme, in asynchronous mode the local programs execute in arbitrary order at arbitrary rate. The partially

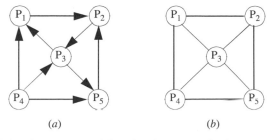

Figure 6.8 Unidirectional and bidirectional communication graphs (*a*) directed communication graph; and (*b*) unidirected communication graph.

synchronous systems work at an intermediate degree of synchrony, where there are restrictions on the relative timing events.

In this section we focus on studying synchronous message passing systems. We outline the basic elements of a formal model of a distributed system as described by Lynch (1996). The models presented here may be more detailed than needed in some cases, but they help give the reader a good idea of the formal representation of different and more general systems. We also discuss the complexity analysis of algorithms described in terms of these formal models as we define the time and message complexity.

6.7.1 Synchronous Message Passing Model

Given a message passing system consisting of n processes, each of which is running on a separate processor, we show how to model such a system in the synchronous mode. As mentioned earlier, the communication among processors is represented using a communication graph $G = (V,E)$. The behavior of this system can be described as follows:

1. System is initialized and set to an arbitrary initial state.
2. For each process $i \in V$, repeat the following two steps in synchronized rounds (lock–step fashion):
   (a) Send messages to the outgoing neighbors by applying some message generation function to the current state.
   (b) Obtain the new state by applying a state transition function to the current state and the messages received from incoming neighbors.

An execution of this synchronized system can be represented as a sequence of (1) states, (2) sent messages, and (3) received messages as follows:

$$\texttt{state}_0, \texttt{sent-msg}_1, \texttt{rcvd-msg}_1, \texttt{state}_1, \texttt{sent-msg}_2, \texttt{rcvd-msg}_2,$$
$$\texttt{state}_2, \ldots, \texttt{sent-msg}_j, \texttt{rcvd-msg}_j, \texttt{state}_j, \ldots$$

The system changes its current state to a new state based on the messages sent and received among the processes. Note that the messages received may not be the same as the messages sent because some of them may be lost as a result of a faulty channel. For example, the system starts at $\texttt{state}_0$ and is changed to $\texttt{state}_1$ after the sending and receiving of $\texttt{sent-msg}_1$ and $\texttt{rcvd-msg}_1$. The system then changes from $\texttt{state}_1$ to $\texttt{state}_2$, and so on.

Thus, a synchronous system can be modeled as a state machine with the following components:

1. $\texttt{M}$, a fixed message alphabet.
2. A process i can be modeled as:
   (a) $\texttt{Q}_i$, a (possibly infinite) set of states. The system state can be represented using a set of variables.

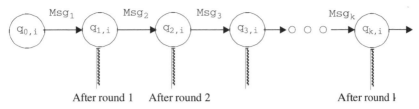

After round 1   After round 2   After round k

Figure 6.9 An example of a state diagram for process i.

(b) $q_{0,i}$, the initial state in the state set Q_i. The state variables have initial values in the initial state.

(c) **GenMsg**$_i$, a message generation function. It is applied to the current system state to generate messages to the outgoing neighbors from elements in M.

(d) **Trans**$_i$, a state transition function that maps the current state and the incoming messages into a new state.

Suppose that the communication links are reliable and the messages received by process i are the same as the ones sent by its incoming neighbors. Figure 6.9 shows a simple example of a state diagram for process i. Starting at state $q_{0,i}$, process i receives the messages Msg_1 from its incoming neighbors and changes to state $q_{1,i}$. Process i at state $q_{1,i}$ now receives the messages Msg_2 from its incoming neighbors and changes its state to $q_{2,i}$. This process is repeated any number of times as shown in the figure. Note that after k rounds process i will be at state $q_{k,i}$.

In order to provide a description for algorithms studied under the synchronous model, the following is a template that we will be using in this chapter. The template, which is referred to as *S_Template*, describes the computation carried out by process $i \in V$. The prefix *S_* in the algorithm's name is meant to indicate that it is synchronous.

Algorithm S_Template
Q_i
     <state variables used by process i>
$q_{0,i}$
     <state variables> ← <initial values>
GenMsg$_i$
     <Send one message to each of a (possibly empty) subset of outgoing neighbors>
Trans$_i$
     <update the state variables based on the incoming messages>

6.7.2 Complexity Analysis

As discussed earlier, complexity analysis of algorithms is usually expressed in terms of the amount of resources needed by the computation to be completed. In addition to the run time, the amount of communication is an important resource in message passing systems. The complexity of algorithms in such systems will be measured quantitatively using time complexity and message complexity. The measures of complexity will be expressed in the usual asymptotic fashion as functions of the number of nodes and edges in the communication graph representing the distributed system.

Message Complexity   The message complexity is defined as the number of messages sent between neighbors during the execution of the algorithm. We usually consider the worst-case message complexity, which is the maximum number of messages.

Time Complexity   The time complexity is defined generally as the time spent during the execution of the algorithm. The definition of the time complexity in the synchronous model is rather simple, and amounts to the number of rounds until the termination of the algorithm. Defining the time complexity of an algorithm in asynchronous executions is not so straightforward. The time complexity in this case only considers messages that happen sequentially. It can be obtained by assigning occurrence times to events in the execution under some restrictions.

Example 3   Consider a synchronous hypercube made of n processors. Assume that each link connecting two adjacent processors can perform communication in both directions at the same time (bidirectional communication). Suppose that each process i has its own data x_i, and we would like to compute the summation of data at all processes. The summation can be computed in $\log n$ rounds. At each round each process sends its data to one of its neighbors along one of the hypercube dimensions. At the end, each process will have the summation stored in its local space. A formal description of this method using the above model is shown below in *Algorithm S_Sum_Hypercube*:

Algorithm S_Sum_Hypercube
Q$_i$
    buff, an integer
    dim, a value in {1, 2, ... , log n}
q$_{0,i}$
    buff ← x$_i$
    dim ← log n
GenMsg$_i$
    If the current value of dim = 0, do nothing. Otherwise,
    send the current value of buff to the neighbor along the
    dimension dim.
Trans$_i$
    if the incoming message is v & dim > 0, then
    buff ← buff + v, dim ← dim - 1

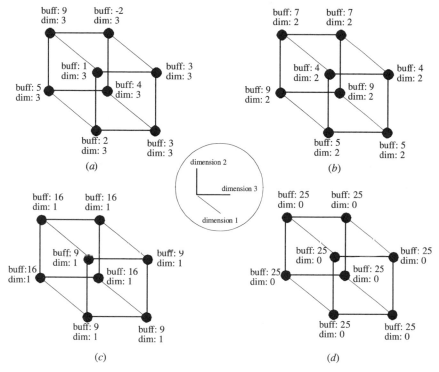

Figure 6.10 Computing the summation synchronously on a three-dimensional hypercube (*a*) initial states; (*b*) after first round; (*c*) after second round; and (*d*) after third round.

Figure 6.10 illustrates the rounds of the algorithm for a hypercube of dimension 3. Assume that the data values 1, 2, 3, 3, 9, 5, 4, −2 are distributed to the eight processes as shown in Figure 6.10*a*. The states after each of the first three rounds are shown in Figures 6.10*b*, *c*, and *d*.

Complexity Analysis Given *n* processors connected via a hypercube, *S_Sum_ Hypercube* needs log *n* rounds to compute the sum. Since *n* messages are sent and received in each round, the total number of messages is $O(n \log n)$.

Therefore, the complexity of Algorithm *S_Sum_Hypercube* is summarized:

1. Time complexity: $O(\log n)$.
2. Message complexity: $O(n \log n)$.

6.8 LEADER ELECTION PROBLEM

A *leader* among *n* processors is the processor that is recognized by all other processors as distinguished to perform a special task. The leader election problem arises when the processors of a distributed system must choose one of them as a leader. Each processor should eventually decide whether or not it is a leader, given that each processor is only aware of its identification and not aware of any other processes.

The problem of electing a leader in a distributed environment is most important in situations in which coordination among processors becomes necessary to recover from a failure or topological change. A leader in such situations is needed, for example, to coordinate the reestablishment of allocation and routing functions. For example, consider a token ring network, in which a token moves around the network giving its current owner the right to initiate communication. If the token is lost, a leader in this case is needed to coordinate the regeneration of the lost token.

The leader election problem is meaningless in the context of anonymous systems. A system is anonymous if the processes on all processors are identical and the processors do not have access to their identifications.

Theorem 6.1   There is no algorithm for leader election in anonymous rings (Angluin).

Proof   For simplicity, we prove this theorem in synchronous rings. Assume that all processes in the anonymous ring start in the same state. Since an algorithm in a synchronous system proceeds in rounds, we use induction on the number of rounds that have been executed (r). It is straightforward to verify that all the processes will be in identical states immediately after r rounds. Consequently, if any process reaches a state where its status is leader, then all other processes will also reach such a state at the same time.

The above result can be extended to hold for any system in which the communication graph is regular such as a complete graph. Moreover, even if the system is not anonymous, the leader election problem can only be solved if every processor's identification is unique.

Now, let us explore the basic idea behind the different leader election algorithms. Suppose that the communication graph is an arbitrary graph $G = (V, E)$. The following two steps summarize our first attempt to solve the problem:

1. Each node in the graph would broadcast its unique identifier to all other nodes.
2. After receiving the identifiers of all nodes, the node with the highest identifier declares itself as the leader.

Let us study the complexity of the above solution for an arbitrary graph. Since each node sends its identifier to all other nodes, the number of messages sent to deliver only one identifier to all other nodes is equal to the number of edges in the graph $|E|$. Since there are $|V|$ identifiers that need to be broadcast, the message complexity (total number of messages) is $O(|V|.|E|)$.

How does this algorithm work under the synchronous model? Suppose that the communication graph is a complete graph. The following two steps summarize the algorithm:

1. At the first round, each node sends its unique identifier to all other nodes.
2. At the end of the first round, every node has the identifiers of all nodes, the node with the highest identifier declares itself as the leader.

Since there is only one round, the time complexity of the synchronous algorithm is $O(1)$. The message complexity is $O(n^2)$ since the number of messages is equal to the number of edges in the graph. In order to decrease the message complexity, a process does not have to send its unique identifier to all of its neighbors during the same round. Instead, a process may first communicate with one neighbor then with two other neighbors, then with four, and so on.

6.9 LEADER ELECTION IN SYNCHRONOUS RINGS

In this section we present two algorithms to solve the leader election problem under the synchronous model in a distributed system whose communication graph is a ring. Let us assume that the process with the largest identifier (ID) is the one that will always be elected as a leader.

6.9.1 Simple Leader Election Algorithm

The idea of this simple algorithm is that each process sends its identifier all the way around the ring. The process that receives its identifier back is declared as a leader. This algorithm was presented in Chang and Roberts (1979), Le Lann (1977) and Lynch (1996). We assume the following:

1. Communication is unidirectional (clockwise).
2. The size of the ring is not known.
3. The identification of each processor is unique.

The algorithm can be summarized as follows:

1. Each process sends its identifier to its outgoing neighbor.
2. When a process receives an identifier from its incoming neighbor, then:
   (a) The process sends null to its outgoing neighbor, if the received identifier is less than its own identifier.
   (b) The process sends the received identifier to its outgoing neighbor, if the received identifier is greater than its own identifier.
   (c) The process declares itself as the leader, if the received identifier is equal to its own identifier.

Assuming that the message alphabet M is the set of identifiers, the above method is described in terms of the synchronous model in *Algorithm S_Elect_Leader_Simple*:

Algorithm S_Elect_Leader_Simple
Q_i
     u, some ID
     buff, some ID or null
     status, a value in {unknown, leader}
$q_{0,i}$
     u ← ID_i
     buff ← ID_i
     status ← unknown
GenMsg$_i$
     Send the current value of buff to clockwise-neighbor
Trans$_i$
     buff ← null
     if the incoming message is v and is not null, then
     case
       v < u: do nothing
       v = u: status ← leader
       v > u: buff ← v
     endcase

Complexity Analysis   Given n processors connected via a ring, *Algorithm S_Elect_Leader_Simple* needs n rounds to elect a leader in the worst case. Since n messages are sent and received in each round, total number of messages is $O(n^2)$.

Therefore, the complexity of *Algorithm S_Elect_Leader_Simple* is summarized:

1. Time complexity: $O(n)$.
2. Message complexity: $O(n^2)$.

Example 4   Suppose that we have four processes running on four processors connected via a synchronous ring. The processes (processors) have the IDs 1, 2, 3, and 4. Message passing is performed in a unidirectional fashion. The ring is oriented such that process i sends messages to its clockwise neighbor. Figure 6.11 illustrates the state of each process after each of the four rounds.

6.9.2   Improved Leader Election Algorithm

In order to decrease the message complexity, a process does not have to send its ID all the way around the ring. Instead, a process may send its messages to neighbors within a certain distance, which will successively increase. This is the idea behind the algorithm described here, which was first introduced by Hirschberg and Sinclair (1980). We assume the following:

   • Communication is bidirectional.
   • The size of the ring is not known.
   • The identification of each processor is unique.

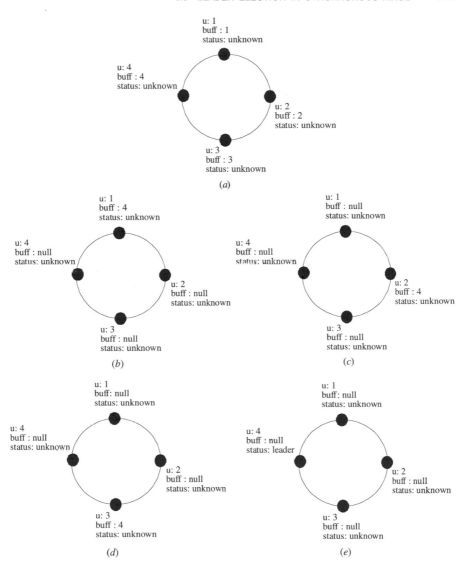

Figure 6.11 Leader election in a synchronous ring using *Algorithm S_Elect_Leader_Simple* (*a*) initial states; (*b*) after first round; (*c*) after second round; (*d*) after third round; and (*e*) after fourth round.

The algorithm can be summarized as follows:

1. $k \leftarrow 0$
2. Each process sends its identifier in messages to its neighbors in both directions intending that they will travel 2^k hops and then return to their origin.

3. If the identifier is proceeding in the outbound direction, when a process on the path receives the identifier from its neighbor, then:
   (a) The process sends null to its outneighbor, if the received identifier is less than its own identifier.
   (b) The process sends the received identifier to its outneighbor, if the received identifier is greater than its own identifier.
   (c) The process declares itself as the leader, if the received identifier is equal to its own identifier.
4. If the identifier is proceeding in the inbound direction, when a process on the path receives the identifier, it sends the received identifier to its outgoing neighbor on the path, if the received identifier is greater than its own identifier.
5. If the two original messages make it back to their origin, then $k \leftarrow k + 1$; Go to Step 2.

Figure 6.12 shows the paths of messages initiated at process i for the different values of k. Note that in this algorithm, we assume that the processors are numbered $1, 2, \ldots, n$. The clockwise neighbor of processor i is processor $(i + 1)$. However, we assume that processor n is also known as 0. That is, processor $(i + 1)$ is 1 when $i = n$; and processor $(i - 1)$ is n, when $i = 1$.

Let us assume that the message alphabet is defined as follows:

M
    The set of triples consisting (ID, F, H) as follows:
    ID, a process identifier
    F, flag value in {in, out}
    H, a positive integer indicating the number of hops.

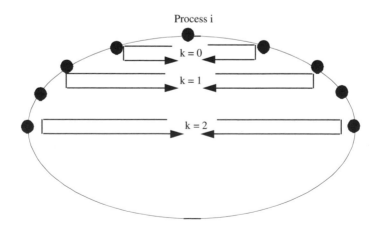

Figure 6.12 Messages initiated at process i using the improved leader election algorithm.

The improved algorithm is described in terms of the synchronous model in *Algorithm S_Elect_Leader_Improved*:

Algorithm S_Elect_Leader_Improved
Q_i

 u, some ID
 buff+, containing either an element of M or null
 buff-, containing either an element of M or null
 status, a value in {unknown, leader}
 k, a non negative integer

$q_{0,i}$

 u ← ID_i
 buff+ ← (ID_i, out, 1)
 buff- ← (ID_i, out, 1)
 status ← unknown
 k ← 0

GenMsg$_i$

 Send the current value of buff+ to clockwise-neighbor
 (process i + 1).
 Send the current value of buff- to counter-clockwise-
 neighbor (process i - 1).

Trans$_i$

 buff+ ← null
 buff- ← null
 if the message from i - 1 is (v, out, h), then
 case
  v > u & h > 1: buff+ ← (v, out, h − 1)
  v > u & h = 1: buff- ← (v, in, 1)
  v = u: status ← leader
 endcase
 if the message from i + 1 is (v, out, h), then
 case
  v > u & h > 1: buff- ← (v, out, h − 1)
  v > u & h = 1: buff+ ← (v, in, 1)
  v = u: status ← leader
 endcase
 if the message from i - 1 is (v, in, 1) & v > u, then
  buff+ ← (v, in, 1)
 if the message from i + 1 is (v, in, 1) & v > u, then
  buff- ← (v, in, 1)
 if both messages from (i−1) and (i+1) are (u, in, 1), then
  k ← k + 1
  buff- ← (u, out, 2^k)
  buff+ ← (u, out, 2^k)

Complexity Analysis Suppose that the ring has n processors. In *Algorithm S_Elect_Leader_Improved*, the value of k at any processor starts at 0 and can go up to $\lceil \log n \rceil$. To simplify our discussion of the time complexity analysis, let us first assume that n is a power of 2. When $k = 0$, there are two rounds before it can be incremented at any of the processes. Similarly, $k = 1$ will last four rounds before it can be incremented by any of the processes. The following table shows the number of rounds associated with each value of k.

k	Rounds
0	2
1	4
2	8
...	...
l	$2 * 2^l$
...	...
$\lceil \log n \rceil - 1$	$2 * 2^{\lceil \log n \rceil - 1}$
$\lceil \log n \rceil$	n

Note that when $k = \log n$, the messages will travel only in the outbound direction, which implies that the number of rounds in this case is only n. From the above table, we compute the total number of rounds R as follows:

$$R = n + 2(1 + 2 + \cdots + 2^{\lceil \log n \rceil - 1}) = n + 2(2^{\log n} - 1)$$
$$R = n + 2(n - 1) = 3n - 2$$

(Note that if n is not a power of 2 then $R = 5n - 2$.) Hence, the total number of rounds R is $O(n)$.

Now, let us analyze the number of messages. When $k = 0$, the number of messages sent by all processes is $4n$. However, when $k = l$ $(l > 0)$, not all processes will initiate messages. Only those processes that received their messages back when $k = l - 1$ will initiate messages for the next value of k. Only one process among the consecutive $2^{l-1} + 1$ processes will be able to do that. This is the process with the highest identifier. Therefore, the number of processes that will initiate messages in this case is

$$\left\lfloor \frac{n}{2^{l-1} + 1} \right\rfloor$$

Note that when $k = l$, the number of messages involved with each process initiating messages is $4 * 2^l$. Thus the total number of messages for $k = l$ is

$$4 \times 2^l \times \left\lfloor \frac{n}{2^{l-1} + 1} \right\rfloor \leq 8n$$

Since there are $\lceil \log n \rceil + 1$ values of k, then the total number of messages is bounded by $8n(\lceil \log n \rceil + 1)$, which is $O(n \log n)$. Therefore, the complexity of *Algorithm S_Elect_Leader_Improved* can be summarized as:

1. Time complexity: $O(n)$.
2. Message complexity: $O(n \log n)$.

Example 5 In this example, we apply *Algorithm S_Elect_Leader_Improved* to a system of four processes running on a synchronous ring with four processors. Figure 6.13 shows the initial states and the states after each of the first three rounds. It is left as an exercise to show the states after each of the remaining rounds until a leader is elected (see Problem 11).

6.10 CHAPTER SUMMARY

The migrations to parallel and distributed platforms have increased the need for a better understanding of computational models and algorithms for such systems. In

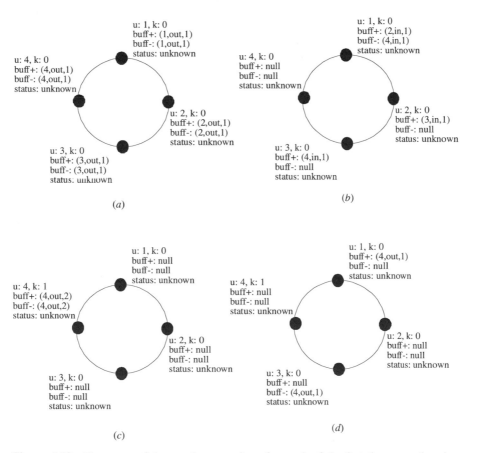

Figure 6.13 The states of the synchronous ring after each of the first three rounds using algorithm *S_Elect_Leader_Improved* (*a*) initial states; (*b*) after first round; (*c*) after second round; and (*d*) after third round.

this chapter, we studied the PRAM model for studying shared memory systems. We also outlined the basic elements of a formal framework of message passing systems under the synchronous model. We designed and discussed the complexity analysis of algorithms described in terms of both models.

The PRAM has played an important role in the introduction of parallel programming paradigms and design techniques that have been used in real parallel systems. Since the PRAM is conceptually easy to work with when developing parallel algorithms, a lot of effort has been spent in finding efficient ways to simulate PRAM computation on other models that do not necessarily follow the PRAM assumptions. This way, parallel algorithms can be designed using the PRAM and then translated into real machines. A large number of PRAM algorithms for solving many fundamental problems have been introduced in the literature and efficiently implemented on real systems.

An important characteristic of a message system is the degree of synchrony, which reflects the different types of timing information that can be used by an algorithm. In this chapter, we focused our attention to synchronous systems, where computation and communication are performed in a lock–step manner. Message passing in such systems happens in synchronized rounds. The complexity of algorithms is measured quantitatively using message complexity and time complexity. The message complexity is defined as the number of messages sent between neighbors during the execution of the algorithm. The time complexity is defined generally as the time spent during the execution of the algorithm.

PROBLEMS

1. Conduct a comparison between the different variations of the PRAM model and the physical models of real parallel and distributed systems.

2. Show that a fully connected topology with n processors is equivalent to an EREW PRAM with n processors and exactly n memory locations.

3. Prove that the best parallel algorithm designed for an EREW PRAM with p processors can be no more than $O(\log p)$ slower than any algorithm for a p-processor CRCW PRAM.

4. Explain why *Algorithm Broadcast_EREW*, which we used to simulate concurrent read, is not appropriate to use in all cases. What are the situations in which the algorithm will not be efficient? Show how to deal with these situations.

5. Indicate whether or not *Algorithm AllSums_EREW* (Section 6.4.2) and *Algorithm MatMult_CREW* after modification (Section 6.5.2) are cost optimal. Justify your answer.

6. Give a PRAM implementation of matrix multiplication of two $n \times n$ matrices using p processors, where $1 < p \leq n^3/\log n$. Use an appropriate variation of the PRAM model to design the fastest algorithm. Obtain the complexity measures.

7. Devise an algorithm to sort n elements in $O(\log n)$ steps on a CREW PRAM. The number of processors should be bounded by a polynomial in n. Is it cost optimal?

8. Devise a PRAM algorithm to merge two sorted lists of length n in $O(\log \log n)$ time.

9. Distributed algorithms arise in a wide range of applications. Make a list of at least five applications that use distributed algorithms.

10. Modify *Algorithm S_Sum_Hypercube* to find the minimum.

11. Given the states shown in Figure 6.13, apply *Algorithm A_Elect_Leader_ Improved* to show the states after each of the remaining rounds until a leader is elected.

REFERENCES

Agrawal, A., Chandra, and Snir, M. Communication complexity of PRAM. *Theory of Computer Science*, 71, 3–28 (1990).

Akl, S. G. *Parallel Computation: Models and Methods*, Prentice-Hall, 1997.

Angluin, D. Local and global properties in networks of processors, *Proc. of the 12th ACM Symposium on Theory of Computing*, pp. 82–93.

Baase, S. *Computer Algorithms: Introduction to Design and Analysis*, 2nd edition, Addison-Wesley, 1988.

Borodian and Hopcroft, J. E. Routing, merging and sorting on parallel models of computation. *Journal of Computer System. Science*, 30, 130–145 (1985).

Brent, R. P. The parallel evaluation of general arithmetic expression. *Journal of ACM*, 21, 201–206 (1974).

Chang and Roberts, R. An improved algorithm for decentralized extrema-finding in circular configurations of processes. *Communication of the ACM*, 22 (5), 281–283 (1979).

Cosnard, M. and Trystram, D. *Parallel Algorithms and Architecture*, International Thomson Computer Press, 1996.

Hirschberg, D. and Sinclair, J. Decentralized extrema-finding in circular configuration of process, *Communication of the ACM*, 23, 627–628, (1980).

JaJa, J. *An Introduction to Parallel Algorithms*, Addison-Wesley, 1992.

Kronsjo, L. PRAM Models, in A. Y. Zomaya, Ed., *Handbook of Parallel and Distributed Computing*, McGraw-Hill, Chapter 6, 1996, pp. 163–191.

Kumar, V., Grama, A., Gupta, A. Karypis. *Introduction to Parallel Computing: Design and Analysis of Algorithms*, Benjamin Cumming, 1994.

Lakshmivarahan, S. and Dhall, S. *Analysis and Design of Parallel Algorithms: Arithmetic and Matrix Problems*, McGraw-Hill, 1990.

Le Lann, G. *Distributed Systems – Towards A Formal Approach*, Information Processing 77 (Toronto, August 1977), Vol. 7 of Proceedings of IFIP Congress, North-Holland, Amsterdam, 1977, pp. 155–160.

Lynch, N. *Distributed Algorithms*, Morgan Kaufmann, 1996.

CHAPTER 7

Network Computing

The proliferation of the Internet has stimulated rapid growth of interest in large-scale network computing that may span the entire globe. The Internet is the most widely used distributed system in the world. Nodes in the Internet may be single-processor workstations, shared-memory MIMD machines, massively parallel SIMD machines, or other types. Links are TCP/IP packet-switched connections and the bandwidth varies with load, number of hops, and underlying communication technology. When one node connects with another, the packets of data may be sent through a wireless link, fiber optical cable, coaxial cable, digital telephone line, and so on. These physical layers introduce delays and may be errors, which must be corrected by retransmission and dynamic reconfiguration of the Internet's links.

In previous chapters, we studied computing systems consisting of multiple processing units connected via some interconnection network. There are two major factors that differentiate such systems: the processing units and the interconnection network that ties them together. We learned that the processing units could communicate and interact with each other using either shared memory or message passing methods. In this chapter we discuss network computing, in which the nodes are stand-alone computers that could be connected via a switch, local area network, or the Internet. The main idea is to divide the application into semi-independent parts according to the kind of processing needed. Different nodes on the network can be assigned different parts of the application. This form of network computing takes advantage of the unique capabilities of diverse system architectures. For example, the fine-grained SIMD part of the application would be shipped off to the SIMD machine and the graphical presentation and I/O portions to one or more single-processor workstations. The overall coordination may be done by a PC on someone's desk. It also maximally leverages potentially idle resources within a large organization. Therefore, unused CPU cycles may be utilized during short periods of time resulting in bursts of activity followed by periods of inactivity. In what follows, we discuss the utilization of network technology in order to create a computing infrastructure using commodity computers.

Advanced Computer Architecture and Parallel Processing, by H. El-Rewini and M. Abd-El-Barr
ISBN 0-471-46740-5   Copyright © 2005 John Wiley & Sons, Inc.

7.1 COMPUTER NETWORKS BASICS

Networks can be divided into the following four categories based on their sizes and the geographic distances they cover:

- Wide area network (WAN);
- Metropolitan area network (MAN);
- Local area network (LAN);
- System or storage area network (SAN).

A WAN connects a large number of computers that are spread over large geographic distances. It can span sites in multiple cities, countries, and continents. A LAN connects a small number of computers in a small area within a building or campus. The MAN is an intermediate level between the LAN and WAN and can perhaps span a single city. A SAN connects computers or storage devices to make a single system. The major factor that distinguishes WAN from other network types is the scalability factor. A WAN must be able to grow as long as there are more computers to be added to the network. A message sent over WAN uses intermediate nodes in its route from the source to the destination. Computers hooked to a LAN often communicate using a shared medium. Also, LAN technologies provide higher speed connections compared to WAN because they cover short distances and hence offer lower delay than WANs.

Network routing schemes can be classified as connection-oriented and connectionless. In connection-oriented, the entire message follows the same path from source to destination. Only the first packet holds routing information such as the destination address. In connectionless schemes, a message is divided into packets. The packets of a given message may take different routes from source to destination. Therefore, the header of every packet holds routing information. Using a serial number, the message can be reassembled in the correct order at the destination as packets may arrive in a different order.

7.1.1 Network Performance

The following are two popular laws that predict the advances in network technologies.

Gilder's Law   George Gilder projected that the total bandwidth of communication systems triples every 12 months.

Metcalfe's Law   Robert Metcalfe projected that the value of a network is proportional to the square of the number of nodes.

Gilder's law tells us that networking speed is increasing faster than processing power. While this remains true for the backbone network, end-to-end performance is likely to be limited by bottlenecks. For example, over about 15 years, LAN technology has increased in speed from 10 Megabits per second (10 Mbps) to 10 Gigabits per second (10 Gbps), which is a factor of 1000 increase. Over a similar time period, advances in silicon technology, driven by Moore's Law, have allowed the CPU clock frequency in an average PC to increase from roughly 25 MHz to 2.5 GHz (a factor of about 100 increase in processing power). Metcalfe's law also explains the prolific growth of the Internet. As a network grows, the value of being connected to it grows exponentially, while the cost per user remains the same or even reduces.

7.1.2 Internet

Internet is the collection of networks and routers that form a single cooperative virtual network, which spans the entire globe. The Internet relies on the combination of the Transmission Control Protocol and the Internet Protocol or TCP/IP. The majority of Internet traffic is carried using TCP/IP packets. Internet has evolved from a research prototype to become the largest communication media in the world. The explosive usage of the Internet and the World Wide Web (WWW) has stimulated rapid growth of interest in electronic publishing, browsing, and distributed computing. Table 7.1

TABLE 7.1 Top Ten Countries with Highest Number of Internet Users

Country	Internet Users Latest Data	Population (2004 Est.)	% of Population	Source of Latest Data	% of World Usage/Users
United States	209,518,183	294,540,100	71.1	Nielsen//NR Mar/04	27.7
China	79,500,000	1,327,976,227	6.0	CNNIC Dec/03	10.5
Japan	63,884,205	127,944,200	49.9	Nielsen//NR Mar/04	8.4
Germany	45,315,166	82,633,200	54.8	Nielsen//NR Mar/04	6.0
United Kingdom	35,089,470	59,157,400	59.3	Nielsen//NR Mar/04	4.6
South Korea	29,220,000	47,135,500	62.0	KRNIC Dec/03	3.9
France	22,534,967	59,494,800	37.9	Nielsen//NR Mar/04	3.0
Brazil	20,551,168	183,199,600	11.2	Nielsen//NR Mar/04	2.7
Italy	19,900,000	56,153,700	35.4	ITU Dec/02	2.6
Canada	16,841,811	32,026,600	52.6	Nielsen//NR May/02	2.2
Top ten countries	542,354,970	2,270,261,327	23.9	IWS–Apr.6/04	71.6
Rest of the world	215,175,767	4,183,049,740	5.1	IWS–Mar.19/04	28.4
Totals	757,530,737	6,453,311,067	11.7	IWS–Apr.6/04	100.0

shows some statistics by Internet World Stats (www.internetworldstats.com) about the top 10 countries with the highest number of Internet users. As you can see from the table, in the United States alone, 71% of the population use the Internet. Also, close to 12% of the entire world population use the Internet. With the projections of Gilder and Metcalfe, the number of users is expected to grow even more.

7.1.3 Other Network Technologies

In addition to the popular TCP/IP protocol, many more protocols and combinations of protocols exist. Some of these protocols are briefly mentioned below. Figure 7.1 shows different network technologies and their speed in relation to the network taxonomy provided above.

Fast Ethernet and Gigabit Ethernet Fast Ethernet (100Base-T) is a high-speed LAN that allows a computer to transmit or receive data at 100 Megabits per second (100 Mbps). The demand for a bandwidth that is even higher than 100 Mbps has motivated the extension of Ethernet to a bit rate of 1 Gbps. Gigabit Ethernet (1000Base-T) has become an attractive choice for corporate backbone networks and high-performance clusters of workstations.

The Fiber Distributed Data Interface (FDDI) The FDDI specifies a 100 Mbps token-passing, dual-ring LAN using fiber-optic cable. The FDDI is frequently used as high-speed backbone technology because of its support for high bandwidth and greater distances than copper.

High-Performance Parallel Interface (HiPPI) The HiPPI is a point-to-point communication channel and it does not support multidrop configurations. HiPPI

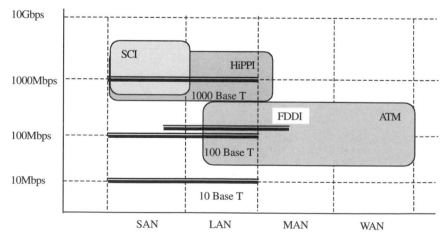

Figure 7.1 Representation of network technologies.

is capable of transferring data at 800 Mbps using 32 parallel line or 1.6 Gbps over 64 parallel lines.

Asynchronous Transfer Mode (ATM) The ATM is a connection-oriented scheme that is suitable for both LANs and WANs. It transfers data in small fixed-size packets called cells. It can handle multimedia in an integrated way. Cells are allowed to transfer using several different media such as both copper and fiber-optic cables. It is designed to permit high-speed data. The fastest ATM hardware can switch data at a gigabit rate.

Scalable Coherent Interface (SCI) The SCI is an IEEE standard that is quite popular for PC clusters. It represents a point-to-point architecture with directory-based cache coherence. It provides a cluster-wide shared memory system. A remote communication in SCI takes place as just part of a simple load or store process in a processor.

7.2 CLIENT/SERVER SYSTEMS

A Client/Server is a distributed system whereby the application is divided into at least two parts: one or more servers perform one part and the other part is performed by one or more clients. Furthermore, the clients are connected to the servers by some kind of network. A client computer may do very little more than simply display data accessed from the server, or a more sophisticated client may run a full application, which uses data provided by the server. Client/Server systems are often categorized as two-tier or three-tier. A two-tier system separates clients from servers: all clients are on one tier, and all servers are on the second tier. For example, client PCs may access a database on one or more servers. A three-tier system separates the clients from the servers as does a two-tier system, but in addition, servers are divided into two more tiers. The application servers fit into a middle level, called the second tier, and the database servers fit into a third level called tier 3. For example, client PCs might be connected to a web server (tier 2) that in turn accesses a database server (tier 3) to handle storage.

Modern programming languages provide constructs for building client/server-based distributed applications. These applications are divided into clients and servers, which are allocated to different computers in a network. A client sends a request to the server and waits for a response. At the other end, when the server receives a request, it processes it and sends the results back to the client. In a traditional client/server environment, a powerful machine acts as a server, serving requests from multiple clients. For example, in a database system, several clients send queries to the server that has access to the database. The server executes the queries on behalf of the clients and sends each client its respective result. A multi-threaded process is considered an efficient way to provide server applications. A server process can service a number of clients as shown in Figure 7.2. Each client request triggers the creation of a new thread in the server.

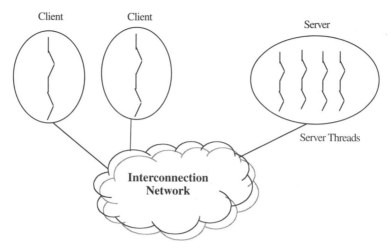

Figure 7.2 A multithreaded server in a client server system.

7.2.1 Sockets

Sockets are used to provide the capability of making connections from one application running on one machine to another running on a different machine. A socket abstraction consists of the data structure that holds the information needed for communication, and the system calls that manipulate the socket structure. Once a socket is created, it can be used to wait for an incoming connection (passive socket), or can be used to initiate connection (active socket).

A client can establish an active connection to a remote server by creating an instance of a socket. To establish a server connection and bind it to a particular port number, we should create an instance of a server socket. A server socket listens on a TCP port for a connection from a client (passive socket). When a client connects to that port, the server accepts the connection. Figure 7.3 visualizes the socket connection. Once the connection is established, the client and server can read from and write to the socket using input and output streams. Streams are ordered sequences of data that have a source (input stream), or destination (output stream). Once the client or server finishes using the socket, the socket structure is de-allocated.

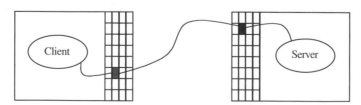

Figure 7.3 A socket connection.

Example 1   In this example, we write a small segment of a simple Client/Server Java program, in which the client reads from the server. This simple example does not require prior knowledge of Java as we will explain the main Java constructs needed in this example.

Java programs, like programs written in other object-oriented languages, are built from classes. You can create any number of objects from a class. These objects are known as instances of that class. Think of a class as a template or blueprint for the creation of objects. When a house is constructed from a blueprint, it is one of many possible instances of the same blueprint. Thus, an object is the actual thing, but a class is only a blueprint. A class contains functions called methods or behavior and states called fields or instance variables. Fields are data belonging to either a class or the objects that belong to a class. Methods are program statements that operate on the field to manipulate the state.

CLIENT/SERVER JAVA STATEMENT

The `Socket` class provides a client-side socket interface. A client can establish an active connection to a remote server by creating an instance of `Socket` as follows:

```
Socket <connection> = new Socket(<hostname>,<portnumber>);
```

The variable `<hostname>` gives the name of the server to connect to; and `<portnumber>` should match the port number at the server end.

The `ServerSocket` class provides a server-side socket interface. To establish a server connection and bind it to a particular port number, we should create an instance of `ServerSocket` as follows:

```
ServerSocket <connection> = new ServerSocket(<portnumber>);
```

Once the connection is established, the client and server can read from and write to the socket using input and output streams. Streams in Java are used for Input/Output. They are ordered sequences of data that have a source (input stream), or destination (output stream). For example, the `DataInputStream` and `DataOutputStream` are classes that provide the implementations for methods to transmit Java primitive types across a stream. Input and output streams can be used to read from and write to a socket connection as follows:

```
DataInputStream in = new DataInputStream(<connection>.
  getInputStream());
DataOutputStream out = new
DataOutputStream(<connection>.getOutputStream());
```

CLIENT STEPS
  1. The client tries to establish a connection with the server.
  2. When the connection is established, the client receives a string from the server.
  3. The client displays the string received.

JAVA MAIN STATEMENTS

. . . . .

```
Socket connect = new Socket (host, 8888);
```

. . . . .

```
DataInputStream in = new DataInputStream(connect.getInput
   Stream());
```

. . . . .

```
msg = in.readByte();
connect.close();
```

SERVER STEPS

1. The server waits for a connection from a client.
2. When the connection is established, the server sends a string to the client.
3. The server closes the connection.

JAVA MAIN STATEMENTS

. . . . .

```
Socket connect = null;
```

. . . . .

```
ServerSocket sconnect = new ServerSocket(8888);
connect = sconnect.accept();
DataOutputStream out = new DataOutputStream(connect.get
   OutputStream());
out.writeByte(message);
sconnect.close();
```

. . . . .

7.2.2   Remote Procedure Call (RPC)

Remote procedure call (RPC) is the basis of most client/server systems. Think of RPC as a procedure call where the procedure is located on a different computer than the caller. Thus, when the procedure is called, its parameters are passed (sent) via the network to the remote computer, and then the remote computer executes the procedure, returns the result(s), and continues on its way.

The RPC can be constructed on top of sockets. That is, the socket mechanism can be used to pass parameters and the name of the procedure to be activated on the remote computer, and so on. The remote procedure call mechanism is simple to use because it looks much like any other procedure call familiar to programmers. However, it covers up many complexities.

The RPC can be blocking or nonblocking. A *blocking RPC* means that the program that places the call is stopped in its tracks while waiting for a reply. The nonblocking RPC, however, allows the calling program to continue without waiting for a reply. In this case, the caller must explicitly ask for the reply at some later time, or else the return value will never get back to the caller.

7.2.3 Middleware

Middleware is an important part of client/server systems because it solves many interoperability problems, opens the door for multiple servers, and in general provides great flexibility. Middleware is an important intermediate layer of software, for the following reasons:

- It makes it possible for new systems to coexist with legacy systems, which means we can use it to glue together new clients with old mainframe databases;
- It solves a number of interoperability problems because it can simultaneously convert formats and gain access without code rewriting;
- It isolates system components so that changes in one component have little effect on other components; and
- It lowers effort and time to develop and deploy systems because programmers do not need to know network and distributed programming details.

7.2.4 A Client Server Framework for Parallel Applications

Parallel applications can be designed using the client/server model. A client may divide a big application into several smaller problems that can be processed by multiple servers simultaneously. All the servers compute the solution to their respective problems and send their results to the client. The client assembles the results from each server and outputs the final result to the user. The client acts as the master (supervisor) while the servers act as the slaves (workers) in the master–slave (supervisor–workers) model as shown in Figure 7.4. The steps taken at the client and each server are summarized as follows.

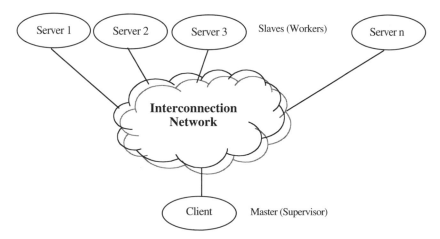

Figure 7.4 Supervisor workers model in client server.

Client (Supervisor)

1. Client creates an array of sockets and input/output data streams with all the servers. Optimally, the client should spawn a thread for each available server, which would then make connections with an individual server.

2. Client passes control to the client body, which contains the code specific to the application being executed in parallel. Mainly, it divides the main task into smaller portions and passes one small portion of the task to each server. It then waits for all the servers to send back the result of their smaller computations. Finally it merges the results of each server and computes the final solution to the big problem.

3. Client closes all the streams and sockets with all the servers.

Server (Worker)

1. Server creates a server socket on an unused port number.

2. Server waits for connections on that port. Once it gets a request from a client, it accepts that connection.

3. Server creates input and output data streams for that socket. This establishes the foundation for communication between the server socket and the client.

4. Server passes control to the server body, which contains the code specific to the application executed in parallel. The main server would accept the connection from the client, create a socket, and invoke the server body thread to handle that client.

5. Server goes back and waits for another connection from a client.

7.3 CLUSTERS

The 1990s have witnessed a significant shift from expensive and specialized parallel machines to the more cost-effective clusters of PCs and workstations. Advances in network technology and the availability of low-cost and high-performance commodity workstations have driven this shift. Clusters provide an economical way of achieving high performance. Departments that could not afford the expensive proprietary supercomputers have found an affordable alternative in clusters.

A cluster is a collection of stand-alone computers connected using some interconnection network. Each node in a cluster could be a workstation, personal computer, or even a multiprocessor system. A node is an autonomous computer that may be engaged in its own private activities while at the same time cooperating with other units in the context of some computational task. Each node has its own input/output systems and its own operating system. When all nodes in a cluster have the same architecture and run the same operating system, the cluster is called *homogeneous*, otherwise, it is *heterogeneous*. The interconnection network could be a fast LAN or a switch. To achieve high-performance computing, the interconnection network must provide high-bandwidth and low-latency communication. The nodes of a cluster may be dedicated to the cluster all the time; hence computation can be performed on the entire cluster. Dedicated clusters are normally packaged compactly in a single room. With the exception of the front-end node, all nodes are headless with no keyboard, mouse, or monitor. Dedicated clusters usually use high-speed networks such as fast Ethernet and Myrinet. Alternatively, nodes owned by different individuals on the Internet could participate in a cluster only part of the time. In this case, the cluster can utilize the idle CPU cycles of each participating node if the owner's permission is granted.

Figure 7.5 shows the architecture of a homogeneous cluster made of similar nodes, where each node is a single-processor workstation. The middleware layer in the architecture makes the cluster appears to the user as a single parallel machine, which is referred to as the single system image (SSI). The SSI infrastructure offers unified access to system resources by supporting a number of features including:

- Single entry point: A user can connect to the cluster instead of to a particular node.
- Single file system: A user sees a single hierarchy of directories and files.
- Single image for administration: The whole cluster is administered from a single window.
- Coordinated resource management: A job can transparently compete for the resources in the entire cluster.

In addition to providing high-performance computing, clusters can also be used to provide high-availability environment. High availability can be achieved when

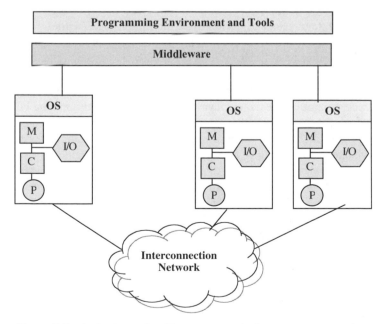

Figure 7.5 A cluster made of homogenous single-processor computers.

only a subset of the nodes is used in the computation and the rest is used as a backup in case of failure. In cases when one of the main objectives of the cluster is high availability, the middleware will also support features that enable the cluster services for recovery from failure and fault tolerance among all nodes of the cluster. For example, the middleware should offer the necessary infrastructure for checkpointing. A checkpointing scheme makes sure that the process state is saved periodically. In the case of node failure, processes on the failed node can be restarted on another working node.

The programming environment and tools layer provide the programmer with portable tools and libraries for the development of parallel applications. Examples of such tools and libraries are Threads, Parallel Virtual Machine (PVM), and Message Passing Interface (MPI). Note that PVM and MPI will be covered in detail in Chapters 8 and 9, respectively.

7.3.1 Threads

An important aspect of modern operating systems is their support for threads within processes. A thread, sometimes called a lightweight process, is a basic unit of processor utilization. It runs sequentially on a processor and is interruptible so that the processor can switch to other threads. A process does nothing if it has no threads in it, and a thread must be in exactly one process. A thread is different from the traditional or heavy-weight process, which is equivalent to a task with one thread. Context switching among peer threads is relatively inexpensive, compared with context switching among heavy-weight processes.

Concurrency among processes can be exploited because threads in different processes may execute concurrently. Moreover, multiple threads within the same process can be assigned to different processors. Threads can be used to send and receive messages while other operations within a task continue. For example, a task might have many threads waiting to receive and process request messages. When a message is received by one thread, it is processed by this thread concurrently with other threads processing other messages. Java has support for multithreading built in the language. Java threads are usually mapped to real operating system threads if the underlying operating system supports multithreads. Thus, applications written in Java can be executed in parallel on a multiprocessor environment.

Example 2: Creating Threads in Java   Here is a simple example of how Java creates multiple threads. This program is the multithreaded version of the program *HelloWorld*, which is normally the first program in most programming languages books. Two threads are created, each of which prints a message of the form "Hello World from thread i", where i is in $\{1, 2\}$, a number of times (three times in this example). Again, this simple example does not require prior knowledge of Java. We will explain the main Java constructs needed in this example.

The class Thread is one of the classes in the standard Java libraries. This class supports a number of methods to handle threads. For example, the method start spawns a new thread of control, which can be stopped or suspended by invoking the methods stop or suspend. The class Thread also supports the method run, which is invoked by start to make the thread active. The standard implementation of Thread.run does nothing, but the class Thread can be extended to provide a new run method. The Java code is shown below:

```
class HelloWorld extends Thread {
  int myId;          // a thread id
  int count;         // how many times
  int sleepTime;     // how long to pause
  HelloWorld (int id, int cnt, int slp){
    myId = id;
    count = cnt;
    sleepTime = slp;
  }
  public void run() {
    while (count-- > 0) {
    System.out.println('Hello World from thread' + id);
    try {
      Thread.sleep(sleepTime);
    catch (Exception e) {
      return;
    }
  }
  public static void main (String[] args) {
    new HelloWorld(1,3,100).start();
    new HelloWorld(2,3,300).start();
  }
}
```

This example illustrates a number of features in Java. The program first creates a class called HelloWorld, which extends the class Thread. The input for this class is an identifier for the thread, how many times the message will be printed, and a time interval to sleep between the times the message is printed. Its run method loops the required number of times, printing its message, and waiting the specified amount of sleep time.

Finally, the main function creates two HelloWorld objects, each with its own identifier and sleep time, and invokes each object's start method. A possible result (remember that the order of the messages is unpredictable) when you run this program is:

```
Hello World from thread 1
Hello World from thread 2
Hello World from thread 1
Hello World from thread 1
Hello World from thread 2
Hello World from thread 2
```

7.4   INTERCONNECTION NETWORKS

The overall performance of a cluster system can be determined by the speed of its processors and the interconnection network. Many researchers argue that the interconnection network is the most important factor that affects cluster performance. Regardless of how fast the processors are, communication among processors, and hence scalability of applications, will always be bounded by the network bandwidth and latency. The bandwidth is an indication of how fast a data transfer may occur from a sender to a receiver. Latency is the time needed to send a minimal size message from a sender to a receiver. In the early days of clusters, Ethernet was the main interconnection network used to connect nodes. Many solutions have been introduced to achieve high-speed networks. Key solutions in high-speed interconnects include Gigabit Ethernet, Myrinet, and Quadrics. While Ethernet resides at the low end of the performance spectrum, it is considered a low-cost solution. Other solutions add communication processors on the network interface cards, which provide programmability and performance. Table 7.2 shows the relative performance and other features of different high-speed networks.

In this section, we will cover the evolution of Ethernet and discuss a sample of switches used in connecting computers to form a cluster. The most important distinguishing factor among the different switches will be the bandwidth and the latency time.

7.4.1   Ethernet

Ethernet is a packet-switched LAN technology introduced by Xerox PARC in the early 1970s. Ethernet was designed to be a shared bus technology where multiple hosts are connected to a shared communication medium. All hosts connected to an Ethernet receive every transmission, making it possible to broadcast a packet to all hosts at the same time. Ethernet uses a distributed access control scheme called *Carrier Sense Multiple Access* with *Collision Detect* (CSMA/CD). Multiple machines can access an Ethernet at the same time. Each machine senses whether a carrier wave is present to determine whether the network is idle before it sends a packet. Only when the network is not busy sending another message can transmission start. Each transmission is limited in duration and there is a minimum

TABLE 7.2   Data Rate, Switching Method, and Routing Scheme for Interconnection Networks

Interconnection Network	Data Rate	Switching	Routing
Ethernet	10 Mbit/s	Packet	Table-based
Fast Ethernet	100 Mbit/s	Packet	Table-based
Gigabit Ethernet	1 Gbit/s	Packet	Table-based
Myrinet	1.28 Gbit/s	Wormhole	Source-path
Quadrics	7.2 Gbyte/s	Wormhole	Source-path

idle time between two consecutive transmissions by the same sender. In the early days of LAN technology, an Ethernet speed of 10 million bits per second (10 Mbps) (*10Base-T*) was quite sufficient. However, with the dramatic increase in CPU speed and advances in network technology, a 10 Mbps Ethernet became an obvious bottleneck. Fast Ethernet, which uses twisted-pair wiring, was later introduced with speed of 100 Mbps (*100Base-T*). Dual-speed Ethernet (10/100 Ethernet) was also introduced to accommodate both 10 or 100 Mbps connections. By the late 1990, demand has increased for even higher speed Ethernet. Therefore Gigabit Ethernet was introduced. Gigabit Ethernet (*1000Base-T*) extended the Ethernet technology to a bit rate of 1 gigabit per second (1 Gbps).

Each computer connected to an Ethernet network is assigned a unique 48-bit address known as its Ethernet address. Ethernet manufacturers assign unique Ethernet addresses as they produce hardware interfaces. The Ethernet address, which is also called a media access (MAC) address, is fixed in a machine-readable form on the host interface hardware. The address can specify the physical address of one network interface, the network broadcast address, or a multicast. In addition to its MAC address, an interface must recognize a broadcast address (all 1s) and the group addresses in the case of multicast. The Ethernet interface hardware is usually given the set of addresses to recognize by the operating system during boot time. The host interface hardware, which receives a copy of every packet that passes by, will use the destination address to determine the packets that should be passed to the host. Other packets addressed to other hosts will be ignored.

In order to achieve an acceptable level of performance and to eliminate any potential bottleneck, there must be some balance between the Ethernet speed and the processor speed. The initial Beowulf prototype cluster in 1994 was built with DX4 processors and 10 Mbit/s Ethernet. The processors were too fast for this kind of Ethernet. In late 1997, a good choice for a cluster system was sixteen 200 MHz P6 processors connected by Fast Ethernet. The network configuration of a high-performance cluster is dependent on the size of the cluster, the relationship between processor speed and network bandwidth and the current price list for each of the components.

7.4.2 Switches

An $n_1 \times n_2$ switch consists of n_1 input ports, n_2 output ports, links connecting each input to every output, control logic to select a specific connection, and internal buffers. Although n_1 and n_2 do not have to be equal, in practice and in most cases they have the same value, which is usually power of two. A switch is used to establish connections from the input ports to the output ports. These connections may be one-to-one, which represent point-to-point connections, or one-to-many, which represent multicast or broadcast. The case of many-to-one should cause conflicts at the output ports and therefore needs arbitration to resolve conflicts if allowed. When only one-to-one connections are allowed, the switch is called crossbar. An $n \times n$ crossbar switch can establish $n!$ connections. The proof is quite simple. To allow only one-to-one connections, the first input port should have n choices of output ports, the second input port will have $(n - 1)$ choices, the third input port will have $(n - 2)$ choices, and so on. Thus, the number of one-to-one connections is $n * (n - 1) * (n - 2) \cdots * 2 * 1 = n!$ If we allow both one-to-one as well as one-to-many in an $n \times n$ switch, the number of connections that can be established is n^n (see Problem 3). For example, a binary switch has two input ports and two output ports. The number of one-to-one connections in a binary switch is two (straight and crossed), while the number of all allowed connections is four (straight, crosses, lower broadcast, and upper broadcast).

Routing can be achieved using two mechanisms: source-path and table-based. In source-path, the entire path to the destination is stored in the packet header at the source location. When a packet enters the switch, the outgoing port is determined from the header. Used routing data is stripped from the header and routing information for the next switch is now in the front. In table-based routing, the switch must have a complete routing table that determines the corresponding port for each destination. When a packet enters the switch, a table lookup will determine the outgoing port. Figure 7.6 illustrates the difference between source-path routing and table-based routing in the case when a packet enters an 8-port switch at port 0. In the source-path case, the header contains the entire path and the next port is port 6. In the table-based case, the destination address dest-id is looked up in the routing table and port 6 is followed.

7.4.3 Myrinet Clos Network

Myrinet is a high-performance, packet-communication and switching technology. It was produced by Myricom as a high-performance alternative to conventional Ethernet networks. Myrinet switches are multiple-port components that route a packet entering on an input channel of a port to the output channel of the port selected by the packet. Myrinet switches have 4, 8, 12, 16 ports. For an n-port switch, the ports are addressed $0, 1, 2, \ldots, n - 1$. For any switching permutation, there may be as many packets traversing a switch concurrently as the switch has ports. These switches are implemented using two types of VLSI chips: crossbar-switch chips and the Myrinet-interface chip.

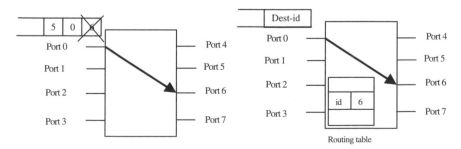

Figure 7.6   Source-path routing vs. table-based routing.

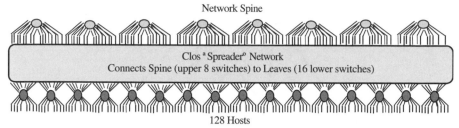

Figure 7.7 A 128-host Clos network using 16-port Myrinet switch.

The basic building block of the Myrinet-2000 network is a 16-port Myrinet cross-bar switch, implemented on a single chip designated as Xbar16. It can be interconnected to build various topologies of varying sizes. The most common topology is the Clos network. Figure 7.7 shows a 128-host Clos network, which includes 24 Xbar16s. Each Xbar16 switch is represented using a circle. The eight switches forming the upper row is the Clos network *spine*, which is connected through a Clos spreader network to the 16 *leaf* switches forming the lower row. The Clos network provides routes from any host to any other host. There is a unique shortest route between hosts connected to the same Xbar16. Routes between hosts connected to different Xbar16s traverse three Xbar16 switches.

Figure 7.8 shows a 64-host Clos network. Please note that a network of 64 hosts or fewer would require eight-port switches for the spine. In the figure, an Xbar16 switch can serve the purpose of two 8-port switches. The thick line connecting a spine switch to a leaf switch represents two links. Similarly, Figure 7.9 shows a 32-host Clos network. Each thick line connecting a spine switch to a leaf switch represents four links.

The routing of Myrinet packets is based on the source routing approach. Each Myrinet packet has a variable length header with complete routing information. When a packet enters a switch, the leading byte of the header determines the

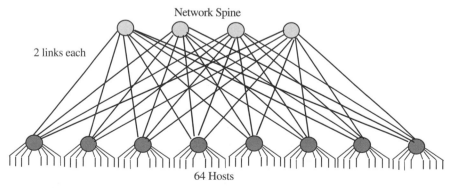

Figure 7.8 A 64-host Clos network using 16-port Myrinet switch (each line represents two links).

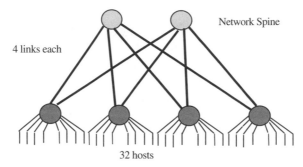

Figure 7.9   A 32-host Clos network using 16-port Myrinet switch (each line represents four links).

outgoing port before being stripped off the packet header. At the host interface, a control program is executed to perform source-route translation.

7.4.4   The Quadrics Network

According to Petrini et al. (2002), the Quadrics network (QsNet) consists of two hardware building blocks: a programmable network interface called Elan and a high-bandwidth, low-latency communication switch called Elite. The Elan network interface connects the Quadrics network to a processing node containing one or more CPUs. In addition to generating and accepting packets to and from the network, Elan provides substantial local processing power to implement high-level message passing protocols such as the Message Passing Interface (MPI), which we will study in Chapter 9.

QsNet connects Elite switches in a quaternary fat-tree topology. A quaternary fat tree of dimension n is composed of 4^n processing nodes and $n \times 4^{n-1}$ switches interconnected as a delta network. It can be recursively built by connecting four quaternary fat trees of dimension $n - 1$. Figures 7.10 and 7.11 show quaternary fat trees of dimensions 1 and 2, respectively. When $n = 1$, the network consists of one switch and four processing nodes. When $n = 2$, the network consists of eight switches and 16 processing nodes.

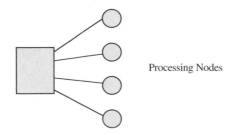

Figure 7.10   Quaternary fat tree of dimension 1.

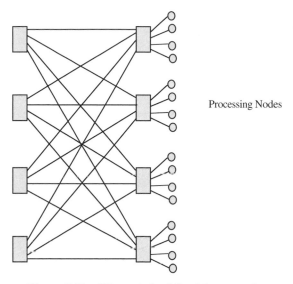

Processing Nodes

Figure 7.11 Elite switch of Quadrics networks.

Elite networks are source routed. The Elan network interface attaches route information to the packet header before transmitting the packet into the network. The route information is a sequence of Elite link tags. As the packet moves inside the network, each switch removes the first route tag from the header and forwards the packet to the next switch in the route or the final destination. The routing tag can identify either a single output link or a group of links. Packets are routed using wormhole routing flow control. As discussed in Chapter 5, each packet is divided into flow control digits (flits). In QsNet, the size of each flit is 16 bits. Network nodes can send packets to multiple destinations using the network's broadcast capability.

7.5 CLUSTER EXAMPLES

7.5.1 Berkeley Network of Workstations (NOW)

The Berkeley Network of Workstations (NOW) is an important representative of cluster systems. In 1997, the NOW project achieved over 10 Gflops on the Linpack benchmark, which made it one of the top 200 fastest supercomputers in the world. The hardware/software infrastructure for the project included 100 SUN Ultrasparcs and 40 SUN Sparcstations running Solaris, 35 Intel PCs running Windows NT or a PC Unix variant, and between 500 and 1000 disks, all connected by a Myrinet switched network. The programming environments used in NOW are sockets, MPI, and a parallel version of C, called Split C. Active Messages is the basic communication primitive in Berkeley NOW. The Active Messages communication is a simplified remote procedure call that can be implemented efficiently on a wide range of hardware. Figure 7.12 shows the different components of NOW.

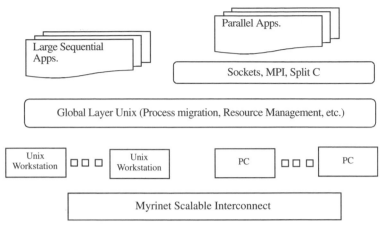

Figure 7.12 Berkeley Network of Workstations (NOW).

7.5.2 The Beowulf Cluster

The idea of the Beowulf cluster project was to achieve supercomputer processing power using off-the-shelf commodity machines. One of the earliest Beowulf clusters contained sixteen 100 MHz DX4 processors that were connected using 10 Mbps Ethernet. The second Beowulf cluster, built in 1995, used 100 MHz Pentium processors connected by 100 Mbps Ethernet. The third generation of Beowulf clusters was built by different research laboratories. JPL and Los Alamos National Laboratory each built a 16-processor machine incorporating Pentium Pro processors. These machines were combined to run a large N-body problem, which won the 1997 Gordon Bell Prize for high performance.

The communication between processors in Beowulf has been done through TCP/IP over the Ethernet internal to the cluster. Multiple Ethernets were also used to satisfy higher bandwidth requirements. Channel bonding is a technique to connect multiple Ethernets in order to distribute the communication traffic. Channel bonding was able to increase the sustained network throughput by 75% when dual networks were used.

Two of the early successful Beowulf clusters are Loki and Avalon. In 1997, Loki was built using 16 Pentium Pro Processors connected using Fast Ethernet switches. It achieved 1.2 Gflops. In 1998, the Avalon was built using one hundred and forty 533 MHz Alpha Microprocessors connected. Avalon achieved 47.7 Gflops.

7.5.3 FlashMob I

In April 2004, the University of San Francisco hosted the first Flash Mob Computing computer; FlashMob I, with the purpose of creating one of the fastest supercomputers on the planet. A FlashMob supercomputer was created by connecting a large number of computers via a high-speed LAN, to work together as a single supercomputer. A FlashMob computer, unlike an ordinary cluster, is temporary and organized ad hoc for the purpose of working on a single problem. It used volunteers and ordinary laptop PCs, and was designed to allow anyone to create a supercomputer in a matter of hours.

Over 700 computers came into the gym and they were able to hook up 669 to the network. The best Linpack result was a peak rate of 180 Gflops using 256 computers; however, a node failed 75% through the computation. The best completed result was 77 Gflops using 150 computers. The biggest challenge was identifying flaky computers and determining the best configuration for running the benchmark. Each of the 669 computers ran Linpack at some point in the day.

7.6 GRID COMPUTING

While clusters are collections of computers tied together as a single system, grids consist of multiple systems that work together while maintaining their distinct identities. In their article "The grid grows up", Fred Douglis and Ian Foster (2003) defined the term Grid to denote middleware infrastructure, tools, and applications concerned with integrating geographically distributed computational resources. Owing to the decentralized and heterogeneous nature of the grid, the middleware that glues the different components is more complicated compared with that of clusters. Resembling an electric power grid, the computing grid is expected to become a pervasive computing infrastructure that supports large-scale and resource-intensive applications. Grid resources, which span the entire globe, include hardware, software, data, and instruments. The significant increase in application complexity and the need for collaboration have made grids an attractive computing infrastructure. Applications will continue to be complex, multidisciplinary, and multidimensional, and collaboration will become the default mode of operation. Thus, the need for the distributed grid infrastructure will continue to be an important resource.

An important concept in grids is the virtual organization, which offers a unified view of resources. Although the resources in a grid might be in separate administrative domains, they are made available as virtual local resources to any node on the grid. A user signing on at one location would view computers at other remote locations as if they were part of the local system. Grid computing works by polling the resources available, and then allocating them to individual tasks as the need arise. Resources are returned to the pool upon completion of the task. Grid gives an illusion of a big virtual computer capable of carrying out enormous tasks. The challenge is to allow meaningful sharing of resources without compromising local autonomy. Support of grids requires innovative solutions to a number of challenging issues including: resource management, resource monitoring, interoperability, security, billing and accounting, communication, and performance.

There are several examples of grid platforms and tools such as Globus and Tera-Grid. The Globus Toolkit is an enabling technology for the grid. It allows users to share computing power, databases, and other tools securely on line across corporate, institutional, and geographic boundaries, without sacrificing local autonomy. The toolkit includes software services and libraries for resource monitoring, discovery, and management, plus security and file management. It also includes software for communication, fault detection, and portability. The Globus Toolkit has grown through an open-source strategy. Version 1.0 was introduced in 1998 followed by the 2.0 release in 2002. The latest 3.0 version is based on new open-standard Grid services.

TeraGrid is a large high-performance computing project headed by the National Center for Supercomputing Applications at the University of Illinois at Urbana-Champaign. The TeraGrid uses thousands of Intel Itanium 2 processors located at four sites in the United States. The TeraGrid is an effort to build and deploy the world's largest, fastest distributed infrastructure for open scientific research. The TeraGrid is expected to include 20 teraflops of computing power, facilities capable of managing and storing nearly 1 petabyte of data, high-resolution visualization environments, and toolkits for grid computing. These components will be tightly integrated and connected through a network that will operate at 40 gigabits per second.

7.7 CHAPTER SUMMARY

The recent migrations to distributed platforms have increased the need for a better understanding of network computing. Distributed platforms may be connected in a variety of ways ranging from geographically dispersed networks to architecture-specific interconnection structures. A processing unit in such systems is an autonomous computer that may be engaged in its own private activities while at the same time cooperating with other units in the context of some computational task. Network computing is concerned with how to use multiple computers to solve single or multiple problems, more or less simultaneously. The infrastructure includes desktop machines connected by a WAN, workstation clusters and Ethernet-connected or switch-connected workstations. A number of models exist to aggregate the resources of multiple compute engines for large-scale processing tasks. Multiprocessor systems incorporate multiple processors into a single machine, whether it is a desktop workstation, a mainframe, or something in between. Clusters aggregate many machines into a large, centrally managed entity. Grid computing allows each node to access resources on other nodes as if they were local. Whatever the choice, it is clear that as processor power becomes less expensive, capable stand-alone commodity processors connected via some type of high-speed network will become a standard part of computing in the future.

PROBLEMS

1. Read the Ethernet Standard and find the details including:
   (a) CSMA/CD.
   (b) What happens when multiple machines access an Ethernet at the same time?
   (c) The minimum idle time between two consecutive transmissions.

2. Explain the following:
    (a) Two-tier client/server.
    (b) Three-tier client/server.
    (c) Thin client.
    (d) Fat client.
    (e) Sockets.
    (f) Port.

3. Prove that the number of one-to-one and one-to-many connections in an $n \times n$ switch is n^n.

4. How many switches are needed in a Clos network in each of the following cases?
    (a) Number of hosts is 256.
    (b) Number of hosts is 192.
    (c) Number of hosts is 1042.

5. Draw a QsNet of dimension 3. How many switches? How many processing units?

6. Find a lower bound on the time it takes to transfer a 100 MB file across a network that operates at 1.5 Mbps, 10 Mbps, 100 Mbps, 1 Gbps, 2.4 Gbps.

7. Which of the following applications are better suited for clusters and which are better for a grid? Justify your answer.
    (a) Parallel computation with minimal interprocess communication and workflow dependencies.
    (b) Interactive.
    (c) Noninteractive (batch jobs).
    (d) Simulation.
    (e) Games.

8. Compare shared memory systems, distributed memory systems, clusters, and grids in the following aspects:
    (a) Advantages and disadvantages.
    (b) Cost and benefits.
    (c) Applications.
    (d) Performance.

9. Draw a block diagram that shows the most important modules in basic grid architecture. Show the main function of each module and the relationship between the different modules.

10. Conduct a literature search to find five grid platforms. Construct a table that shows the similarities and differences among the platforms you found. What is the most distinguishing feature of each platform?

REFERENCES

Becker, D. J., Sterling, T., Savarese, D., Dorband, J. E., Ranawake, U. A. and Packer, C. V. BEOWULF: A parallel workstation for scientific computation. *Proceedings of the 1995 International Conference on Parallel Processing (ICPP)*, 1995, pp. 11–14.

Boden, N. J., Cohen, D., Felderman, R. E., Kulawik, A. E., Seitz, C. L., Seizovic, J. N. and Su, W.-K. Myrinet – A gigabit-per-second local-area network. *IEEE Micro* (1995).

Comer, D. E. *Internetworking with TCP/IP: Principles, Protocols, and Architectures*, 4th edition, Prentice-Hall, 2000.

Douglis, F. and Foster, I. The Grid Grows Up. *IEEE Internet Computing* (2003).

Foster, I. The Grid: A new infrastructure for 21st century science. *Physics Today*, 55 (2), 42–47 (2002).

Foster, I., Kesselman, C. and Tuecke, S. The anatomy of the Grid: Enabling scalable virtual organizations. *International Journal of Supercomputer Applications*, 15 (3) (2001).

Hwang, K. et al. Designing SSI clusters with hierarchical checkpoints and single I/O space. *IEEE Concurrency*, 7 (1), (1999).

Petrini, F., Feng, W.-C., Hoisie, A., Coll, S. and Frachtenberg, E. The Quadrics network: High performance clustering technology. *IEEE Micro* (2002).

Warren, M. S., Germann, T. C., Lomdahl, P. S., Beazley, D. M. and Salmon, J. K. Avalon: An Alpha/Linux cluster achieves 10 Gflops for $150k. In *Supercomputing '98*, Los Alamitos, 1998, IEEE Comp. Soc.

Websites

http://www.flashmobcomputing.org/
http://www.beowulf.org/
http://www.ieeetfcc.org/
http://www.myricom.com/myrinet/overview/
http://www.internetworldstats.com
http://now.cs.berkeley.edu/
http://www.teragrid.org
http://www.globus.org/

CHAPTER 8

Parallel Programming in the Parallel Virtual Machine

The Parallel Virtual Machine (PVM) was originally developed at Oak Ridge National Laboratory and the University of Tennessee. It makes it possible to develop applications on a set of heterogeneous computers connected by a network that appears logically to the users as a single parallel computer. The PVM offers a powerful set of process control and dynamic resource management functions. It provides programmers with a library of routines for the initiation and termination of tasks, synchronization, and the alteration of the virtual machine configuration. It also facilitates message passing via a number of simple constructs. Interoperability among different heterogeneous computers is a major advantage in PVM. Programs written for some architecture can be copied to another architecture, compiled and executed without modification. Additionally, these PVM executables can still communicate with each other. A PVM application is made from a number of tasks that cooperate to jointly provide a solution to a single problem. A task may alternate between computation and communication with other tasks. The programming model is a network of communicating sequential tasks in which each task has its own locus of control, and sequential tasks communicate by exchanging messages.

8.1 PVM ENVIRONMENT AND APPLICATION STRUCTURE

The computing environment in PVM is the virtual machine, which is a dynamic set of heterogeneous computer systems connected via a network and managed as a single parallel computer. The computer nodes in the network are called hosts, which could be uniprocessor, multiprocessor systems, or clusters running the PVM software. PVM has two components: a library of PVM routines, and a daemon that should reside on all the hosts in the virtual machine. Before running a PVM application, a user should start up PVM and configure a virtual machine. The PVM console allows the user to interactively start and then alter the virtual machine at any time during system operation. The details of how to set up the

Advanced Computer Architecture and Parallel Processing, by H. El-Rewini and M. Abd-El-Barr
ISBN 0-471-46740-5   Copyright © 2005 John Wiley & Sons, Inc.

PVM software, how to configure a virtual machine, and how to compile and run PVM programs can be found at http://www.epm.ornl.gov/pvm and in Geist et al. (1994).

The PVM application is composed of a number of sequential programs, each of which will correspond to one or more processes in a parallel program. These programs are compiled individually for each host in the virtual machine. The object files are placed in locations accessible from other hosts. One of these sequential programs, which is called the *initiating task*, has to be started manually on one of the hosts. The tasks on the other hosts are activated automatically by the initiating task. The tasks comprising a PVM application can all be identical but work on different ranges of data. This model of parallel programming is called SPMD, which stands for Single Program Multiple Data. Although SPMD is common in most PVM applications, it is still possible to have the tasks perform different functions. A pipeline of parallel tasks that perform input, processing, and output is an example of parallel tasks that are performing different functions. Parallel virtual machine parallel applications can take different structures. One of the most common structures is the *star* graph in which the middle node in the star is called the supervisor and the rest of the nodes are workers. The star structure is often referred to as a *supervisor–workers* or a *master–slaves* model. In this model, the supervisor is the initiating task that activates all the workers. A tree structure is another form of a PVM application. The root of the tree is the top supervisor and underneath there are several levels in the hierarchy. We will use the terms *supervisor–workers* and *hierarchy* to refer to the star and the tree structures, respectively.

8.1.1   Supervisor–Workers Structure

There is only one level of hierarchy in this structure: one supervisor and many workers. The supervisor serves as the initiating task that is activated manually on one of the hosts. The supervisor, which is also called the master, has a number of special responsibilities. It normally interacts with the user, activates the workers on the virtual machine, assigns work to the workers, and collects results from the workers.

The workers, which are also called slaves, are activated by the supervisor to perform calculations. The workers may or may not be independent. If they are not independent, they may communicate with each other before sending the result of the computation back to the supervisor.

For example, a simple idea to sort an array of numbers using the supervisor–workers structure can be described as follows. The supervisor creates a number of workers and divides the array elements among them such that each worker gets an almost equal number of elements. Each worker independently sorts its share of the array and sends the sorted list back to the supervisor. The supervisor collects the sorted lists from the workers and merges them into one sorted list. Figure 8.1 shows an example of sorting an array of elements using one supervisor (S) and four workers (W1, W2, W3, and W4). Note that in this example the workers are entirely independent and communicate only with the supervisor that performs the merge procedure on the four sorted sublists while the workers remain idle.

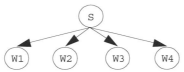

(*a*) The supervisor creates four workers and send them four sublists to sort

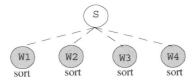

(*b*) The supervisor is idle and the four workers are sorting their sublists

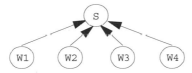

(*c*) The four workers are sending their sorted sublists to the supervisor

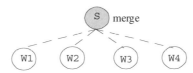

(*d*) The supervisor is merging the four sorted sublists and the four workers are idle

Figure 8.1 Supervisor–workers structure of sorting using a supervisor S and four independent workers W1, W2, W3, and W4. The solid edges indicate message passing. The dashed edges between S and W1, W2, W3, and W4 indicate that the workers were created by S.

Another way of sorting a list using the supervisor–workers structure is to make the workers help in the merge process and let the supervisor eventually merge only two sorted sublists. Figure 8.2 illustrates how this procedure works using one supervisor (S) and four workers (W1, W2, W3, and W4). First, the supervisor divides the list among the four workers. Each worker sorts its sublist independently. Workers W2 and W4 then send their sorted sublists to W1 and W3, respectively. Worker W1 will merge its sorted sublist with the one received from W2. Similarly, W3 will merge its sorted sublist with the one received from W4. Eventually the supervisor receives two sorted sublists from W1 and W3 to perform the final merge.

8.1.2 Hierarchy Structure

Unlike the supervisor–workers structure, the hierarchy structure allows the workers to create new levels of workers. The top-level supervisor is the initiating task, which creates a set of workers at the second level. These workers may create other sets of

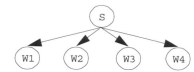

(*a*) The supervisor creates four workers and send them four sublists

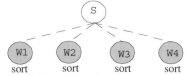

(*b*) The supervisor is idle and the four workers are sorting their sublists

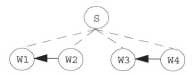

(*c*) Workers W2 and W4 send their sorted sublists to W1 and W3, respectively

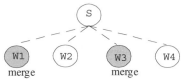

(*d*) Workers W1 and W3 are merging two sublists each and W2 and W4 are idle

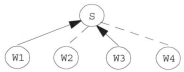

(*e*) Workers W1 and W3 send two sorted sublists to the supervisor

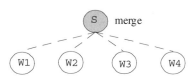

(*f*) The supervisor is merging two sorted sublists and the four workers are idle

Figure 8.2 Supervisor–workers sorting using the supervisor S and four communicating workers W1, W2, W3, and W4. The dashed lines indicate that W1, W2, W3, and W4 were created by S.

workers at the next level, and so on. (A task that creates another task is also called its parent.) This task creation process can continue to any number of levels, forming a tree structure. The leaves of the tree are the workers at the lowest level. This structure matches very well with the organization of divide and conquer applications.

For example, sorting an array of elements using the hierarchy structure can be performed as follows. The top supervisor creates two workers and passes to each of them one-half of the array to sort. Each worker will in turn create two new workers and send to each of them one-half of the already halved array to sort. This process will continue until the leaf workers have an appropriate number of elements to sort. These leaf workers will independently sort their lists and send them up to their parent to perform the merge operation. This process will continue upward until finally the top supervisor merges two sorted lists into the final sorted array. Figure 8.3 illustrates the sorting algorithm using the hierarchy structure when eight leaf workers are used for sorting. Note that dashed edges in the tree signify a parent–child relationship between the tasks.

8.2 TASK CREATION

A task in PVM can be started manually or can be spawned from another task. The initiating task is always activated manually by simply running its executable code on one of the hosts. Other PVM tasks can be created dynamically from within other tasks. The function pvm_spawn() is used for dynamic task creation. The task that calls the function pvm_spawn() is referred to as the parent and the newly created tasks are called children. To create a child from a running parent, a programmer must at least specify the following:

1. The machine on which the child will be started.
2. A path to the executable file on the specified machine.
3. The number of copies of the child to be created.
4. An array of arguments to the child task(s).

As all PVM tasks are identified by an integer task identifier, when a task is created it is assigned a unique identifier (TID). Task identification can be used to identify senders and receivers during communication. They can also be used to assign functions to different tasks based on their TIDs.

8.2.1 Task Identifier Retrieval

Parallel virtual machine provides a number of functions to retrieve TID values so that a particular task can identify itself, its parent, and other tasks in the system.

Task's TID A running task can retrieve its own TID by calling the PVM function pvm_myid() as follows:

```
mytid = pvm_mytid();   /* get my own tid */
```

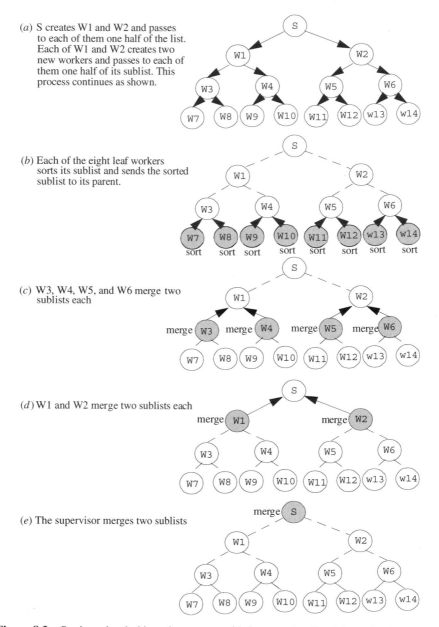

(a) S creates W1 and W2 and passes to each of them one half of the list. Each of W1 and W2 creates two new workers and passes to each of them one half of its sublist. This process continues as shown.

(b) Each of the eight leaf workers sorts its sublist and sends the sorted sublist to its parent.

(c) W3, W4, W5, and W6 merge two sublists each

(d) W1 and W2 merge two sublists each

(e) The supervisor merges two sublists

Figure 8.3 Sorting using the hierarchy structure with the supervisor S and the workers W1–W14.

Child's TID When a task calls the function pvm_spawn(), an array containing the TIDs of the children created by this call will be returned. For example, the array tid in the following pvm_spawn() call will have the TIDs of all the children.

```
pvm_spawn(...,...,...,...,...,&tid)
/* The TIDs of the children created by this call are saved in
   the array tid */
```

Parent's TID A task can retrieve the TID of its parent (the task from which it was spawned) by calling the function pvm_parent() as follows:

```
my_parent_tid = pvm_parent();   /* get my parent's tid */
```

The value PvmNoParent will be returned if the calling task is the one that was created manually and does not have a parent. This is an easy way to distinguish the supervisor from the workers in an application.

Daemon's TID A task can retrieve the TID of the daemon running on the same host as another task whose TID is id by calling the function pvm_tidtohost() as follows:

```
daemon_tid = pvm_tidtohost(id);
/* get tid of daemon running on the same host as the task whose
   TID is id*/
```

This function is useful for determining on which host a given task is running.

8.2.2 Dynamic Task Creation

The pvm_spawn() function is used to create one task or more on the same or a different machine in the PVM configuration. The format of this function is given as follows:

```
num = pvm_spawn(Child,Arguments,Flag,Where,HowMany,&Tids)
```

This function has six parameters and returns the actual number of the successfully created tasks in the variable num. The first two parameters are the executable file name of the program to be activated and the arguments to be passed to the executable (in standard argv format, terminated with a NULL).

The next two parameters specify where to start the process. The Flag parameter controls the target of the spawn operation. A value of zero lets PVM decides on the appropriate machine on which to start the task. Other values specify that the where parameter signifies a machine name, or an architecture type. Specifying a machine name gives the programmer ultimate control over the task allocation process. Specifying an architecture type may be more appropriate in some cases, especially when the virtual machine is configured from a widely dispersed set of architectures. One of the requirements of the spawn command is that the executable must already exist on whatever machine it is to run on.

TABLE 8.1   Parameters for Dynamic Task Creation

Parameter	Meaning
Child	The executable file name of the program to be started. The executable must reside on the host on which it will run.
Arguments	A pointer to an array of arguments to the program. If the program takes no arguments this pointer should be NULL.
Flag	A flag value of zero lets the PVM system decides what machine will run the spawned task(s). Other values signify that a particular host name or architecture type will be specified to run the spawned tasks.
Where	A host name or an architecture type to run the created tasks depending on the value of the above flag.
HowMany	The number of identical children to be started.
Tids	The TIDs of the children created by this call.

The final two parameters contain control information, such as the number of processes to spawn with this call, and an array in which to return information, such as task identifiers and error codes. The different parameters and their meanings are summarized in Table 8.1.

Example 1   Suppose that we want to create two and four copies of the program "worker" on the two hosts: homer and fermi, respectively. Assume that the executable file "worker" resides in the directory "/user/rewini" in both machines. The following two statements in the initiating task should create the required tasks:

```
n1 = pvm_spawn("/user/rewini/worker", 0, 1, "homer", 2, &tid1)
n2 = pvm_spawn("/user/rewini/worker", 0, 1, "fermi", 4, &tid2)
```

The second parameter is 0 when there is no arguments to "worker". The third parameter is the spawn type flag, which was set to 1 so that we can specify homer and fermi as our target hosts. The TID values of the created tasks are returned in $tid1$ and $tid2$. Finally $n1$ and $n2$ are the actual number of created tasks on homer and fermi, respectively.

8.3   TASK GROUPS

PVM allows running tasks to belong to named groups, which can change at any time during computation. Groups are useful in cases when a collective operation is performed on only a subset of the tasks. For example, a broadcast operation, which sends a message to all tasks in a system, can use a named group to send a message to only the members of this group. A task may join or leave a group at any time without informing other tasks in the group. A task may also belong to multiple groups. PVM provides several functions for tasks to join and leave a group, and retrieve information about other groups.

A task can join a group by calling the function pvm_joingroup() as follows:

i = pvm_joingroup(group_name)

This function adds the task that calls it to the group named group_name. It returns the instance number of the task that just joined the group. The group itself is created when pvm_joingroup is called for the first time. In this case, the first caller gets 0 as instance number. The returned instance number starts at 0 and is incremented by 1 every time a new task joins the group. However, this set of instance numbers may have gaps as a result of having one or more tasks leave the group. When a task joins a group with gaps in the set of instance numbers, this new member will get the lowest available instance number. Maintaining a set of instance numbers without gaps is the programmer's responsibility.

A member of a group may leave the group by calling the function pvm_lvgroup() as follows:

info = pvm_lvgroup(group_name)

The task that successfully calls this function will leave the group group_name. In case of an error, info will have a negative value. If this task decides to rejoin this group at a later time, it may get a different instance number because the old number may have been assigned to another task that may have joined.

There are a number of other functions that can be called by any task to retrieve information without having to be a member of the specified group. For example, the function pvm_gsize() can be used to retrieve the size of a group. It takes as input the group name and returns the number of members in the group. The function pvm_gettid() is provided to retrieve the TID of a task given its instance number and its group name. Similarly, the function pvm_getinst() retrieves the instance number of a task given its TID and the name of a group to which it belongs.

Example 2 Suppose that tasks T0, T1, T2, and T3 have TIDs 200, 100, 300, and 400, respectively. Let us see what happens after the execution of each of the following statements.

1. Task T0 calls the function i1 = pvm_joingroup("slave")
   The group "slave" is created, T0 joins this group and T0 is assigned the instance number 0 (i1 = 0).
2. Task T1 calls the function i2 = pvm_joingroup("slave")
   T1 joins the group "slave" and is assigned instance number 1 (i2 = 1).
3. Task T2 calls the function i3 = pvm_joingroup("slave")
   T2 joins the group "slave" and is assigned the instance number 2 (i3 = 2).
4. Task T1 calls the function info = pvm_lvgroup("slave")
   T1 leaves the group "slave" and the instance number 1 becomes available to other tasks that may wish to join the group "slave" in the future.

5. Some task calls the function size = pvm_gsize("slave")
    The variable size will be assigned the value 2, which is the number of tasks that currently belong to the group "slave".

6. Task T3 calls the function i4 = pvm_joingroup("slave")
    T3 joins the group "slave" and is assigned instance number 1 (i4 = 1).

7. Task T1 calls the function i5 = pvm_joingroup("slave")
    T1 rejoins the group "slave" and is now assigned the instance number 3 (i5 = 3).

8. Some task calls the function tid = pvm_gettid("slave",1)
    The variable tid will be assigned the value 400, which is the TID of the task T3 whose instance number is 1.

9. Some task calls the function inst = pvm_getinst("slave",100)
    The variable inst will be assigned the value 3, which is the instance number of the task T1 whose TID is 100.

8.4   COMMUNICATION AMONG TASKS

Communication among PVM tasks is performed using the message passing approach, which is achieved using a library of routines and a daemon. During program execution, the user program communicates with the PVM daemon through the library routines. The daemon, which runs on each machine in the PVM environment, determines the destination of each message. If the message is sent to a task on the local machine, the daemon routes the message directly. If the message is for a task on a remote host, the daemon sends the message to the corresponding daemon on the remote machine. The remote daemon then routes the message to the right receiving task.

The operations Send and Receive are the heart of this communication scheme, which is generally asynchronous. A message can be sent to one or more destinations by calling one of the PVM send functions. A message can be received by calling either a blocking or nonblocking receive function. Figure 8.4 schematically illustrates communication in PVM. The arrows from the user applications to the daemons represent communication calls (crossing the API boundary). The arrows from the daemons back to the user applications represent the return from the API calls. The thread of control of the user task briefly blocks on the daemon.

Using standard PVM asynchronous communication, a sending process issues a send command (point 1 in Fig. 8.4). The message is transferred to the daemon (point 2), then control is returned to the user application (points 3 and 4). The daemon will transmit the message on the physical link sometime after returning control to the user application (point 3). At some other time, either before or after the send command, the receiving task issues a receive command (point 5 in Fig. 8.4). In the case of a blocking receive, the receiving task blocks on the daemon waiting for a message (point 6). After the message arrives, control is returned to the user application (points 7 and 8). In the case of nonblocking receive, control is returned to the user application immediately (points 7 and 8) even if the message has not yet arrived.

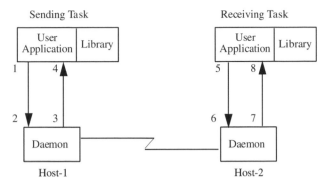

Figure 8.4 Communication in PVM.

A sender task can send a message to one or more receivers in three steps as follows:

1. A send buffer must be initialized.
2. The message is packed into this buffer.
3. The completed message is sent to its destination(s).

Similarly, receiving a message is done in two steps as follows:

1. The message is received.
2. The received items are unpacked from the receive buffer.

8.4.1 Message Buffers

Before packing a message for transmission, a send buffer must be created and prepared for data to be assembled into it. PVM provides two functions for buffer creation; pvm_initsend() and pvm_mkbuf(). These two functions agree on the input and output parameters. They take as input an integer value to specify the next message's encoding scheme, and they return an integer value specifying the message buffer identifier. The two functions are listed below.

```
bufid = pvm_initsend(encoding_option)
bufid = pvm_mkbuf(encoding_option)
```

There are three encoding options in creating the buffer. The default encoding option is XDR, which is useful when a message is sent to a different machine that may not be able to read the message native format. However, if this is not the case, another option is to skip the encoding step and a message is sent using its original format. A third option is to leave data in place and to make the send operation copy items directly from the user's memory. The buffer is used only to store the message size and pointers to the data items in this case. Clearly, the third option saves time by reducing the copying time but it requires that the user does not modify

TABLE 8.2   Encoding Options for Buffer Creation

encoding_option	Meaning
0	XDR
1	No encoding
2	Leave data in place

data before they are sent. The different values and the meanings of the different encoding options are summarized in Table 8.2.

If the user is using only one send buffer, pvm_initsend() should be the only required function. It clears the send buffer and prepares it for packing a new message. The function pvm_mkbuf(), on the other hand, is useful when multiple message buffers are required in an application. It creates a new empty send buffer every time it is called. In PVM 3, there is only one active send buffer and one active receive buffer at any time. All packing, sending, receiving, and unpacking functions affect only the active buffer. PVM provides the following functions to set the active send (or receive) buffers to bufid. They save the state of the previous buffer and return its identifier in oldbuf.

oldbuf = pvm_setsbuf(bufid)
oldbuf = pvm_setrbuf(bufid)

PVM also provides the functions pvm_getsbuf() and pvm_getrbuf() to retrieve the identifier of the active send buffer and the active receive buffer, respectively.

8.4.2 Data Packing

PVM provides a variety of packing functions pvm_pk*() to pack an array of a given data type into the active send buffer. Each of the packing functions takes three arguments as input. The first argument is a pointer to where the first item is, and the second argument specifies the number of items to be packed in an array. The third argument is the stride to use when packing (that is, how many items to skip between two packed items). For example, a stride of 1 means a contiguous array is packed, a stride of 2 means every other item is packed, and so on. The packing functions return a status code, which will have a negative value in case of an error.

There are several packing functions for all kinds of data types such as byte, double, string, and so on. All the functions have the same number of arguments except the string packing function pvm_pkstr(), which takes only one argument (a pointer to the string). PVM also provides the function pvm_packf() that uses a printf like format expression to specify what to pack in the buffer before sending. Packing functions can be called multiple times to pack data into a single message. Other packing functions for the different data types include: pvm_pkbyte(), pvm_pkcplx(), pvm_pkdcplx(), pvm_pkdouble(), pvm_pkfloat(), pvm_pkint(), pvm_pklong(), pvm_pkshort(), pvm_pkuint(), pvm_pkushort(), pvm_pkulong().

Example 3 The following function calls pack a string followed by an array, called my_array, of *n* items into the message buffer:

```
info = pvm_pkstr("This is my data");
info = pvm_pkint(my_array, n, 1)
```

First, the string is packed and then *n* integers from the array list are packed into the send buffer. Note that there is no limit to the complexity of the packed message, but it should be unpacked exactly the same way at the receiving end.

8.4.3 Sending a Message

Sending messages in PVM is done in an asynchronous fashion. The sending task will resume its execution once the message is sent (points 3 and 4 in Fig. 8.4). It will not wait for the receiving task to execute the matching receive operation as in synchronous communication. Note that synchronous communication constructs for PVM were suggested in Lundell et al. (1996).

After the buffer is initialized and the packing process is completed, the message is now ready to be sent. A message can be sent to one or multiple receivers. All we need to specify at this point are an identifier for each task that should receive the message and a label (tag) for the message.

Sending to One Receiver The function pvm_send() performs a point-to-point send operation. It takes two arguments: the TID of the destination task and an integer message identifier (tag). For example, the function call

```
info = pvm_send(tid, tag)
```

will label the message packed in the send buffer with the label tag that is supplied by the programmer and send it to the task whose TID is tid. The call returns integer status code info. A negative value of info indicates an error.

Sending to Multiple Receivers To send the message to multiple destinations, the function pvm_mcast() should be used. The TIDs of the tasks that will receive the message should be saved in an array. A pointer to the TIDs array, the number of recipient tasks, and the message label are the arguments to pvm_mcast(). For example, the function call

```
info = pvm_mcast(tids, n, tag)
```

will label the message with the integer tag and send it to the n tasks whose TIDs are specified in the array tids. Again the status code info indicates whether the call was successful. Note that the message will never be sent to the caller task even if its TID was included in the array tids.

Sending to a Group   A message can be broadcast to all members of a group using the function `pvm_bcast()`. Any task can call this function without having to be a member of the group. The arguments of this function are the group name and the message tag. It first determines the TIDs of the group members and then uses `pvm_mcast()` to broadcast the message. For example, the function call

```
info = pvm_bcast(group_name, tag)
```

will label the message with the integer `tag` and send it to all members of the group `group_name`. Note that if the group changes during the broadcast, the change will not be reflected. Since group changes are not collective operations over the group, the result of collective operations cannot be predicted unless synchronization is done by hand.

Packing and Sending in One Step   PVM also provides another function to send messages without the need to prepare and pack the buffer manually. The operation `pvm_psend()` does the packing automatically for the programmer. In addition to the destination TID and the message label, `pvm_psend()` takes a pointer to a buffer, its length, its data type as arguments. For example, the call

```
info = pvm_psend(tid, tag, my_array, n, int)
```

packs an array of n integers called `my_array` into a message labeled `tag`, and sends it to the task whose TID is `tid`.

8.4.4   Receiving a Message

PVM supports three types of message receiving functions: blocking, nonblocking, and timeout. When calling a blocking receive function, the receiving task must wait until the expected message arrives in the receive buffer. A nonblocking receive immediately returns with either the expected data or a flag that the data have not arrived. Timeout receive allows the programmer to specify a period of time for which the receive function should wait before it returns. If the timeout period is very large, this function will act like the blocking receive. On the other hand, if the timeout period is set to zero, it acts exactly like the nonblocking case. Figure 8.5 illustrates the three types of receive operations.

Blocking Receive

```
bufid = pvm_recv(tid, tag)
```

This function will wait until a message with label `tag` is received from a task with TID = `tid`. A value of -1 can be used as a wild card to match anything in either one of the arguments: `tid` or `tag`. A successful receive will create a receive buffer and return the buffer identifier to be used in unpacking the message.

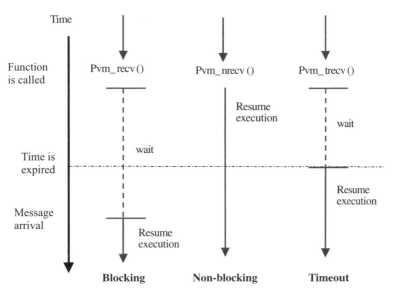

Figure 8.5   The three types of receive operations.

Nonblocking Receive

bufid = pvm_nrecv(tid, tag)

If the message has arrived successfully when this function is called, it will return a buffer identifier similar to the case of blocking receive. However, if the expected message has not arrived, the function will return immediately with bufid = 0.

Timeout Receive

bufid = pvm_trecv(tid, tag, timeout)

This function blocks the execution of its caller task until a message with a label tag has arrived from tid within a specified waiting period of time. If there is no matching message arriving within the specified waiting time, this function will return with bufid = 0, which indicates that no message was received. The waiting time argument (timeout) is a structure with two integer fields tv_sec and tv_usec. With both fields set to zero, this function will act as a nonblocking receive. Passing a null pointer as timeout makes the function act like a blocking receive. If pvm_trecv() is successful, bufid will have the value of the new active receive buffer identifier.

Receive and Unpack in One Step   Similar to the pvm_psend() function, PVM provides the function pvm_precv(), which combines the functions of blocking receive and unpacking in one routine. It does not return a buffer identifier; instead it returns the actual values. For example, the following call

```
info = pvm_precv(tid, tag, my_array, len, datatype, &src,
  &atag, &alen)
```

will block until a matching message is received. The contents of the message will be saved in `my_array` up to length `len`. In addition to the status code `info`, the actual TID of the sender, actual message tag, and the actual message length are returned in `src`, `atag`, and `alen`, respectively. Again the value -1 can be used as a wild card for the arguments: `tag` or `tid`.

8.4.5 Data Unpacking

When messages are received, they need to be unpacked in the same way they were packed in the sending task. Unpacking functions must match their corresponding packing functions in type, number of items, and stride.

PVM provides many unpacking functions `pvm_upk*()`, each of which corresponds to a particular packing function. Similar to packing functions, each of the unpacking functions takes three arguments as input. These arguments are address of the first item, number of items, and stride. PVM also provides the two functions `pvm_upkstr()` and `pvm_unpackf()` to unpack the messages packed by `pvm_pkstr()` and `pvm_packf()`, respectively.

Other unpacking functions for the different data types include: `pvm_upkbyte()`, `pvm_upkcplx()`, `pvm_upkdcplx()`, `pvm_upkdouble()`, `pvm_upkfloat()`, `pvm_upkint()`, `pvm_upklong()`, `pvm_upkshort()`, `pvm_upkuint()`, `pvm_upkushort()`, `pvm_upkulong()`.

Example 4   The following function calls unpack a string followed by an array of *n* items from the receive buffer:

```
info = pvm_upkstr(string)
info = pvm_upkint(my_array, n, 1)
```

Note that the string and the array must have been packed using the corresponding packing functions.

8.5   TASK SYNCHRONIZATION

Synchronization constructs can be used to force a certain order of execution among the activities in a parallel program. For example, a task that uses certain variables in its computation must wait until these variables are computed (possibly by other tasks) before it resumes its execution. Even without data dependence involvement, parallel tasks may need to synchronize with each other at a given point in the execution. For example, members of a group that finish their work early may need to wait at a synchronization point until those tasks that take a longer time reach the same point. Synchronization in PVM can be achieved using several constructs, most notably blocking receive and barrier operations.

8.5.1 Precedence Synchronization

Message passing can be used effectively to force precedence constraints among tasks. Using the blocking receive operation (pvm_recv()) forces the receiving task to wait until a matching message is received. The sender of this matching message may hold its message as long as it wants the receiver to wait. For example, consider the two tasks; T0 and T1 in Figure 8.6. Suppose that we want to make sure that the function g() in T1 is not executed until T0 has completed the execution of the function f(). This particular order of execution can be guaranteed using a send operation after calling f() in T0, and a matching blocking receive operation before calling g() in T1.

8.5.2 Barriers

Parallel tasks can be synchronized through the use of synchronization points called barriers. No task may proceed beyond a barrier until all participating tasks have reached that barrier. Members of a group can choose to wait at a barrier until a specified number of group members check in at that barrier. PVM provides barrier synchronization through the use of the function pvm_barrier(). This function takes two inputs: the group name, and the number of group members that should call this function before any of them can proceed beyond the barrier as follows.

```
info = pvm_barrier(group_name, ntasks)
```

Again the status code info will return a negative integer value in case of an error. The number of members specified could be set to any number less than or equal to

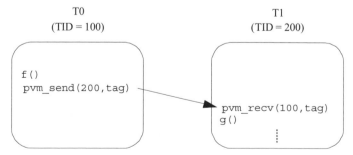

Figure 8.6 Precedence synchronization using message passing. The function f() in T0 is guaranteed to be executed before the function g() in T1.

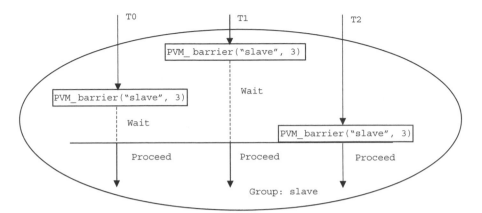

Figure 8.7   Three tasks in the group slave are waiting on a barrier.

the total number of members. However, it is typically the total number of members in the group. In any case, the value of this argument should match across a given barrier call. If this argument is set to −1, PVM will use the value of pvm_gsize(), which returns the total number of members. Since it is possible for tasks to join the group after other tasks have already called pvm_barrier(), it is necessary to specify the number of tasks that should check in at the barrier. It is not allowed for a task to call pvm_barrier() with a group to which it does not belong.

Example 5   Figure 8.7 shows three members of the group slave (T0, T1, T2) using a barrier to synchronize at a certain point in their execution. Each of the three tasks should call the following function:

info = pvm_barrier("slave", 3)

The execution will block until three members of the group slave have issued the call to function pvm_barrier() as shown in the figure. Task T1 calls the function first, followed by T0, and then finally T2. Tasks T0 and T1 wait at the barrier until T2 reaches the barrier before they can all proceed.

8.6   REDUCTION OPERATIONS

Reduction is an operation by which multiple values are reduced into a single value. This single value could be the maximum (minimum) value, the summation (product) of all elements, or the result of applying an associative binary operator that yields a single result. PVM supports reduction through the use of the function pvm_reduce(). The format of this function is given as follows:

info = pvm_reduce(func, data, n, datatype, tag, group_name,
  root)

TABLE 8.3 Parameters for Reduction Operations

Parameter	Meaning
func	The function that defines the operation to be performed.
data	An array of data elements.
n	The number of elements in the data array.
datatype	The type of entries in the data array.
tag	Message tag.
group_name	The name of an existing group.
root	Instance number of a group member who gets the result.

The function returns an integer status code (info). The different parameters and their meanings are summarized in Table 8.3.

The reduction operation is performed on the corresponding elements in the data array across the group. The reduced value for each element in the array across the group will be returned to the root specified in the parameters. In fact, the data array on the root will be overwritten with the result of the reduction operation over the group. Users can define their own functions or can use several PVM predefined functions such as PvmMin, PvmMax, PvmSum, and PvmProduct for the minimum, maximum, summation, and product, respectively.

Example 6 Figure 8.8 shows an example of a reduction summation of the entries of data_array over the group "slave", which has three members: T0, T1, and T2. The reduced values are returned to the root, which is assumed to be task T1 in this example. The following function must be called by the three tasks.

```
info = pvm_reduce(PvmSum,   data_array,   5,PVM_INT,   tag,
   "slave", root)
```

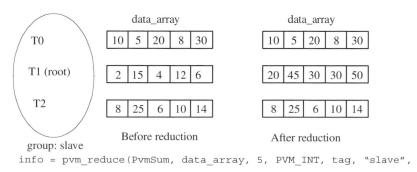

Figure 8.8 Reduction operation on the members of the group slave.

8.7 WORK ASSIGNMENT

Assigning work to workers can be done either by writing a separate program for each worker or writing a single program for all workers. If the workers perform the same computation on different sets of data concurrently, it is appropriate to use a single program for all workers. On the other hand, if the workers perform different functions, it is possible to do it either way. In this section, we show how to assign work to the parallel tasks.

8.7.1 Using Different Programs

If the workers forming the parallel application perform completely different operations, they can be written as different programs. These different workers can be activated by the initiating task (supervisor) using `pvm_spawn()`. The supervisor can communicate with the workers since it knows their TIDs, which are returned when `pvm_spawn()` is called. To communicate with the supervisor, the workers need to know the supervisor's TID. The function `pvm_parent()` returns the supervisor's TID when called by the workers.

Example 7 Suppose that we want to activate four different tasks: "worker1", "worker2", "worker3", and "worker4" on the hosts cselab01, cselab02, cselab03, and cselab04, respectively. Assume that the executable files reside in the directory "/user/rewini" in all machines. The following statements in the initiating task will create the required tasks.

```
info1 = pvm_spawn("/user/rewini/worker1", 0, 1, "cselab01",
   1, &tid1)
info2 = pvm_spawn("/user/rewini/worker2", 0, 1, "cselab02",
   1, &tid2)
info3 = pvm_spawn("/user/rewini/worker3", 0, 1, "cselab03",
   1, &tid3)
info4 = pvm_spawn("/user/rewini/worker4", 0, 1, "cselab04",
   1, &tid4)
```

8.7.2 Using the Same Program

Assigning work to parallel tasks running the same program can be done easily if we know in advance the identification numbers assigned by the system. For example, if we know that the identification numbers of $n - 1$ workers running the same program are $1, 2, \ldots, n - 1$, we can assign work to these tasks as follows:

```
switch (my_id) {
  case 1:
    /* Work assigned to the worker whose id number is 1 */
    break;
```

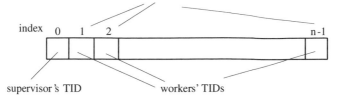

Figure 8.9   The task ID array sent to all workers by the supervisor.

```
case 2:
   /* Work assigned to the worker whose id number is 2 */
   break;
......
case n - 1:
   /* Work assigned to the worker whose id number is n - 1 */
   break;
default:;}/* end switch */
```

Unfortunately, a task in PVM is assigned any integer as its identification number. Tasks are not necessarily identified by the integers 1, 2, 3, and so on, as shown in the above example. In what follows, we show how to overcome this problem.

Using Task Groups   In this method, all the tasks join one group and the instance numbers are used as the new task identifiers. The supervisor is the first one to join the group and gets 0 as its instance number. The workers will get instance numbers in the range from 1 to $n - 1$.

Using Task ID Array   In this method, the supervisor sends an array containing the TIDs of all the tasks to all the workers. The supervisor TID is saved in the zeroth element of the array, and the workers' TIDs are saved in elements 1 to $n - 1$. Each worker searches for its own TID in the array received from the supervisor and the index can be used to identify the corresponding worker as shown in Figure 8.9.

8.8   CHAPTER SUMMARY

Message passing libraries have been effective in parallel programming environments for clusters and other distributed memory systems. The parallel virtual machine is one of the most popular high-level message passing systems for scientific and engineering applications. PVM started as a research project in 1989 to provide a framework for exploring ideas in heterogeneous distributed computing. It has achieved enormous popularity and has evolved over the years to satisfy the need for additional features. The PVM libraries are defined for C, C++, Fortran, and Java. Also, many tools such as debugger and performance visualization tools are available. In this chapter, we studied a variety of PVM constructs in C and showed how to use them in writing parallel programs.

PROBLEMS

1. What are the differences between the functions `pvm_initsend()` and `pvm_mkbuf()`?
2. Discuss some situations in which nonblocking receive is preferred over blocking receive?
3. Consider the precedence constraints in Figure 8.10 among the tasks T0, T1, T2, T3, T4. Note that an arc from T_i to T_j implies that T_i must be completed before T_j can start. Show how to enforce these precedence in PVM.
4. Consider the four tasks in Figure 8.11, which are synchronized using barriers corresponding to the synchronization points shown. Show how to implement the given barrier structure in PVM.

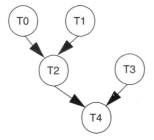

Figure 8.10   Precedence constraints for Problem 3.

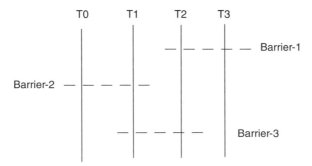

Figure 8.11   Tasks and barriers for Problem 4.

5. Suppose that we want to extend PVM to support fully synchronized communication among processes. What parts of PVM should be altered to provide a fully synchronous send operation? Discuss all possible methods to achieve this goal.

6. Suppose that you were hired to develop techniques for assigning tasks to machines in a PVM environment. What performance measures should you optimize? What parameters should be considered? Should the assignment be done statically or dynamically? Why?

7. Devise a static algorithm for task allocation that can be used to schedule a PVM application on a given virtual machine. Devise another dynamic method to balance the load among the PVM hosts.

8. A task can be partitioned at different levels of granularity: fine-grain, medium-grain, and large-grain. Which level of granularity fits the PVM programming approach the most? Justify your answer.

9. Develop a matrix multiplication program in PVM. This program multiplies two $n \times n$ matrices in parallel ($C = A \times B$). The program consists of a supervisor and $n - 1$ workers. The supervisor sends each worker one row of the first matrix and the entire second matrix. Each worker calculates one row in the resulting matrix and sends it to the supervisor.

10. Rewrite the program of Problem 9 such that each task calculates (a) exactly one cell in the matrix C, (b) part of a row in C, (c) more than one row in C. Contrast all the methods. Discuss the advantages and disadvantages of each method.

REFERENCES

Geist, A. and Sunderam, V. Network-based concurrent computing on the PVM system. *Concurrency: Practice & Experience*, 4 (4), 293–311 (1992).

Geist, A., Beguelin, A., Dongarra, J., Jiang, W., Manchek, R. and Sunderam, V. *PVM: Parallel Virtual Machine – A User's Guide and Tutorial for Network Parallel Computing*, MIT Press, 1994.

Lundell, S., Smith, D. and El-Rewini, H. Synchronous Communication for PVM. *Proceedings of the 8th IASTED International Conference on Parallel and Distributed Computing and Systems*, Chicago, October 1996, pp. 278–282.

Sunderam, V. PVM: A framework for parallel distributed computing. *Concurrency: Practice & Experience*, 2 (4), 1990.

Website

http://www.epm.ornl.gov/pvm

CHAPTER 9

Message Passing Interface (MPI)

The goal of the Message Passing Interface (MPI) is to provide a standard library of routines for writing portable and efficient message passing programs. Message passing interface is not a language; it is a specification of a library of routines that can be called from programs. It provides a rich collection of point-to-point communication routines and collective operations for data movement, global computation, and synchronization. The MPI standard has evolved with the work around MPI-2, which extended MPI to add more features, including: dynamic processes, client–server support, one-sided communication, parallel I/O, and nonblocking collective communication functions. In this chapter, we discuss a number of the important functions and programming techniques. An MPI application can be visualized as a collection of concurrent communicating tasks. A program includes code written by the application programmer that is linked with a function library provided by the MPI software implementation. Each task is assigned a unique rank within a certain context: an integer number between 0 and $n-1$ for an MPI application consisting of n tasks. These ranks are used by MPI tasks to identify each other in sending and receiving messages, to execute collective operations, and to cooperate in general. The MPI tasks can run on the same processor or on different processors concurrently.

9.1 COMMUNICATORS

An important requirement in all message passing systems is to guarantee a safe communication space in which unrelated messages are separated from one another. For example, library messages can be sent and received without interference from other messages generated in the system. In PVM, as explained in Chapter 8, daemon processes on all hosts in the virtual machine maintain a system-wide unique context for safe communication.

In MPI, where there is no virtual machine, using just a message tag is not enough to safely distinguish library messages from user messages. The concept of *communicator* is introduced in MPI to achieve this safe communication requirement. A

Advanced Computer Architecture and Parallel Processing, by H. El-Rewini and M. Abd-El-Barr
ISBN 0-471-46740-5   Copyright © 2005 John Wiley & Sons, Inc.

communicator can be thought of as a binding of a communication context to a group of tasks. A communicator is an object that can be accessed via a handle of type `MPI_COMM`.

Communicators can be classified into intracommunicators for operations within a single group of tasks, and intercommunicators for operations between different groups of tasks. When an MPI application starts, all tasks are associated to a "world" communicator. When a new context is needed, the program makes a synchronizing call to derive the new context from an existing one.

9.1.1   Task Groups

Tasks in MPI are allowed to belong to named groups. A group in MPI is an object that can be accessed via a handle of the predefined type `MPI_Group`. Task groups provide contexts through which MPI operations can be restricted to only the members of a particular group. The members of a group are assigned unique identifiers within the group called ranks. A group is an ordered set of ranks that are contiguous and start from zero.

MPI provides a number of functions to create new groups from existing ones. It does not provide functions to create groups from scratch. At the beginning, all tasks belong to one base group from which other groups can be formed. The members of a new group can be solicited from one or more groups. Given an existing group, a new group can be formed by either excluding a set of tasks or by only including a set of tasks from the existing group. A new group can also be formed using two existing groups using set operations: union, intersection, and difference.

9.1.2   Default Communicator

MPI provides the predefined communicator `MPI_COMM_WORLD` as the default communicator. Once `MPI_Init()` is called, this default communicator defines a single context including the set of all MPI tasks available for the computation. The communicator `MPI_COMM_WORLD` has the same value in all processes and cannot be changed during the lifetime of a task. MPI also provides the predefined communicator `MPI_COMM_SELF`, which includes only the calling process itself.

9.1.3   Task Rank

The tasks involved in a communicator are assigned consecutive integer identifiers between zero and the size of the communicator's group minus one. These identifiers, which are called ranks, are used to distinguish the different tasks within the same group. For example, tasks with different ranks can be assigned different types of work to perform. A task can find out its rank within a communicator by calling the function `MPI_Comm_rank()` as follows:

```
MPI_Comm communicator;/* communicator handle */
int my_rank;/* the rank of the calling task */
MPI_Comm_rank(communicator, &my_rank);
```

This function takes an existing communicator `communicator` and returns the rank of the calling task (`my_rank`) in this communicator's group.

9.1.4 Communicator's Group

The group associated with a communicator can be retrieved using the function `MPI_Comm_group()`. This function takes an existing communicator and returns its corresponding group of tasks. Since MPI does not provide functions to create groups from scratch, `MPI_Comm_group()` is important to create a base group from which other groups can be formed. The format of this function is given as follows:

```
MPI_Comm communicator;/*communicator handle */
MPI_Group corresponding_group;/*group handle */
MPI_Comm_group(communicator, &corresponding_group)
```

The size of the group associated with a communicator can be determined by calling the function `MPI_Comm_size()`. This function takes an existing communicator and returns the size of its corresponding group as follows:

```
MPI_Comm communicator;/*communicator handle */
int number_of_tasks;
MPI_Comm_size(communicator, &number_of_tasks)
```

Example 1 Suppose that an MPI application has started with five tasks: T0, T1, T2, T3, T4 having ranks 0, 1, 2, 3, 4, respectively. At the beginning, all five tasks are referenced by the communicator `MPI_COMM_WORLD`.

Suppose that task T3 calls the following function

```
MPI_Comm_rank(MPI_COMM_WORLD, &me);
```

The variable me will be assigned the value 3, which is the rank of the T3 within the group that corresponds to `MPI_COMM_WORLD`.

To create a group of all tasks in the application, the following function should be called:

```
MPI_Comm_group(MPI_COMM_WORLD, &world_group)
```

It uses the default communicator `MPI_COMM_WORLD` to form the matching group `world_group` that will include the tasks T0, T1, T2, T3, T4.

If the following function is called

```
MPI_Comm_size(MPI_COMM_WORLD, &n)
```

the variable n will be assigned 5, which is the size of the group that corresponds to the communicator `MPI_COMM_WORLD`.

9.1.5   Creating New Communicators

In MPI, an existing communicator is needed to create a new one. The base communicator for all MPI communicators is the default communicator `MPI_COMM_WORLD`. We present three collective functions that can be used to create new communicators. It is required that these functions be called by all tasks that belong to the existing communicator even if some tasks will not belong to the new one.

1. `MPI_Comm_dup(oldcomm, &newcomm)`   This function duplicates the existing communicator `oldcomm`. It returns in `newcomm` a new communicator with the same group of tasks but in a new context.

2. `MPI_Comm_create(oldcomm, group, &newcomm)`   This function creates a new communicator `newcomm` with a corresponding group of tasks `group`. Note that `group` must be a subset of the set of tasks associated with `oldcomm`.

3. `MPI_Comm_split(oldcomm, split_key, rank_key, &newcomm)` This function partitions the group associated with `oldcomm` into disjoint subgroups, one for each value in the argument `split_key`. Each subgroup contains all tasks of the same `split_key`. Within each subgroup, the tasks are ranked in the order defined by the value of the argument `rank_key`, with ties broken according to their rank in the group associated with the old communicator. A new communicator is created for each subgroup and returned in `newcomm`. This is a collective function and must be called by all tasks in `oldcomm` even if the user does not wish to assign every task to a new communicator. If a task provides `MPI_UNDEFINED` as the argument `split_key`, it will get the predefined value `MPI_COMM_NULL` as `newcomm`.

Example 2   Suppose that an MPI application has started with five tasks: T0, T1, T2, T3, T4 having ranks 0, 1, 2, 3, 4, respectively. Suppose that we were able to form a group named `small_group`, which has only two members: tasks T0 and T1. A communicator corresponding to this new group can be created when the following function is called by all tasks:

`MPI_Comm_create(MPI_COMM_WORLD, small_group, &small_comm)`

Now, suppose that tasks T0, T1, T2, T3, T4 call the function `MPI_Comm_split()` as follows.

- T0 calls the following function with $x = 8$ and $me = 0$:
  `MPI_Comm_split(MPI_COMM_WORLD, x, me, &newcomm)`

- T1 calls the following function with $y = 5$ and $me = 1$

  `MPI_Comm_split(MPI_COMM_WORLD, y, me, &newcomm)`
- T2 calls the following function with $x = 8$ and $me = 2$

  `MPI_Comm_split(MPI_COMM_WORLD, x, me, &newcomm)`
- T3 calls the following function with $y = 5$ and $me = 3$

  `MPI_Comm_split(MPI_COMM_WORLD, y, me, &newcomm)`
- T4 calls the following function with `MPI_UNDEFINED` and $me = 4$

  `MPI_Comm_split(MPI_COMM_WORLD, MPI_UNDEFINED, 4, &newcomm)`

The group associated with `newcomm` will consist of the tasks {T0,T2} in the tasks T0 and T2. In the tasks T1 and T3, the group associated with `newcomm` will consist of {T1,T3}. The predefined value `MPI_COMM_NULL` will return in the task T4. The new rank of the tasks in each subgroup will follow their rank in `MPI_COMM_WORLD`.

9.1.6   Intercommunicator

The MPI provides a more general type of communicator, specifically targeted towards group-to-group communication, called intercommunicators. Each inter-communicator contains a local group and a remote group. The local group, for which the owner of the intercommunicator is always a member, is accessible using functions such as `MPI_Comm_group()` and `MPI_Comm_size()` to retrieve, the local group associated with the intercommunicator and its size, as discussed above. Information about the remote group can also be accessed using `MPI_Comm_remote_group()` and `MPI_Comm_remote_size()`. Intercommunicator can be used in creating tasks dynamically as will be discussed in Section 9.6. New tasks in MPI can be started using spawn functions to start new tasks and establish communication with them.

9.2   VIRTUAL TOPOLOGIES

The logical communication patterns among tasks may not be adequately reflected using the linear ranking of tasks in a group that we have seen so far. The logical arrangement of tasks in the group associated with a communicator may need to take different shapes such as two-dimension or three-dimension grids, for example. In this section, we show how to add a topology attribute to a communicator.

In addition to binding a context to a group of tasks, a communicator may be associated with a topology. The topology can be used to associate some addressing scheme to the tasks within a group. Information about the topology is said to be cashed with the communicator. There are two different types of virtual topologies in MPI: Cartesian topology and graph topology.

9.2.1   Cartesian Topology

The collective function `MPI_Cart_create()` shown below can be used to create Cartesian structures of arbitrary dimension. It takes as input the following specifications and returns a handle to a communicator with the new Cartesian structure:

- An existing communicator, which defines the set of tasks on which the topology is to be mapped.
- The number of dimensions in the Cartesian structure.
- The size of each dimension.
- Whether or not the structure is periodic at each dimension.
- Whether or not the system is allowed to optimize the mapping of the virtual topology on the underlying physical processors. This may result in a change in the original task ranking in the group associated with the existing communicator:
  `MPI_Cart_create(oldcomm, ndims, sizeofdims, periods, mapping, newcomm)`

The parameters of this function and their meanings are summarized in Table 9.1. The tasks in a Cartesian structure are ranked in a row-major order and task coordinates begin their numbering at zero.

Example 3   Suppose that an MPI application has started with six tasks: T0, T1, T2, T3, T4, T5 having ranks 0, 1, 2, 3, 4, 5, respectively. At the beginning, all six tasks are referenced by the communicator `MPI_COMM_WORLD`. Now, suppose that we want to associate a 2 × 3 grid structure with the tasks in `MPI_COMM_WORLD`. We can do that by creating a new communicator `gridcomm` as shown below. Note that we set `mapping` to false so that the system will not change the task ranking.

```
MPI_Comm gridcomm; /*new communicator */
int sizeofdims[2];
int periods[2];
```

TABLE 9.1   Parameters of Function `MPI_Cart_create()`

Parameter	Meaning
oldcomm	Input communicator (handle).
ndims	Number of dimensions of Cartesian structure (integer).
sizeofdims	Integer array of size ndims specifying the number of tasks in each dimension.
periods	Boolean array of size ndims specifying whether the structure is periodic (true) or not (false) in each dimension.
mapping	Boolean specifying whether the system is allowed to reorder the ranks (true) or not (false).
newcomm	New communicator with Cartesian structure (handle).

```
int mapping = 0;
sizeofdims[0] = 2;
sizeofdims[1] = 3;
periods[0] = periods[1] = 0;
MPI_Cart_create(MPI_WORLD_COMM, 2, sizeofdims, periods,
  mapping, gridcomm);
```

The relation between the original task ranks and the task coordinates in the 2×3 grid structure is illustrated in Table 9.2.

9.2.2 Retrieval of Task Coordinates and Ranks

MPI provides functions that allow a task to inquire about its rank and its coordinates in a Cartesian structure. Inquiring about the task's rank is particularly important if the system was permitted to change the task ranking during the creation of the Cartesian structure (mapping was set to true). This can be done using the following function:

```
MPI_Cart_rank(communicator, coords, &rank)
```

This function returns the rank rank in the Cartesian structure communicator of the task with Cartesian coordinates coords. Note that coords is an array with order equal to the number of dimensions in the Cartesian topology associated with communicator.

Similarly, the function MPI_Cart_coords() can be used to retrieve the coordinates of a task as follows:

```
MPI_Cart_coords(communicator, rank, ndims, &coords)
```

This function returns the coordinates coords of the task with rank rank in the Cartesian structure communicator in which the number of dimensions is ndims.

TABLE 9.2 Relation Between Task Ranks and Task Coordinates

Task Ranks in the Group	Task Coordinates in gridcomm
0	(0,0)
1	(0,1)
2	(0,2)
3	(1,0)
4	(1,1)
5	(1,2)

9.2.3 Graph Topology

The function `MPI_Graph_create()` shown below can be used to create a new communicator to which a graph topology information is attached. It takes as input the following specifications and returns a handle to a communicator with the new graph topology:

- An existing communicator, which defines the set of tasks on which the topology is to be mapped.
- The number of nodes in the graph.
- Information about the degree (number of neighbors) of each node.
- The edges in the graph.
- Whether or not the system is allowed to optimize the mapping of the virtual topology on the underlying physical processors. This may result in a change in the original task ranking in the group associated with the existing communicator.

  `MPI_Graph_create(oldcomm, nnodes, index, edges, mapping, newcomm)`

The parameters of this function and their meanings are summarized in Table 9.3.

Example 4 Suppose that an MPI application has started with six tasks: T0, T1, T2, T3, T4, T5 having ranks 0, 1, 2, 3, 4, 5, respectively. Suppose that we want to associate the graph shown in Figure 9.1 to the communicator covering all the tasks (`MPI_WORLD_COMM`). The following segment of code shows how to associate the above graph to the new communicator `graphcomm` using the function `MPI_Graph_create()`:

```
MPI_Comm graphcomm; /* new communicator */
int nnodes = 6;
```

TABLE 9.3 Parameters of Function `MPI_Graph_create()`

Parameter	Meaning
Oldcomm	Input communicator (handle).
nnodes	Number of nodes in the graph (integer). Nodes are numbered $0, 1, \ldots$, nnodes -1.
index	Array of integers describing node degrees. The ith entry is the total number of neighbors of the first i graph nodes.
edges	Array of integers describing graph edges. The list of neighbors of nodes 0, $1, \ldots$, nnodes -1 are stored in consecutive locations in this array.
mapping	Boolean specifying whether the system is allowed to reorder the ranks (true) or not (false).
newcomm	New communicator with graph topology (handle).

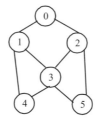

Figure 9.1 Graph for Example 4.

```
int index[6] = {2,5,8,12,14,16};
int edges[16] = {1,2,0,3,4,0,3,5,1,2,4,5,1,3,2,3};
int mapping = 0;
MPI_Graph_create(MPI_WORLD_COMM, nnodes, index, edges,
  mapping, graphcomm)
```

9.3 TASK COMMUNICATION

Communication among MPI tasks is based on the message passing paradigm. MPI utilizes a rich set of functions for sending and receiving messages. Communication between two tasks involves the following components:

1. Sender, which is usually identified by its rank.
2. Receiver, which is usually identified by its rank.
3. Message data.
4. Message tag, which helps multiple messages between two tasks be handled in order.
5. Communicator, which provides a context for communication.

In this section, we study how to use the above components in several functions to perform different types of communication between tasks.

9.3.1 Communication Modes

The basic functions to send and receive messages in MPI are the blocking send and blocking receive. There are several variations of functions that facilitate different kinds of communication modes. MPI supports the following modes.

Standard Send In this mode, the sender will block until its message has been safely copied into either a matching receive buffer or a temporary system buffer. It is up to the MPI implementation to decide whether or not a message should be buffered. Once the send call returns, the send buffer can be overwritten and reused for other purposes by the sender. The following function is the standard send in MPI:

```
MPI_Send(buf, count, data_type, to_whom, tag, communicator)
```

This function will send the message stored starting at address buf to the task whose rank is given as to_whom. The message is consisting of count elements, each of which is of type data_type. The message tag is given as tag. Both the sender and the receiver must be parts of the same communicator communicator. If the buffer is used to store the outgoing message, the sender will continue without having to wait for a matching receive to be posted.

Blocking Receive   The standard receive function in MPI is the blocking receive. A call to this function will not return until it receives the message it is expecting in its buffer. The following function is the blocking receive in MPI:

```
MPI_Recv(buf, count, data_type, from_whom, tag, communicator,
    &status)
```

This receive will select a message with a matching sender (from_whom) and a matching message tag (tag) for receipt into the buffer (buf). Additional status information will be returned in (status).The status field is useful, particularly when the source and/or the tag of the received message is not known to the receiver as a result of using wild cards. The status is normally a structure consisting of two fields MPI_SOURCE and MPI_TAG for the rank of the sender and the tag of the received message, respectively. Again, the sender and the receiver should be participants in communicator.

Buffered Send (B)   In the standard send described above, an outgoing message may or may not be buffered based on the MPI system decision. Using buffered mode, message buffering is guaranteed. That is, a buffered send may return whether or not a matching receive call has been posted. Once the message information is buffered, the send call will return and the send buffer becomes reusable. The format of the buffered send is the same as in the standard send. The only difference is the addition of the letter B to the name of the send function as MPI_Bsend().

Synchronous Send (S)   Synchronous communication can be accomplished if both the sender and the receiver block until the send and receive calls are posted and the communication is complete. Since the standard receive is already blocking, we just need a blocking send to be able to accomplish synchronous communication. MPI provides the function MPI_Ssend() for this purpose. It has the same format as the standard send and it can start without having to wait for a matching receive call to be posted. However, it will not complete until a matching receive has been posted and the receiver has started to receive the message.

Ready Send (R)   A send in the ready mode can be started only after a matching receive has been posted. The function `MPI_Rsend()` is provided for this purpose. The completion of the ready send however does not depend on the status at the receiving end.

9.3.2 Nonblocking Communication

Message passing interface supports nonblocking communication in which a task can begin a send or receive operation, move on to perform other work, and then return to check the completion status of the messaging operation. These nonblocking send/receive capabilities can be used interchangeably with the normal send/receive capabilities and need not be paired. The use of nonblocking send (receive) can be accomplished in three steps:

1. Initiate a send (receive) using `MPI_Isend()` (`MPI_Irecv()`).
2. Do some computation during the communication time.
3. Complete the communication using `MPI_Wait()` and `MPI_Test()`.

Initiating Nonblocking Communication   Initiating a send operation in the standard mode described above can be performed using the following function:

```
MPI_Isend(buf, count, data_type, to_whom, tag, communicator,
    &request)
```

A call to `MPI_Isend()` will return before the message is copied out of the send buffer. All the arguments of this function except one carry the same meaning of the arguments of other send functions. The last argument, `request`, is a system object that is returned when the function is called and can be accessed via a handle. It is used to identify communication operations and match the operations that initiate and complete a nonblocking communication. Similarly, initiating a nonblocking receive operation can be performed using the following function:

```
MPI_Irecv(buf, count, data_type, from_whom, tag, communi-
    cator, &request)
```

Calling `MPI_Irecv()` will initiate the receive operation. It will return immediately without having to wait for a message to be stored in the receive buffer. As in the send case, the returned argument `request` can be used later to query the status of the communication or wait for its completion. Note that `MPI_Irecv()` does not return status information as it was shown in the blocking receive. The status can be obtained when a call to complete the receive operation is made.

Initiating a send operation can also be done in the other send modes. In addition to the letter I, a prefix of b, s, or r can be used for buffered, synchronous, or ready mode, respectively (Table 9.4).

TABLE 9.4

Initiate Send	Mode
MPI_Isend()	Standard
MPI_Ibsend()	Buffered
MPI_Issend()	Synchronous
MPI_Irsend()	Ready

Completing Nonblocking Communication MPI provides functions for testing for the completion of nonblocking communication operations that have already been initiated. One can either check the status of a send (receive) operation or just wait until the operation is completed. The completion of a nonblocking send operation implies that the data has been copied out of the send buffer and the sender can reuse the buffer for other purposes. The completion of a nonblocking receive operation indicates that the data has already been placed in the receive buffer and it is ready for access by the receiver.

The following function is used to check the completion of a communication operation:

```
MPI_Test(request, &flag, &status)
```

Calling this function returns the current standing of the communication operation identified by `request`. The argument `flag` will be set to true if the communication operation is complete and false otherwise. The `status` field will return additional status information.

The following function will wait for a communication operation to complete:

```
MPI_Wait(request, &status)
```

A call to `MPI_Wait()` will return after the completion of the communication operation identified by `request`.

In some cases, one may wish to test or wait for multiple nonblocking operations. MPI provides functions to test or wait for all or any of a collection of nonblocking operations using the following functions:

```
MPI_Testall(count, array_of_requests, &flag, &array_of_
   statuses)
MPI_Testany(count, array_of_requests, &flag, &status)
MPI_Waitall(count, array_of_requests, &array_of_statuses)
MPI_Waitany(count, array_of_requests, &status)
```

9.3.3 Persistence Communication

MPI provides persistent communication requests constructs to help reduce the communication overhead between a task and the communication controller. For example, suppose that communication with the same argument list is repeatedly executed in a program. It is possible to bind the list of communication arguments to a persistent communication request once, and then repeatedly use that request to initiate and complete messages. A persistent communication request is created in MPI using one of the following functions: `MPI_Send_init()`, `MPI_Bsend_init()`, `MPI_Ssend_init()`, `MPI_Rsend_init()`, and `MPI_Recv_init()`. A persistent communication request is inactive after it is created. This means that no active communication is associated with the request yet. A communication that uses a persistent request is initiated by one of the following two functions:

`MPI_Start(request)`

which starts the communication associated with `request`; and

`MPI_startall(count, array_of_requests)`

which starts all communication associated with requests in the array `array_of_requests`.

Once communication is started, it is treated like other nonblocking communication operations. Recall that all nonblocking functions that we have seen so far have a request argument, which is used to identify the nonblocking operations. This argument is a system object that is returned when the function is called and can be accessed via a handle.

9.4 SYNCHRONIZATION

As we discussed in the chapter on PVM, synchronization constructs are used to force a certain order of execution among the activities of parallel tasks. In some cases parallel tasks are required to synchronize with each other at a given point during the execution. Members of a group may need to wait at a synchronization point until all tasks reach the same point. Synchronization in MPI can be achieved using message passing and barrier operations.

Precedence Synchronization   Using the blocking receive operation (`MPI_Recv()`) forces the receiving task to wait until a matching message is received. The sender of this matching message may hold its message as long as it wants the receiver to wait.

Communication Rendezvous Using the synchronous mode of communication, two tasks can rendezvous at a synchronization point. If both send and receive operation are blocking, the communication will not complete at either end until both sender and receiver meet as shown in Figure 9.2.

Barriers Tasks in a group can synchronize at a synchronization point using a barrier. No task can proceed beyond the barrier until all tasks have checked in at that barrier. The group may include all tasks or only a subset of the tasks depending on the communicator. The construct `MPI_Barrier()` takes a communicator as input as follows:

```
MPI_Barrier(communicator)
```

Barrier synchronization is achieved by having all tasks in the communicator's group call the function `MPI_Barrier()`. A task waits at the barrier until all tasks referenced by the communicator reach the barrier before continuing. A call to `MPI_Barrier()` returns after all the communicator's group members have executed their calls to this function.

Example 5 Suppose that an MPI application has started with five tasks (T0, T1, T2, T3, T4) having ranks 0, 1, 2, 3, 4. At the beginning, all five tasks are referenced by the communicator `MPI_COMM_WORLD`. Thus, using the construct

```
MPI_Barrier(MPI_COMM_WORLD)
```

will force each task to wait at the barrier until the rest of the tasks reach their barriers as shown in Figure 9.3.

Example 6 Consider the five tasks in the previous example. Suppose that we want to use a barrier only for the tasks T2 and T3 as shown in Figure 9.4. To form a group from a subset of tasks to check in at a barrier, one can exclude certain process ranks

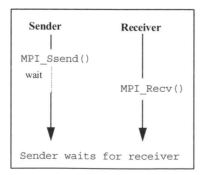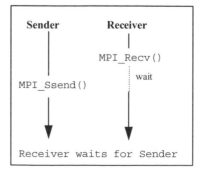

Figure 9.2 Communication rendezvous.

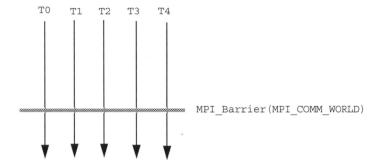

Figure 9.3   Barrier synchronization for all tasks in `MPI_COMM_WORLD`.

from an existing group. In this case, we need to exclude the tasks whose ranks are 0, 1, 4 from the current group and then create a new communicator for the new group. The following four steps show how this can be done:

1. We use the following function to form a group of all tasks (`world_group`) from the default communicator:

   `MPI_Comm_group(MPI_COMM_WORLD,&world_group)`

2. We save the ranks 0, 1, 4 in the array `exclude_ranks` of size 3. We then call the following function, which will create the new group (`small_group`):

   `MPI_Group_excl(world_group,3,exclude_ranks,&small_group)`

3. We use the existing communicator `MPI_COMM_WORLD` and the newly formed group `small_group` to form a new communicator `new_comm` that matches the new group as follows:

   `MPI_Comm_create(MPI_COMM_WORLD,small_group,&new_comm)`

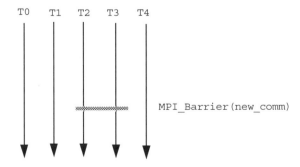

Figure 9.4   Barrier synchronization for a subset of the tasks.

4. Finally, we use the following construct to force only T2 and T3 to wait at the barrier:

```
MPI_Barrier(new_comm)
```

9.5 COLLECTIVE OPERATIONS

Collective operations in MPI are those operations that are applied to all members of a communicator's group. A collective operation is usually defined in terms of a group of tasks. The operation is executed when all tasks in the group call the collective routine with matching parameters. There are three types of collective operations: task control, global computation, and data movement. The barrier function MPI_Barrier() that was discussed in the previous section can be classified as a task control collective operation. In the remainder of this section, we will cover global computation and data movement operations.

9.5.1 Global Computation

We discuss a number of global reduction and scan operations. In reduction, an associative, commutative operation is applied across data items provided by members of a group of tasks. A reduction operation could be user-defined function or MPI predefined operation such as sum, minimum, maximum, and so on. The result of applying a reduction operation may be sent to every task in the group, or it may be returned to only a single task, called the root. There are two types of scan operations: prefix and postfix scan. The result of a scan operation is different at each task based on the rank of the task. Given members of a group T0, T1, T2, $\ldots$, T$n-1$ holding data items d0, d1, d2, $\ldots$, d$n-1$ and an operator $\propto$. In a prefix scan, the result at task Ti is T0 $\propto$ T1$\propto \cdots \propto$ Ti. In a postfix scan, the result at task Ti is T$i \propto$ T$i+1$ T$\propto \cdots \propto$ T$n-1$.

Global Combine MPI provides the following reduction function in which the result returns only to the root:

```
MPI_Reduce(sbuf, rbuf, n, data_type, op, rt, communicator)
```

The parameters of this function and their meanings are summarized in Table 9.5.

The reduction operator is applied to the data given in the send buffer of each task in the communicator's group. The result will be returned only to the receive buffer of the root. Note that the receive buffer is only meaningful to the root (see Fig. 9.5). MPI provides a number of predefined reduction operations as in Table 9.6.

Many-to-Many Reduction A variant of the global combine operation is the many-to-many reduction operation in which the result is returned to all members

TABLE 9.5

Parameter	Meaning
sbuf	Address of the send buffer.
rbuf	Address of the receive buffer.
n	Number of data elements in the send buffer.
data_type	Type of each element in the send buffer.
op	Reduction operator.
rt	Rank of the root task.
communicator	Communicator.

of the group as shown in Figure 9.6. MPI provides the following function for this operation:

MPI_Allreduce(sbuf, rbuf, n, data_type, op, communicator)

As in MPI_Reduce(), the arguments are the address of the send buffer, address of the receive buffer, number of data elements in the send buffer, type of each element, reduction operator, and a communicator. The result of the reduction appears in the receive buffers of all members of the communicator's group.

Scan   MPI provides the following function to perform a prefix reduction on data associated with group members:

MPI_Scan(sbuf, rbuf, n, data_type, op, communicator)

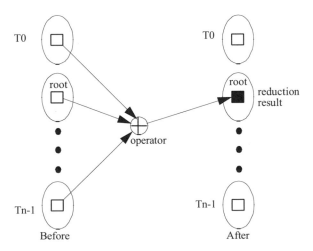

Figure 9.5   Reduce operation.

TABLE 9.6 **Predefined Reduction Operations**

MPI Name	Operation	MPI Name	Operation
MPI_SUM	Sum	MPI_LOR	Logical or
MPI_PROD	Product	MPI_LXOR	Logical exclusive or
MPI_MIN	Minimum	MPI_BAND	Bitwise and
MPI_MAX	Maximum	MPI_BOR	Bitwise or
MPI_LAND	Logical and	MPI_BXOR	Bitwise exclusive or

This function has the same six arguments of MPI_Allreduce(). The arguments are the address of the send buffer, address of the receive buffer, number of data elements in the send buffer, type of each element, reduction operator, and a communicator. After the execution of this function, the receive buffer of the task of rank i will have the reduction of the values in the send buffer of the tasks of ranks $0, 1, \ldots, i$, as shown in Figure 9.7.

9.5.2 Data Movement Operation

MPI supports a broad variety of data movement collective functions. The basic operations supported are broadcast, scatter, and gather. In a broadcast, one process sends the same message to every member in the group. A scatter operation allows one process to send a different message to each member. In gather, which is the dual operation of scatter, one process will receive a message from each member in the group. These basic operations can be combined to form more complex operations.

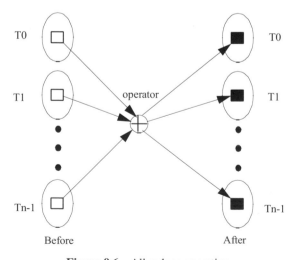

Figure 9.6 All reduce operation.

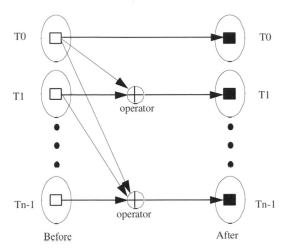

Figure 9.7 Prefix scan operation.

Broadcasting   MPI provides the following function to broadcast a message from the root task to all tasks of the communicator's group:

```
MPI_Bcast(buffer, n, data_type, root, communicator)
```

The parameters and their meanings are summarized in Table 9.7.

This function must be called by all members of the communicator's group using the same arguments for the root and communicator. The contents of the root's buffer will be copied to the buffers of all tasks (see Fig. 9.8).

Scatter and Gather   Scatter and gather operations are dual to each other. While the scatter function allows one task to distribute its buffer to each member in a group, the gather function allows a task to build its buffer from pieces of data collected from other members in a group. The MPI provides the following two functions for scatter and gather:

```
MPI_Scatter(sbuf, n, stype, rbuf, m, rtype, rt, communicator)
MPI_Gather(sbuf, n, stype, rbuf, m, rtype, rt, communicator)
```

TABLE 9.7   Parameters for Broadcasting

Parameter	Meaning
buffer	Starting address of the buffer.
n	Number of data elements in the buffer.
data_type	Type of each element in the buffer.
root	Rank of the root task.
communicator	Communicator.

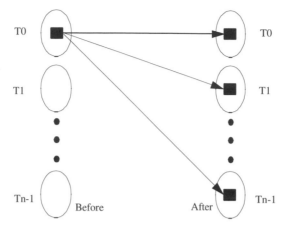

Figure 9.8 A broadcast from task T0 (root).

In scatter, the send buffer at the root is divided into a number of segments, each of size n. The first n elements in the root's send buffer are copied into the receive buffer of the first member in the group, the second n elements in the root's send buffer are copied into the receive buffer of the second member, and so on (see Fig. 9.9a).

In gather, each task (including the root) sends the contents of its send buffer to the root task. The root receives the messages and stores them in rank order. The send buffer of the first member in the group is copied into the first m locations in the receive buffer of the root. The send buffer of the second member in the group is copied into the second m locations in the receive buffer of the root, and so on (see Fig. 9.9b). The parameters and their meanings are summarized in Table 9.8.

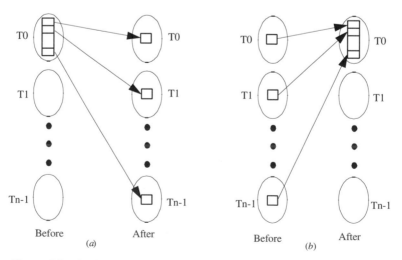

Figure 9.9 (a) Scatter from the root task T0; (b) Gather at the root task T0.

TABLE 9.8 Parameters for Scatter and Gather

Parameter	Meaning
sbuf	Starting address of the send buffer.
n	Number of elements sent to each task by the root (scatter case) or number of elements in the send buffer (gather case).
stype	Type of each element in the send buffer.
rbuf	Starting address of the receive buffer.
m	Number of data elements in the receive buffer (scatter case) or number of elements received by the root from each task (gather case).
rtype	Type of each element in the receive buffer.
rt	Rank of the sending task (scatter case) or receiving task (gather case).
communicator	Communicator.

These functions must be called by all members of the communicator's group using the same arguments for the root and communicator. The send buffer parameters are ignored at all tasks except the root in the case of a scatter operation, whereas in gather the receive buffer parameters are ignored at nonroot tasks. In scatter, n and stype at the root must be equal to m and rtype at all other receiving tasks. Similarly, m and rtype at the root must be equal to n and stype at all other receiving tasks in gather.

9.6 TASK CREATION

In this section we show how an MPI application could spawn new tasks and establish communication among them in MPI-2. We will refer to the spawning tasks as parents and the spawned as children. In what follows, we present two functions MPI_Comm_spawn() and MPI_Comm_spawn_multiple(). Each of these two functions is a collective operation that must be called by the parent tasks. The outcome of a successful execution of these functions is another group of child tasks. Both the parents and children share a new intercommunicator as shown in Figure 9.10.

9.6.1 Bridging Between Spawned and Spawning Tasks

Allowing dynamic tasks in MPI-2 does not only imply the creation of new tasks. It may also require the establishment of communication between the new and the previously existing tasks. We need a way to provide a bridging communicator between the old and the new tasks. This is achieved in MPI-2 using intercommunicators. Figure 9.11 illustrates the use of intercommunicators to establish communication between parent and child tasks. On the spawning side, the local group of the intercommunicator is the group that did the spawning; and the remote group is the group that was spawned. On the spawned side, the local group is set to the MPI_COMM_WORLD of the new tasks and the remote group is set to the group that did the spawning.

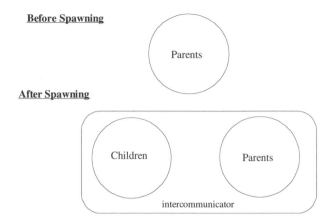

Figure 9.10 Creating children and establishing communication with them via intercommunicator.

9.6.2 Starting Identical Tasks

The `MPI_Comm_spawn()` function is used to create a number of identical copies of a given program and establish communication with them. The format of this function is given as:

```
MPI_Comm_spawn(command, argv, maxprocs, info, root, comm,
    &inter_comm, &array_error_codes)
```

This function has six input parameters and returns an intercommunicator `inter_comm` and an array of error codes `array_error_codes`. The first parameter

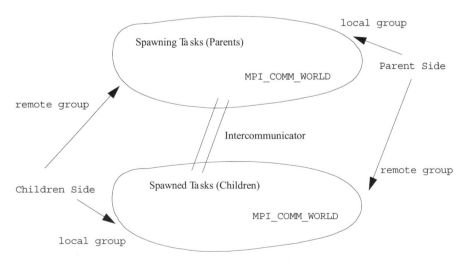

Figure 9.11 Establishing communication using intercommunicators.

command is a string containing the name of the program to be spawned. The parameter argv is an array of strings specifying the arguments that are passed to the spawned program. MPI tries to create maxprocs copies of the program specified in the first parameter. The parameter root specifies the rank of the root task in the group corresponding to the communicator comm. This function must be called by all the tasks in the group corresponding to comm. However, the first four parameters are meaningful only at the root.

Unlike PVM, MPI-2 does not specify how to find the executable code. It is left to the implementation to decide how this is done. The parameter info is a set of key–value pairs of type MPI_Info that tells the runtime system where and how to start the tasks. MPI reserves several keys and requires that if an implementation uses a reserved key, it must provide the specified functionality. Table 9.9 summarizes the reserved keys related to spawn functions. Note that the format of the different values is determined by the implementation. Note also that the info parameter could be set to an empty string to get the implementation defaults.

This function returns an intercommunicator inter_comm in the parent. This intercommunicator contains the parent tasks in the local group and the newly spawned child tasks in the remote group. The intercommunicator can be obtained in the children through the function MPI_Comm_get_parent(), which has only one argument of type MPI_Comm that returns the parent intercommunicator.

The parameter array_error_codes is an array of size maxprocs in which MPI reports the status of each task that MPI requested to start. If the spawning was successful and all tasks were launched, the array array_error_codes will be filled with the value MPI_SUCCESS. Otherwise, only the number of elements equal to the number of successful tasks will contain MPI_SUCCESS, while the rest will have error codes indicating why these tasks did not start.

9.6.3 Starting Multiple Executables

In this section, we show how to spawn different executable codes in MPI using MPI_Comm_spawn_multiple. This function makes it possible to start multiple

TABLE 9.9 Keys Related to Spawn Functions

Key	Value
host	Host name.
arch	Architecture name.
dir	Name of a directory on the remote machine in which the spawned tasks execute.
path	Set of directories on remote machine where the implementation should look for the executable.
file	Name of a file in which additional information is specified.
soft	A set of numbers which are allowed values for the number of tasks that the different versions of spawn functions may create.

programs or the same program with multiple sets of arguments. The format of this function is given as:

```
MPI_Comm_spawn_multiple(count, command_array, argv_array,
    maxprocs_array, info_array, root, comm, &inter_comm,
    &array_error_codes)
```

The parameters of `MPI_Comm_spawn_multiple` are similar to those of `MPI_Comm_spawn`. The first parameter gives the number of commands. Each of the next four parameters is simply an array of the corresponding argument in `MPI_Comm_spawn`. All the spawned tasks will have the same `MPI_COMM_WORLD`. The ranks of the spawned tasks will correspond directly to the order in which the commands are specified in the second parameter.

For example, suppose that the function `MPI_Comm_spawn_multiple` is invoked with `count = 5`; and the five commands would generate 4, 3, 7, 5, and 2 tasks, respectively. A successful execution of this function will spawn 21 tasks, the tasks corresponding to the five command lines have the ranks 0–3, 4–6, 7–13, 14–18, and 19–20, respectively. Note that the array `array_error_codes` will have 21 elements filled with `MPI_SUCCESS`.

Note that using `MPI_Comm_spawn_multiple` is not equivalent to calling `MPI_Comm_spawn` multiple times. In addition to the difference in performance, all the tasks generated by `MPI_Comm_spawn_multiple` belong to the same `MPI_COMM_WORLD`, where as in `MPI_Comm_spawn` would create multiple sets of children with different `MPI_COMM_WORLDs`.

9.7 ONE-SIDED COMMUNICATION

MPI provides constructs for Remote Memory Access (RMA), in which a task is allowed to access the remote memory of another task. These constructs are useful in applications with dynamically changing data access patterns but where the data distribution is fixed or slowly changing. The traditional send/receive communication constructs covered earlier require the explicit involvement of two or more tasks in the data transfer. Both sender and receiver should issue matching operations in order for the data transfer to take place. In the RMA model, only one task is supposed to issue the data transfer operation; either the source or the destination. We will use *origin* and *target* to denote the task that issues the RMA operation and the other involved task, respectively. Remote memory access is supported via two main operations, *put* and *get*. The execution of a put operation is equivalent to the execution of a send by the origin task and a matching receive by the target task. Clearly, all the parameters are issued in only one call in the put case. Similarly, the get operation is equivalent to a receive by the origin task and a matching send by the target task (see Fig. 9.12).

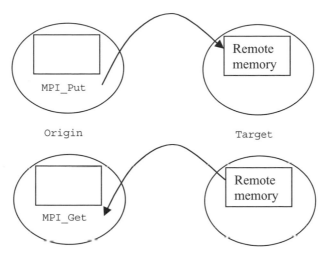

Figure 9.12   Put and get RMA operations.

9.7.1 Specifying Target Windows

Before RMA operations are issued, each task must specify a memory window that is made available for access by remote tasks. This can be achieved using a collective operation that returns a window object, which will be used by tasks in their RMA operations. The window object represents the group of tasks that own and access a set of windows, and the attributes of each window as specified by each task. The function MPI_Win_init() is provided by MPI for this purpose as follows:

```
MPI_Win_init(base, size, disp_unit, info, comm, &win)
```

This function must be executed by all tasks sharing the communicator comm. Each task specifies a window of existing memory for remote access by other tasks. This window consists of size bytes, starting at address base. The parameter disp_unit facilitates the computation of displacements in a heterogeneous environment. Since the size of a certain data type may be different in different architectures, each task should provide the proper disp_unit for its particular machine. This way, array entries of a given type, for example, can be specified by their indices, with the scaling done automatically by MPI. Again, the parameter info provides optimization information to the run time system.

The different tasks can specify completely different target windows with different starting locations, sizes, and displacement units. Additionally, if a task chooses not to make any memory available for remote access, it should specify size = 0.

The returned window object win will carry information about the group associated with the already existing communicator comm and the set of target windows specified by the MPI_Win_init() operation.

9.7.2 Put and Get Operations

The `MPI-Put()` function transfers a number of successive elements from a buffer at the origin task to a remote buffer in the target task. Both the origin and target tasks must share a communicator whose group and other window attributes are carried in a window object created using the collective operation `MPI_Win_init()`. The function takes eight input arguments as follows.

```
MPI_Put(origin_addr, origin_count, origin_datatype, target_
    rank, target_disp, target_count, target_datatype, win)
```

The first three arguments: `origin_addr`, `origin_count`, and `origin_datatype` provide information about the data elements to be transferred. They specify the address of the input buffer, how many elements to be transferred, and data type of these elements at the origin task.

Calling this function transfers the data from the origin task with rank `target_rank` in the group associated with the window object `win`. Note that the target task may be indentical to the origin task. In this case the function is used to move data within the origin task's memory.

The data is written in the target buffer at the following address: (`window_base` + `Target_disp` * `disp_unit`), where `window_base` and `disp_unit` are the base address and window displacement unit specified by the target task using `MPI_Win_init()`. The target buffer is specified by the arguments `target_count` and `target_datatype`.

Similarly, the `MPI_Get()` function transfers a number of successive elements from a buffer at the target task to a buffer in the origin task. The data transfer in this case is done in the opposite direction compared to the data transfer in the put case.

```
MPI_Get(origin_addr, origin_count, origin_datatype, target_
    rank, target_disp, target_count, target_datatype, win)
```

The arguments of this function are similar to those in `MPI_Put()`. A summary of the parameters and their meanings is given in the following table:

Parameter	Meaning
origin_addr	Address of buffer at the origin task.
origin_count	Number of elements to be received.
origin_datatype	Data type of elements to be received.
target_rank	Rank of the target task.
target_disp	Displacement from start of window to the receive buffer at the target task.
target_count	Number of elements to be sent.
target_datatype	Data types of elements to be sent.
win	Window object created by `MPI_Win_init()`.

It is also possible in a put operation to combine the data transferred to the target task with the data that is already there. Instead of replacing the contents of the target buffer, an accumulate operation can use a reduction operation to combine its contents with the data transferred. MPI provides the following function:

```
MPI_Accumulate(origin_addr, origin_count, origin_datatype,
    target_rank, target_disp, target_count, target_datatype,
    op, win)
```

This function accumulates the contents of the origin buffer to the contents of the target buffer using the operation `op`, which is a reduce operation.

9.8 CHAPTER SUMMARY

The Message Passing Interface (MPI) is a standard for writing message passing programs. It was developed during 1993 and 1994 by an international group of application scientists, computer vendors, and software writers called the MPI Forum. The experience gained from the wide use of the original MPI standard has helped the MPI forum expand the standard in MPI-2. Starting in 1995, the MPI forum identified areas of great interest for MPI extension. The forum expanded the scope of MPI to encompass a wider set of distributed and parallel programming constructs. MPI-2 was necessitated by a number of new trends in distributed and parallel computing. The advances in network technology and the revolution in the way distributed systems have been used have created a need for dynamic task management in MPI. The new wave of shared-memory and NUMA architectures led to the introduction of one-sided communication operations. Currently, MPI is widely used in clusters and other message passing system due to its rich functionality. In this chapter, we only tried to touch on some of the important functions in MPI and their relation to one another.

PROBLEMS

1. Explain the following terms:
   - (a) Synchronous versus asynchronous message passing;
   - (b) Blocking versus nonblocking communication;
   - (c) Message buffers;
   - (d) Deadlock;
   - (e) Collective operations;
   - (f) Barriers and precedence relations;
   - (g) Communication contexts;
   - (h) Virtual topologies;
   - (i) Derived datatypes.

2. Explain how MPI send operation is different from the send operation in other message passing systems (PVM, for example);

3. Explain how nonblocking communication can be used to improve performance.

4. Simulate the following functions using other MPI functions:
   `MPI_Allreduce()`, `MPI_Bcast()`, `MPI_Scatter()`, `MPI_Gather()`.

5. Given a number of MPI tasks, write MPI code to perform the following:
   (a) Broadcast 100 integers from the task with rank 10 to all tasks;
   (b) Gather 10 integers from tasks with ranks 0–3, 5–10, 17, 20 to the task with rank 4;
   (c) Scatter five integers from task with rank 4 to tasks with ranks 0–9;
   (d) Have each task send 100 integers to task 0 but place each set of 10 integers apart at the receiving end;
   (e) Compute the dot product of two arrays that are distributed to all tasks and return the answer to task 0.

6. Consider the precedence graph of Figure 9.13 for three MPI tasks T0, T1, and T2, where T0 = {f1, f2, f3}, T1 = {g1, g2, g3, g4}, and T2 = {h1, h2, h3}. Write the necessary MPI synchronization code to enforce the given precedence relations among the functions forming the three tasks.

7. Simulate the PVM task creation model using MPI constructs. Provide a template that can be used to convert PVM programs to MPI.

8. Contrast the send/receive operations versus the one-sided communication operations in MPI.

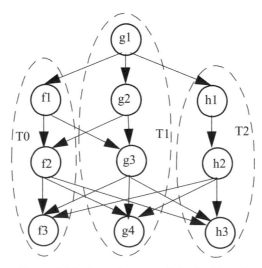

Figure 9.13 Precedence graph for Problem 6.

9. Simulate the following functions using other MPI communication functions:
   `MPI_Get()`, `MPI_Put()`.

10. The traveling salesman problem is to find the shortest route connecting a set of cities, visiting each city only once. This problem is known to be NP-complete and the simulating annealing method has been used to solve it heuristically. Write an MPI parallel program to solve the problem for a fixed number of cities.

REFERENCES

Geist, A., Gropp, W., Huss-Lederman, S., Lumsdaine, A., Lusk, E., Saphir, W., Skjellum, A. and Snir, M. *MPI-2: Extending the Message-Passing Interface, Euro-Par '96 Parallel Processing*, Lecture Notes in Computer Science, Vol. 1, No. 1123, Springer Verlag, 1996, pp. 128–135.

Gropp, W. and Lusk, E. *User's Guide for MPICH, a Portable Implementation of MPI*. Technical Report ANL-96/6, Argonne National Laboratory, 1994.

Gropp, W., Lusk, E. and Skjellum, A. *Using MPI: Portable Parallel Programming with the Message-Passing Interface*. MIT Press, Cambridge, 1994.

Gropp, W., Lusk, E., Doss, N. and Skjellum, A. A high-performance, portable implementation of the MPI message passing interface standard. *Parallel Computing Journal*, 22, 789–828 (1996).

Message Passing Interface Forum. MPI: A message-passing interface standard. *International Journal of Supercomputer Applications*, 8 (3/4), 165–416 (1994).

Pacheco, P. *Parallel Programming with MPI*, Morgan Kaufmann, 1997.

Snir, M., Otto, S., Huss-Lederman, S., Walker, D. and Dongarra, J. *MPI: The Complete Reference*, MIT Press, Cambridge, 1995.

CHAPTER 10

Scheduling and Task Allocation

After a computational job is designed and realized as a set of tasks, an optimal assignment of these tasks to the processing elements in a given architecture needs to be determined. This problem is called the scheduling problem and is known to be one of the most challenging problems in parallel and distributed computing. The goal of scheduling is to determine an assignment of tasks to processing elements in order to optimize certain performance indexes. Performance and efficiency are two characteristics used to evaluate a scheduling system. We should evaluate a scheduling system based on the quality of the produced task assignment (schedule) and the efficiency of the scheduling algorithm (scheduler). The produced schedule is judged based on the performance criterion to be optimized, while the scheduling algorithm is evaluated based on its time complexity. For example, if we try to optimize the completion time of a program, the less the completion time, the better the schedule will be. Also, if two scheduling algorithms produce task assignments that have the same quality, the less complex algorithm is clearly the better.

The scheduling problem is known to be computationally intractable in many cases. Fast optimal algorithms can only be obtained when some restrictions are imposed on the models representing the program and the distributed system. Solving the general problem in a reasonable amount of time requires the use of heuristic algorithms. These heuristics do not guarantee optimal solutions to the problem, but they attempt to find near-optimal solutions.

This chapter addresses the scheduling problem in many of its variations. We survey a number of solutions to this important problem. We cover program and system models, optimal algorithms, heuristic algorithms, scheduling versus allocation techniques, and homogeneous versus heterogeneous environments.

10.1 THE SCHEDULING PROBLEM

10.1.1 A Classical Problem

The general scheduling problem has been described in a number of different ways in different fields. The classical problem of job sequencing in production management

Advanced Computer Architecture and Parallel Processing, by H. El-Rewini and M. Abd-El-Barr
ISBN 0-471-46740-5 Copyright © 2005 John Wiley & Sons, Inc.

has influenced most of the solutions to this problem, which generally assumes a set of resources that could provide service to a set of consumers. The main objective is to find an efficient policy for managing the access to the resources by the consumers to optimize some desired performance measures. A task in a program, a job in a factory, or a customer in a bank are examples of consumers that need service from resources such as a processor in a computer system, a machine in a factory, or a teller in a bank, respectively.

In distributed systems, the scheduling problem arises because the concurrent parts of a program or set of programs must be arranged in time and space so that the overall performance of the system is optimized. A program can be viewed as a collection of tasks, which may run serially or in parallel. Normally, there are some precedence constraints among the tasks that must be enforced. The goal of scheduling is to determine an assignment of tasks to processing elements and an order in which tasks are executed. If there are no precedence relations among the tasks forming a program, this problem is known as the task allocation problem. Task allocation has been studied extensively for the past two decades and is not quite the same as scheduling. The task allocation problem will be studied in detail in Section 10.7. The problem of scheduling program tasks on multiprocessor systems is known to be NP-complete in general as well as in several special cases. There are only a few known polynomial–time scheduling algorithms. The intractability of the cheduling problem has led to a large number of heuristics, each of which may work under different circumstances.

Scheduling techniques can be classified based on the availability of program task information as deterministic and nondeterministic. In deterministic scheduling, all the information about tasks to be scheduled and their relations to one another is entirely known prior to execution time. In nondeterministic scheduling, some information may not be known before the program executes. Conditional branches and loops are two program constructs that may cause nondeterminism. Scheduling non deterministic programs can be achieved using static or dynamic methods. The distinction indicates the time at which the scheduling decisions are made. With static scheduling, information regarding the task graph representing the program must be estimated prior to execution, while in dynamic scheduling, the parallel processor system schedules tasks on the fly. Dynamic scheduling is usually implemented as some kind of load-balancing heuristic. The disadvantage of dynamic scheduling is the overhead incurred to determine the schedule while the program is running. In deterministic (static) scheduling, each task in the program has a static assignment to a particular processor, and each time that task is submitted for execution, it is assigned to that processor. A combination of static and dynamic methods is referred to as hybrid method. All the techniques presented in this chapter can be classified as static scheduling techniques.

10.1.2   Scheduling Model

A scheduling system consists of: program tasks, target machine, and a schedule in which a specific performance criterion is optimized.

Program Tasks   The characteristics of a parallel program can be defined as the system $(T, <, D, A)$ as follows:

- $T = \{t_1, \ldots, t_n\}$ is a set of tasks to be executed.
- $<$ is a partial order defined on T which specifies operational precedence constraints. That is $t_i < t_j$ means that t_i must be completed before t_j can start execution.
- D is an $n \times n$ matrix of communication data, where $D_{ij} \geq 0$ is the amount of data required to be transmitted from task t_i to task t_j, $1 \leq i, j \leq n$.
- A is an n vector of the amount of computations; that is, $A_i > 0$ is a measure of the amount of computation at task t_i, $1 \leq i \leq n$.

The relationship among tasks in distributed systems may or may not include precedence constraints. When some precedence constraints need to be enforced, the partial order $<$ is conveniently represented as a directed acyclic graph (DAG) called a task graph. In this case, scheduling these tasks is usually referred to as Precedence Constrained Scheduling. A task graph $G = (T, E)$ has a set of nodes T and a set of directed edges E. A directed edge (i, j) between two tasks t_i and t_j specifies that t_i must be completed before t_j can begin. Associated with each node t_i is its computational needs A_i (how many instructions or operations, for example). Associated with each edge (i, j) connecting tasks t_i and t_j is the data size D_{ij}, that is, the size of a message from t_i to t_j.

Note that when there is no precedence constraints among the tasks, the relationships are only communication among tasks, which can be represented in a undirected graph called a Task Interaction Graph, as will be shown in Section 10.7.

Target Machine   The target machine consists of a set of m heterogeneous processing elements connected using an arbitrary interconnection network. Associated with each processing element P_i is its speed S_i. The connectivity of the processing elements can be represented using an undirected graph called the network graph. Associated with each edge (i, j) connecting two processing elements P_i and P_j in the network graph is the transfer rate R_{ij}, that is, how many units of data can be transmitted per unit of time over the link.

The Schedule   A schedule of the task graph $G = (T, E)$ on a system of m processing elements is a function f that maps each task to a processing element and a starting time. Formally, $f: T \rightarrow \{1, 2, \ldots, m\} \times [0, \infty)$. If $f(v) = (i, t)$ for some $v \in T$ we say that task v is scheduled to be processed by processor i starting at time t. The function f can be illustrated as a Gantt chart where the start and finish times for all tasks can be easily shown. A Gantt chart consists of a list of all processing elements in a distributed system, and for each processing element, a list of all tasks allocated to that processing element ordered by their execution time, including task start and finish times.

Our scheduling goal is to minimize the total completion time of a parallel program. This performance measure is known as the schedule length or the maximum finishing time of any task.

Execution and Communication Time   Once the parameters of the task graph and the target machine are known, the execution and communication times can always be obtained as follows. The execution time of task t_i when executed on processor P_j is

$$\frac{A_i}{S_j} \quad \text{units of time}$$

The communication delay (over a free link) between tasks t_i and t_j when they are executed on adjacent processing elements P_k and P_l is

$$\frac{D_{ij}}{R_{kl}} \quad \text{units of time}$$

10.2 SCHEDULING DAGs WITHOUT CONSIDERING COMMUNICATION

In this section, we present polynomial time-optimal algorithms for some restricted versions of the scheduling problem. We present optimal algorithms in the following three cases: (1) when the task graph is an in-forest or out-forest; (2) when the task graph is an interval order; and (3) when there are only two processors available. In the three cases, we assume the following:

- A task graph consists of n tasks;
- A target machine is made of m processors;
- The execution time of each task is one unit of time;
- Communication between any pair of tasks is zero;
- The goal is to find an optimal schedule that minimizes the total execution time.

The three algorithms belong to a class of scheduling algorithms called list scheduling, under which many other schedulers are classified. In list scheduling, each task is assigned a priority, and a list of tasks is constructed in a decreasing priority order. A task becomes ready for execution when its immediate predecessors in the task graph have already been executed or if it does not have any predecessors. When a processor has no work to do, it starts the execution of the first ready task in the list (the task with the highest priority). If more than one processor attempt to execute the same task, the processor with the lowest index executes the task and the other processors look for the next ready task. The schedulers in this class differ in the way they assign priorities to tasks.

10.2.1 Scheduling In-Forests/Out-Forests Task Graphs

We present one of the first polynomial–time algorithms to solve the scheduling problem when the task graph is either an in-forest, that is, each node has at most one immediate successor, or an out-forest, that is, each node has at most one immediate predecessor. Algorithm 1, which was introduced by Hu, finds an optimal schedule in time $O(n)$ (Hu, 1961). The general strategy used in the algorithm is the highest level first, where the level of a node x in a task graph is the maximum number of nodes (including x) on any path from x to a terminal node. This should work fine for the in-forest case, but it needs simple modification to be used in the out-forest case.

Algorithm 1
1. The level of each node in the task graph is calculated as given above, and used as each node's priority.
2. Whenever a processor becomes available, assign it the unexecuted ready task with the highest priority.

This algorithm will not produce an optimal solution in the case of an opposing forest. An opposing forest is the disjoint union of an in-forest and an out-forest. Scheduling an opposing forest is proven to be NP-complete.

Example 1   Consider the in-forest task graph shown in Figure 10.1. The level of a given node in the task graph can be computed as the number of nodes on the path from this node to the only terminal node m. For example, the level of node d is the number of nodes on the path d, i, k, m, which is 4. The level of each node is calculated and used as its priority as shown in Figure 10.1. When more than one task have the same priority, ties are broken alphabetically. For example, tasks a, b, and c have the same priority 5, but task a is selected for scheduling first, followed by b, and finally c.

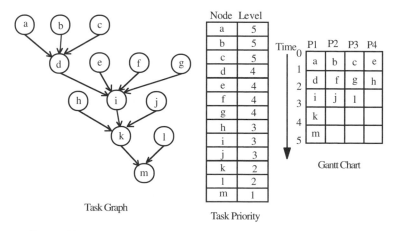

Figure 10.1   In-forest task graph and its schedule on four processors.

The Gantt chart in the figure shows the scheduling of the task graph on four processors. The schedule length is five units of time, which is the optimal schedule. Note that the length of the longest path from a source node to a terminal node (critical path) is also 5, which means that regardless of the number of processors that we may use, we will not be able to achieve schedule length shorter than five units of time.

10.2.2 Scheduling Interval Ordered Tasks

In this section, we deal with a special class of system tasks called *interval ordered tasks*. The term interval ordered tasks is used to indicate that the task graph that describes the precedence relations among the system tasks is an interval order. A task graph is an interval order when its elements can be mapped into intervals on the real line and two elements are related if and only if the corresponding intervals do not overlap. The interval order has a special structure that is established by the following property. For any interval ordered pair of tasks u and v, either the successors of u are also successors of v, or the successors of v are also successors of u.

The following algorithm was introduced by Papadimitriou and Yannakakis (1979) to solve the problem in $O(n + e)$ time complexity, where n is the number of tasks and e is the number of arcs in the interval order.

Algorithm 2
1. The number of all successors of each node is used as each node's priority.
2. Whenever a processor becomes available, assign it the unexecuted ready task with the highest priority.

Example 2 Consider the interval order task graph shown in Figure 10.2. Using Algorithm 2, the number of successors of a node will be used as its priority. For example, the priority of task a is 8 while the priority of task b is 6, which implies that task a will be considered for scheduling first. The Gantt chart in Figure 10.2

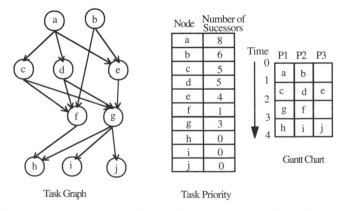

Figure 10.2 Scheduling an interval order without communication on three processors.

shows the scheduling of the task graph on three processors. The schedule length is four units of time, which is the optimal schedule. Note that the length of the longest path from a source node to a terminal node (critical path) is also 4, which means regardless of the number of processors that we may use, we will not be able to achieve schedule length shorter than four units of time.

10.2.3 Two-Processor Scheduling

In this case the number of processors is limited to only two ($m = 2$). The precedence relations in the task graph could have an arbitrary structure. The first polynomial time algorithm for this problem, based on matching techniques, was introduced by Fujii et al. (1969). The time complexity of Fujii's algorithm is $O(n^{2.5})$. Improved algorithms have been obtained by Coffman (1976), Fujii et al. (1969), Sethi (1976) and Gabow (1982). The time complexities of these three algorithms are $O(n^2)$, $O(\min(en, n^{2.61}))$, and $O(e + n\alpha(n))$, respectively, where n is the number of nodes and e is the number of arcs in the task graph. In this section, the algorithm introduced by Coffman and Graham is presented.

Algorithm 3

1. Assign 1 to one of the terminal tasks.
2. Let labels $1, 2, \ldots, j - 1$ have been assigned. Let S be the set of unassigned tasks with no unlabeled successors. We next select an element of S to be assigned label j. For each node x in S define $l(x)$ as follows: Let $L(y_1)$, $L(y_2), \ldots, L(y_k)$ be the labels already assigned to the immediate successors of x. Then $l(x)$ is the decreasing sequence of integers formed by ordering the set $\{L(y_1), L(y_2), \ldots, L(y_k)\}$. Let x be an element of S such that for all x' in S, $l(x) \leq l(x')$ (lexicographically). Assign j to x ($L(x) = j$).
3. Use $L(v)$ as the priority of task v and ties are broken arbitrarily.
4. Whenever a processor becomes available, assign it the unexecuted ready task with the highest priority. Ties are broken arbitrarily.

Since each task executes for one unit of time, processors 1 and 2 both become available at the same time. We assume that processor 1 is scheduled before processor 2.

Example 3   Figure 10.3 shows a task graph and its schedule without communication on two processors using Algorithm 3. The two terminal nodes j and k are assigned the labels 1 and 2, respectively. At this point the set S of unassigned tasks with no unlabeled successors becomes $\{h, i\}$. It can be noticed that $l(h) = \{2, 1\}$ and $l(i) = \{2\}$. Since $\{2\} \leq \{2, 1\}$ (lexicographically), we assign labels 3 and 4 to tasks i and h, respectively. The algorithm continues until all tasks are labeled. The reader is encouraged to try to label the rest of the nodes in the task graph. The labels of all the nodes in the task graph are given in the table of Figure 10.3. Task a with the highest label gets scheduled first on P1, then task b on P2, and so on until all tasks are scheduled.

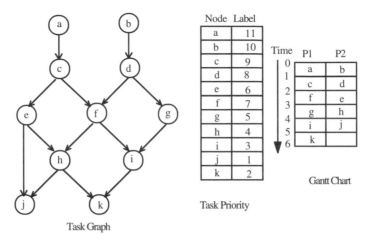

Figure 10.3   Scheduling arbitrary task graphs on two processors.

10.3   COMMUNICATION MODELS

There are two main components that contribute to the program completion time: computing time and communication delay. In this section, we present two methods that can be used to compute the program completion time. In these two methods, communication delay is computed differently according to three models. In this section, we illustrate the different communication models and their role in computing the program completion time.

10.3.1   Completion Time as Two Components

Given a task graph $G = (T, E)$ and the allocation of its tasks on m processors. We use $proc(v)$ to refer to the processor on which task v is allocated. This allocation can be easily represented using a Gantt chart in which communication is not considered. The Gantt chart does not reflect the communication delay, but it shows that the precedence relations between tasks are preserved.

The execution time component of the program completion time can be determined from the Gantt chart as the maximum finishing time of any task, which is also called the schedule length. Now, if we can also determine the total communication delay, we should be able to compute the program completion time as follows:

Program Completion Time = Execution Time + Total Communication Delay

The total communication delay can be computed as follows:

Total Communication Delay = Total Number of Messages
* Communication Delay per Message.

The total number of messages can be obtained according to two models as follows.

Model A   The total number of messages is defined as the number of node pairs (u, v) such that $(u, v) \in E$ and $proc(u) \neq proc(v)$.

Model B   The total number of messages is defined as the number of processor–task pairs (P, v) such that processor P does not compute task v but computes at least one immediate successor of v.

10.3.2   Completion Time from the Gantt Chart

The existence of an I/O processor implies that a processing element can execute a task and communicate with another processing element at the same time. Consequently, tasks can be scheduled for execution in the communication holes in a Gantt chart. The communication delay is reflected in the Gantt chart representing the schedule. Therefore, the program completion time can be determined directly from the Gantt chart as follows:

$$\text{Program Completion Time} = \text{Schedule Length}$$

The communication delay should be considered in the Gantt chart according to the following communication model.

Model C   This model assumes the existence of an I/O processor that is associated with every processor in the system. A task can be assigned to a processor for execution while this processor is performing communication.

Communication delay between two tasks allocated to the same processor is negligible. Communication delay between two communicating tasks allocated to two different processors is a function of the size of the message, the route, and the communication speed.

Example 4   Consider the task graph shown on Figure 10.4a. Suppose that each of the five tasks takes one unit of execution time on either P1 or P2, and task a sends messages to tasks b, c, d, and e. In this example we try to illustrate the differences between the three communication models.

In Models A and B, let us assume that tasks a, b, and d are allocated to processors P1 while tasks c and e are assigned to P2 as shown in Figure 10.4b. Using Model A, the total number of messages $= |(a, c), (a, e)| = 2$. On the other hand if we follow Model B, the total number of messages $= |(a, P2)| = 1$. If we assume that each message takes one unit of time, the program completion time can be obtained as follows:

- Using Model A, Program Completion Time $= 3 + 2 = 5$ units of time.
- Using Model B, Program Completion Time $= 3 + 1 = 4$ units of time.

In Model C, we assume that the communication delay between two communicating tasks allocated to two different processors is one unit of time. Figure 10.4c

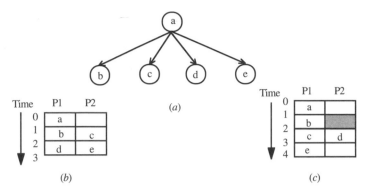

Figure 10.4 The three models of communication (*a*) task graph; (*b*) allocation (Models A & B); and (*c*) schedule (Model C) communication.

shows that task *b* is assigned to the same processors as *a*, which implies no delay. Task *d* cannot start on P2 before the arrival of its message from *a* after one unit of time. Therefore, the program completion time is:

- Program Completion Time = schedule length = 4 units of time.

10.4 SCHEDULING DAGs WITH COMMUNICATION

When communication cost is considered, we present two algorithms to schedule in-forests/out-forests, and interval orders. In these two cases, we assume the following:

- A task graph consisting of *n* tasks;
- A target machine made of *m* processors;
- The execution time of each task is one unit of time;
- Communication according to Model C;
- The communication delay between two communicating tasks scheduled on two different processors is one unit of time;
- The communication delay between two communicating tasks scheduled on the same processor equals zero;
- The goal is to find an optimal schedule that minimizes the total execution time.

10.4.1 Scheduling In-Forests/Out-Forests on Two Processors

The algorithm presented here was introduced by El-Rewini and Ali (1994). The algorithm is based on the idea of adding new precedence relations to the task graph in order to compensate for communication. The task graph after adding the new precedence relations is called the augmented task graph. Scheduling the augmented task graph without considering communication is equivalent to scheduling the original task graph with communication. Algorithm 4 produces an optimal schedule when the task graph is an in-forest. It can be used in the out-forest case with simple modification. We provide the following definitions:

1. *Node Depth*   The depth of a node is defined as the length of the longest path from any node with depth zero to that node. A node with no predecessors has a depth of zero. In other words, $depth(u) = 1 + \max\{depth(v)\}$, $\forall \ v \in predecessors(u)$; and $depth(u) = 0 \ \forall \ u, predecessors(u) = \phi$.

2. *Operation Swapall*   Given a schedule f, we define the operation $Swapall(f, x, y)$, where x and y are two tasks in f scheduled to start at time t on processors i and j, respectively. The effect of this operation is to swap all the task pairs scheduled on processors i and j in the schedule f at time t_1, $\forall \ t_1, t_1 \geq t$.

Algorithm 4

1. Given an in-forest $G = (V, A)$, identify the sets of siblings: $S1, S2, \ldots , Sk$, where Si is the set of all nodes in V with a common child child(Si).

2. $A1 \leftarrow A$.

3. For every set Si

    (a) Pick node $u \in Si$ with the maximum depth

    (b) $A1 \leftarrow A1 - (v, child(Si)) \ \forall \ v \in Si$ and $v \neq u$

    (c) $A1 \leftarrow A1 \ U \ (v, u) \ \forall \ v \in Si$ and $v \neq u$.

4. Obtain the schedule f by applying Algorithm 1 on the augmented in-forest $F = (V, A1)$.

5. For every set Si in the original in-forest G
    if node u (with the maximum depth) is scheduled in f in the time slot immediately before child(Si) but on a different processor, then apply the operation swapall(f, child(Si), x), where x is the task scheduled in the time slot immediately after u on the same processor.

Algorithm 4 selects the node u that has the maximum depth from every set of siblings S_i and places it after the other members of S_i, but before the common child of S_i, $child(S_i)$. In other words, Algorithm 4 adds an arc from every node v, $v \in S_i$ and $v \neq u$ to the node u. Note that the augmented task graph constructed is also an in-forest. These added arcs compensate for communication delay. Thus, Algorithm 1 is applied to this augmented in-forest to obtain a schedule where communication delays are not considered. The operation swapall is applied when communication restrictions are violated in the output schedule. The time complexity of the algorithm is $O(n^2 + nm)$.

Example 5   This example illustrates how to schedule the in-forest task graph shown in Figure 10.5a on two processors using Algorithm 4. Assume that each of the tasks in the task graph takes one unit of time on either one of the two processors, and Model C of communication is followed. The communication delay between two

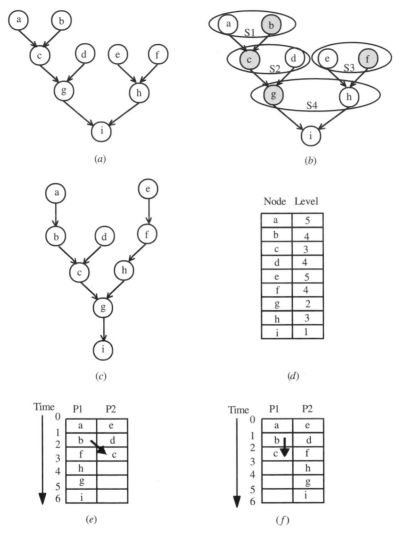

Figure 10.5 Scheduling in-forests with communication (*a*) original task graph (*G*); (*b*) node *u* in each set S_i in *G*; (*c*) augmental task graph (*F*); (*d*) task priority in F; (*e*) optimal schedule of *F* (without communication); and (*f*) optimal schedule of *G* (with Model C communication).

communicating tasks is one unit of time if allocated to two different processors, otherwise the delay is ignored.

- We identify the sets of siblings with a common child. Figure 10.5*b* shows four sets as follows: $S_1 = \{a, b\}$, $S_2 = \{c, d\}$, $S_3 = \{e, f\}$, $S_4 = \{g, h\}$.
- We pick the node that has the maximum depth from each set. Since *a* and *b* in S_1 and *e* and *f* in S_3 have the same depth, we select *b* from S_1 and *f* from S_2 at random. Nodes *c* and *g* are the ones that have the maximum depth in S_2 and S_4, respectively. These selected nodes are shaded in Figure 10.5*b*.

- The augmented task graph (F) is constructed as shown in Figure 10.5c.
- Algorithm 1 for scheduling in-forests without considering communication can be applied to the augmented task graph (F). Figures 10.5d and e show the task priorities and the optimal schedule when communication is ignored.
- The schedule shown in Figure 10.5e is not correct when communication is considered because the communicating tasks b and c are allocated to different processors but there is no delay left for communication according to Model C. The operation swapall is applied to fix this problem.
- Figure 10.5f shows the final optimal schedule on two processors when communication is considered.

10.4.2 Scheduling Interval Orders with Communication

We introduce an optimal algorithm to schedule interval orders on an arbitrary number of processors when communication delay is considered. This algorithm was introduced by Ali and El-Rewini (1995) to solve the problem when execution time is the same for all tasks and is identical to communication delay. We first provide the following definitions:

- start-time(v,i,f)   The earliest time at which task v can start execution on processor P_i in schedule f.
- task(i,t,f)   The task scheduled on processor P_i at time t in schedule f. If there is no task scheduled on processor P_i at time t in schedule f, then task(i,t,f) returns the empty task ϕ. Note that the priority of the empty task is less than the priority of any other task.

Algorithm 5

1. The number of all successors of each node is used as each node's priority.
2. Nodes with the highest priority are scheduled first.
3. Each task v is assigned to processor P_i with the earliest start time.
4. If start-time(v,i,f) = start-time(v,j,f), $1 \leq i,j \leq m$, task v is assigned to processor P_i if task(i, start-time(v,i,f)-1, f) has the smaller priority (smaller number of successors).

The time complexity of the algorithm is $O(e + nm)$ where n is the number of tasks, e is the number of arcs in the interval order, and m is the number of processors.

Example 6   In this example, we use Algorithm 5 to schedule an interval order with communication according to Model C on three processors. Figure 10.6 shows an interval order consisting of 12 nodes. The steps of the algorithm can be summarized as follows:

- The number of successors for each node is obtained and used as each task's priority as shown in the table of Figure 10.6. For example, the priority of task d is 8.

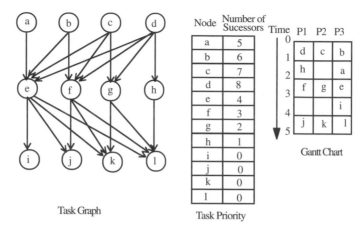

Figure 10.6 Scheduling interval orders with communication according to Model C on three processors.

- Tasks d, c, and b are considered for scheduling in that order and are scheduled to start at time 0 on processors P_1, P_2, and P_3, respectively.
- Task a can start execution at time 1 on any of the three processors. But according to the algorithm it is allocated to processor P_3 after task b with the smallest priority.
- Task e is considered next and it is scheduled to start at time 2 on processor P_3. Note that there is one unit of communication delay between e and its predecessors d and c that are scheduled on different processors (P_1 and P_2).
- This process continues until all tasks are assigned processors.

10.5 THE NP-COMPLETENESS OF THE SCHEDULING PROBLEM

NP-complete problems are the problems that are strongly suspected to be computationally intractable. An intuitive definition of NP-complete problems is introduced here, for a formal definition and comprehensive presentation, refer to Ullman (1975). There is a host of important problems that are roughly equivalent in complexity and form the class of NP-complete problems. This class includes many classical problems in combinatorics, graph theory, and computer science, such as the traveling salesman problem, the Hamilton circuit problem, and integer programming. The best-known algorithms for these problems could take exponential time on some inputs. The exact complexity of these NP-complete problems has yet to be determined and it remains the foremost open problem in theoretical computer science. Either all these problems have polynomial–time solutions, or none of them does.

In this section we list some of the NP-complete results in the scheduling problem. It has been proven that the problem of finding an optimal schedule for a set of tasks is NP-complete in the general case, and in several restricted cases.

10.5.1 NP-Completeness Results when Communication is not Considered

In what follows, we give the formal definition of some versions of the scheduling problem that were proven to be NP-complete when communication among tasks is not considered.

1. *General Scheduling Problem*   Given a set T of n tasks, a partial order $<$ on T, weight W_i, $1 \le i \le n$, and m processors, and a time limit k, does there exist a total function h from T to $\{0, 1, \ldots, k-1\}$ such that:
   - if $i <. j$, then $h(i) + W_i \le h(j)$
   - for each i in T $h(i) + W_i \le k$
   - for each t, $0 \le t < k$, there are at most m values of i for which $h(i) \le t < h(i) + W_i$.

The following problems are special cases of the General Scheduling Problem.

2. *Single Execution Time Scheduling*   The General Scheduling Problem is restricted by requiring $W_i = 1$, $1 \le i \le n$. (All tasks require one time unit.)
3. *Two Processor, One or Two Time Units Scheduling*   The General Scheduling Problem is restricted by requiring $m = 2$, and W_i in $\{1, 2\}$, $1 \le i \le n$. (All tasks require one or two time units, and there are only two processors.)
4. *Two Processor, Interval Order Scheduling*   The General Scheduling Problem is restricted by requiring the partial order $<$ to be an interval order and $m = 2$.
5. *Single Execution Time, Opposing Forests*   The General Scheduling Problem is restricted by requiring $W_i = 1$, $1 \le i \le n$, and the partial order $<$ to be an opposing forest.

The General Scheduling Problem was proven to be NP-complete by Karp in 1972. Problems 2 and 3 were proven to be NP-complete by Ullman in 1975. Problem 4 was proven to be NP-complete by Papadimitriou and Yannakakis in 1979. Garey, Johnson, Tarjan and Yannakakis proved that problem 5 is also NP-complete in 1983. References to the proofs are listed in El-Rewini et al. (1994).

10.5.2 NP-Completeness Results when Communication is Considered

The complexity of the scheduling problem changes based on which cost model is used to compute communication. The following is a summary of the NP-complete results using the different communication models. Using Model A, Afrati et al. showed that scheduling a tree with communication on an arbitrary number of processors is an NP-complete problem. Using Model B, Prastein proved that by taking communication into consideration, even when the execution time for all tasks is identical and equal to the communication cost between any pair of processors, the problem of scheduling an arbitrary precedence program graph on two processors is NP-complete and scheduling a tree-structured program on arbitrarily many processors is also NP-complete. Prastein also indicated that the problem of scheduling a tree-structured task graph on two processors, using model B, is an open problem in general. Using Model C, Papadimitriou and Yannakakis proved that the problem of optimally scheduling unit-time task graphs with communication on an unlimited number of processors is NP-complete when the communication between any pair of processors is the same and greater than or equal to one. References to the above NP-complete results are listed in El-Rewini et al. (1994).

10.6   HEURISTIC ALGORITHMS

In order to provide solutions to real-world scheduling problems, restrictions on the parallel program and the target machine representations must be relaxed. However, because of the computational complexity of optimal solution strategies, a need has arisen for a simplified suboptimal approach to this scheduling problem. Recent research in this area has emphasized heuristic approaches. A heuristic produces an answer in less than exponential time, but does not guarantee an optimal solution. Intuition is usually used to come up with heuristics that make use of special parameters that affect the system in an indirect way. A heuristic is said to be better than another heuristic if solutions fall closer to optimality more often, or if the time taken to obtain a near-optimal solution is less. The effectiveness of these scheduling heuristics is dependent upon several parameters of the program and the distributed system. A heuristic that can optimally schedule a particular task graph on a certain target system may not produce optimal schedules for other task graphs on other systems. As a result, a number of heuristics have been proposed, each of which may work under different circumstances.

In what follows, we present some of the principle issues encountered when designing schedulers of the General Scheduling Problem. We also study a number of the ideas used in developing scheduling heuristics.

10.6.1   Parallelism Versus Communication Delay

In the cases when the communication delay among tasks is negligible, all ready tasks can be allocated to all available processors simultaneously so that the overall execution time is reduced. This situation may occur in a shared memory environment where communication is performed at memory cycle speeds. In fact, this is the basis of a number of heuristic algorithms that do not consider communication delays in making scheduling decisions. On the other hand, when communication delay cannot be overlooked, scheduling heuristics must consider the communication delay before allocating tasks to processors. It is possible for ready tasks with long communication delays to end up assigned to the same processor as their immediate predecessors.

For example, let us consider the task graph shown in Figure 10.7. Since the communication delay between tasks a and b is greater than that between a and c ($y > x$),

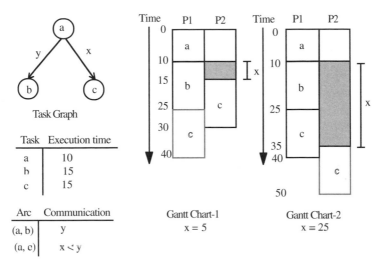

Figure 10.7 Communication delay vs. parallelism.

task b is assigned to the same processor as task a (P1). Now, if the communication delay between tasks a and c (x) is less than the execution time of task b, it is logical to assign task c to P2 since it will produce a shorter schedule. Otherwise, task c must be scheduled on P1. When x equals five units of time, c must be allocated to P2 as shown in Gantt Chart-1, which will produce a schedule length equal to 30 units of time. (Note that if c was allocated to P1, the schedule length would have been 40.) On the other hand if x was 25 units of time, c must be allocated to P1 as shown in Gantt Chart-2, which will produce a schedule length of 40 units of time. (Note that if c was allocated to P2, the schedule length would have been 50.) Hence, considering communication delay constraint increases the difficulty of arriving at an optimal schedule because a scheduler must examine the start time of each node on each available processor in order to select the one with the earliest start time.

As shown above, it would be a mistake to always increase the amount of parallelism available by simply starting each task as soon as possible. Distributing parallel tasks to as many processors as possible tends to increase the communication delay, which contributes to the overall execution time. In short, there is a trade-off between taking advantage of maximal parallelism and minimizing communication delay.

10.6.2 Grain Size and Data Locality

Another issue closely related to the trade-off between parallelism and communication delay is the grain size problem. This issue must be dealt with during the partitioning of the program into grains. The challenge is to determine the best grain size for each node in a task graph representing the program. A grain is defined as one or more sequential instructions, packed together to make a module that is sequentially executed on a single processor. The size of a grain is altered by adding or removing instructions. A grain can be as small as a single operation or as large as a whole program. If a grain is too large, parallelism is reduced because potentially concurrent tasks are grouped together and executed sequentially by one processor. On the other hand, when the grain size is too fine, more overhead in the form of context switching, scheduling time, and communication delay is added to the overall execution time.

With the increasing success and utilization of developing programming models on top of physically distributed computers, it has become very important to partition programs so that the data used by a grain is kept local to the greatest degree possible. The idea is to reduce data movement between the grains running on different processors. Even at high data transfer rates, there is still latency that is many times longer than the local memory latency. Again, there is a trade-off between maximizing locality and maximizing parallelism. At one extreme, considering the whole program as a single grain running sequentially on one processor maximizes locality but does not exploit the parallelism in the program. The parallel execution time of a program can be minimized at an optimal intermediate grain size in which locality is maximized and potential parallelism is also exploited.

10.6.3 Nondeterminism

In deterministic scheduling, all the information about program tasks and their relations to one another is entirely known prior to execution time. When some information may not be known before the program starts its execution, we have to deal with nondeterminism. The problem of scheduling nondeterministic task graphs arises in several situations in programming, particularly in the cases of loops and conditional branching. Nondeterminism arises in loops because the number of loop iterations may not be known before the execution of the program. Since loops form a restricted class of conditional branching, there is a higher degree of nondeterminism associated with scheduling conditional branching. In this case, the direction of every branch remains unknown before run time. Consequently, entire subprograms may or may not be executed, which in turn increases the amount of nondeterminism and complicates the scheduling process. Also, having conditional branching within a node in the task graph may cause variable task execution time and communication delay.

Scheduling nondeterministic programs can be achieved dynamically on the fly. However, dynamic scheduling consumes time and resources, which leads to overhead during program execution. The overhead of extra communication delays, additional memory, and time for the scheduler itself to work, detract from dynamic scheduling. In addition, dynamic scheduling can lead to task thrashing where a task is moved back and forth between processors, consuming yet more time. Therefore, we must be careful when applying dynamic scheduling techniques. In order to eliminate (or reduce) the overhead involved with dynamic scheduling, static methods can be applied. In this case, we must try to predict the behavior of the nondeterministic program during run time prior to execution. This approximation may affect the quality of the produced schedule. A hybrid approach that combines both static and dynamic methods can also be applied.

10.6.4 Priority-Based Scheduling

The list scheduling algorithm discussed in Section 10.2 can be generalized to handle the general scheduling problem. In list scheduling, tasks are considered for scheduling according to their priorities. The task with the highest priority is scheduled first. Once a task is selected for scheduling, a processor selection criterion must be followed to find a processor to run the task. There are a number of heuristics that follow this method and they differ in how they assign priorities to tasks and/or in the processor selection criterion. For example, one heuristic may assign priorities based on the length of the longest path to a terminal node in a task graph. The number of successors could be used as the task priority by another heuristic. Similarly, the earliest start time and the earliest finish time are examples of processor selection criteria. A number of list scheduling heuristics can be found in El-Rewini and Ali (1995), El-Rewini et al. (1994), El-Rewini and Lewis (1990) and Lewis and El-Rewini (1993). Algorithm 6 summarizes the general list scheduling algorithm.

Algorithm 6
1. Each node in the task graph is assigned a priority. A priority queue is initialized for ready tasks by inserting every task that has no immediate predecessors. Tasks are sorted in decreasing order of task priorities.
2. As long as the priority queue is not empty do the following:
   (a) A task is obtained from the front of the queue.
   (b) An idle processor is selected to run the task using the processor-selection criterion.
   (c) When all the immediate predecessors of a particular task are executed, that successor is now ready and can be inserted into the priority queue.

10.6.5 Clustering

The idea behind this type of scheduling heuristic is to partition the scheduling process into two phases: processor assignment, which is the process of allocating tasks to the system processors; and task ordering, which is the process of scheduling the tasks allocated on each processor. Clustering of task graphs can be used as an intermediate phase to solve the allocation problem of the scheduling process. Clustering can be defined as the process of mapping the nodes of a task graph onto labeled clusters. All the tasks that belong to the same cluster must execute on the same processor. If two independent tasks are mapped to the same cluster, then the resulting clustering is called a nonlinear clustering; otherwise, it is called a linear clustering.

Clustering algorithms start with an initial clustering and then perform a sequence of clustering refinements in order to achieve some specific objective. Clusters are not tasks, since tasks that belong to a cluster are permitted to communicate with the tasks of other clusters immediately after the completion of their execution. Clustering heuristics are nonbacktracking heuristics in order to avoid high complexity; that is, once the clusters are merged in a refinement step, they cannot be unmerged afterwards. At the initial step, each task is assumed to be in a separate cluster. A typical refinement step is to merge two clusters and zero the edge that connects them. Zeroing the communication cost on the edge between the two merged clusters is carried out due to the fact that the start and end nodes of this edge will be scheduled on the same processor, and hence, the communication cost between the two nodes becomes negligible. A typical criterion to select an edge for zeroing is to reduce the parallel time of the schedule. The parallel time of a given schedule is equal to its completion time, if we assume that the number of clusters never exceeds the number of processors. There are two other important parameters in performing the refinement steps; the critical path of a clustered task graph and the dominant sequence of a scheduled task graph. The critical path is the longest path in the task graph, while the dominant sequence is the longest path of the scheduled task graph or the path whose length equals the actual parallel time of the schedule. In other words, the critical path is a parameter of the task graph only, while the dominant sequence, as well as the parallel time, are parameters of the schedule of the task graph. A comparison of clustering heuristics and other related results can be found in Gerasoulis and Yang (1992) and Sarkar (1991). Task clustering has been used in a two-phase method for scheduling tasks on distributed systems as shown in Algorithm 7.

Algorithm 7

1. Cluster the tasks assuming an unlimited number of fully connected processors. Two tasks in the same cluster are scheduled in the same processor.
2. Map the clusters and their tasks onto the given number of processors (m). In this step, the following optimizations are performed:
   (a) Cluster merging. If the number of clusters is greater than the number of available processors, the clusters are merged into m clusters.
   (b) Physical mapping. The actual architecture is not fully connected. A mapping must be determined such that overall communication between clusters is minimized.
   (c) Task execution ordering. After the processor assignment of tasks is fixed, the execution ordering is determined to assure the correct dependence order between tasks.

Example 7   Consider the task graph shown in Figure 10.8. Suppose that tasks a, b, c, d, e, f, and g can run on any processor in a distributed system in 1, 5, 1, 2, 2, 1, and 1 units of time, respectively. The communication delays between tasks if assigned to different processors are shown in Table 10.1. The figure also shows four different clusterings of the task graph. Scheduling the two clusters of Figure 10.8a on two

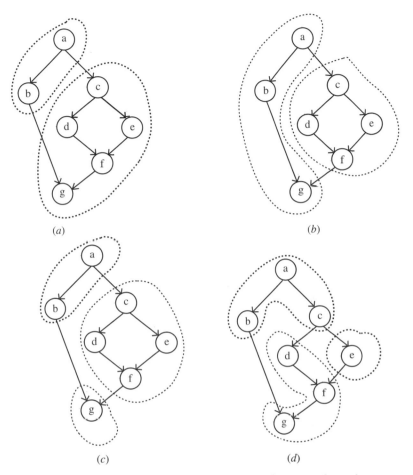

Figure 10.8 Example of different ways to cluster a task graph.

processors will produce a completion time of 9 units of time. In the clustering of Figure 10.8b, the completion time on two processors is 10 units of time. The clustering of Figure 10.8c will produce a schedule of 9 and 10 units of time on two and three processors, respectively. Finally, the completion time is 10.5 units of time if we schedule the clustering of Figure 10.8d on three processors.

10.6.6 Task Duplication

Task duplication can be used in scheduling heuristics to reduce the effect of communication delay. Since the cost of message passing between different processors is significantly higher than that within the same processor, the goal is to reduce the exchange of messages between tasks assigned to different processors. The idea is to execute multiple copies of the sender task on the processors running the

TABLE 10.1   Communication Delay Times for Example 7

Graph Arc	Communication Delay (Units of Time)
(a, b)	5
(a, c)	1
(b, g)	2
(c, d)	4
(c, e)	3
(d, f)	1.5
(e, f)	1.5
(f, g)	1

receiving tasks whenever possible. This task duplication will help change interprocessor communication into communication within the same processor. For example, consider the task graph shown in Figure 10.9. It can be seen that the duplication of task a on both P1 and P2 decreases the starting time of task c on P2. Thus, the parallelism of tasks b and c is fully exploited with zero communication delay.

It is important to make sure that the cost of initiating multiple copies of a task on a number of processors is not going to dominate the communication cost we are trying to offset. Note that the communication cost is usually greater than task duplication cost for small-grain task graphs, which makes the duplication idea very suitable in such cases.

10.7   TASK ALLOCATION

The problem of task allocation arises when specifying the order of executing the system tasks is not required. In other words, system tasks might interact or communicate without imposed precedence relations. In a distributed computing system

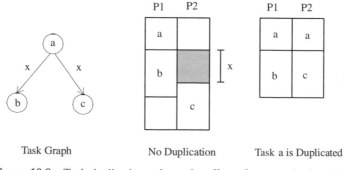

| Task Graph | No Duplication | Task a is Duplicated |

Figure 10.9   Task duplication reduces the effect of communication delay.

made up of several processors, the interacting tasks comprising a distributed program must be assigned to the processors so as to make use of the system resources efficiently.

In the assignment of tasks to processors there are two types of cost: the cost of execution of a task on a processor and the cost of interprocessor communication. In order to improve the performance of a distributed system, two goals need to be met: interprocessor communication has to be minimized and the execution cost needs to be balanced among different processors. These two goals seem to conflict with one another. On one hand, having all tasks on one processor will remove interprocessor communication cost but results in poor balance of the execution load. On the other hand, an even distribution of tasks among processors will maximize the processor utilization but might also increase interprocessor communication. Thus, the purpose of a task allocation technique is to find some task assignment in which the total cost due to interprocessor communication and task execution is minimized.

10.7.1 Task Allocation Model

The model we describe here assumes a set on n tasks forming a program which is supposed to run on a distributed system consisting of m heterogeneous processors. The goal is to minimize the total cost (execution and communication).

The interaction among tasks in the distributed program can be represented by a task interaction graph. Each task in the program is represented by a node in the task interaction graph. An edge between two nodes indicates that the corresponding tasks may interact with each other. Associated with each edge is the communication cost between the corresponding tasks if they are assigned to different processors. It is assumed that the communication cost of two tasks assigned to the same processor is negligible.

Associated with each task t_i is a vector of m values which provides the execution time of this task on each of the m processors $[x_{i1}, x_{i2}, \ldots, x_{im}]$. Note that when the execution cost of a task on a particular processor is set to ∞, it implies that this processor cannot execute the task. Figure 10.10 shows the task interaction graph and the execution time of six tasks on two processors.

10.7.2 Optimal Task Allocation on Two Processors

This optimal algorithm introduced by Harold Stone (1977) is based on the well-known network flow algorithms in the related two-terminal network graphs. Before introducing the optimal algorithm, we briefly introduce the basic definition of minimum cuts in two-terminal networks.

Background In a two-terminal network graph $G = (V, E)$, it is assumed that there are two specific nodes, a source node S and a sink node T, and a weight function $W(e)$ for each edge $e \in E$. A cutset of the two-terminal network graph G is a set of edges C, which, when removed, disconnects the set of nodes V into two sets:

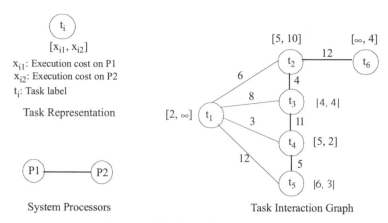

Figure 10.10   Task allocation model.

a source set VS that contains the node S, and a sink set VT that contains the node T, such that $VS \cap VT = \phi$ and $VS \cup VT = V$. The weight of each cutset $W(C)$ is equal to the sum of the weight of all edges in C. A cutset $C0$ is called an optimal cutset or a minimum cutset if $W(C0) \leq W(C)$, for any cutset C of the two-terminal network. This problem has been proven to have polynomial–time solutions. The complexity of the most efficient algorithm to solve this problem is $O(ne \log n)$, where n and e are equal to the number of nodes and edges in the network, respectively.

The Optimal Algorithm   This algorithm assumes a restricted case of a distributed system made of only two processors, which may not need to be identical. The solution of the allocation problem is obtained as follows. A related two-terminal network graph is constructed from the relationships of the tasks in the task interaction graph. The network is constructed in a way such that each cutset in the two-terminal network graph corresponds in a one-to-one fashion to a task assignment, and that the weight of each cutset carries the total cost for the corresponding assignment. The network flow algorithm can then be applied on the two-terminal network. The minimum weight cutset obtained from the solution determines the task assignment that is optimal in terms of the total cost.

Algorithm 8

1. Construct a two-terminal network as follows:
    (a) Add a source node labeled $S1$ and a sink node labeled $S2$ to represent processors $p1$ and $p2$, respectively.
    (b) For every node t in the original task interaction graph, add an edge from t to each of $S1$ and $S2$. The weight on the edge $(t, S1)$ is the cost of executing t on $p2$, while the weight on the edge $(t, S2)$ is the cost of executing t on $p1$.
2. A max-flow min-cut algorithm is applied to the obtained network and a minimum cut C is determined.

3. An optimal solution of the task assignment problem is obtained from the cut such that a task t is assigned to processor Pi if and only if the corresponding nodes t and Si belong to the same partition in C.

Example 8   Consider the system illustrated in Figure 10.10. To construct the two-terminal network, we add the nodes S_1 and S_2 and add an edge from each of the six nodes in the task interaction graph to S_1 and S_2. The weights on the added edges are shown in the Figure 10.11.

Each cutset of the new graph partitions the nodes into two disjoint subsets, with S_1 and S_2 in distinct subsets. Clearly, a task assignment can be associated with each cutset. All the tasks in the same partition with S_1 will be allocated to P_1, and the rest of the tasks, which exist in the same partition with S_2, are allocated to P_2. The optimal cut shown in the figure corresponds to the allocation of tasks t_1, t_2, t_3, t_4, and t_5 to P_1 and task t_6 to processor P_2.

In this case, the execution cost is equal to $2 + 5 + 4 + 5 + 6 + 4 = 26$, and the communication cost is equal to 12, which is the communication cost between tasks t_2 and t_6.

10.7.3   Optimal Task Allocation on Array of Processors

The optimal algorithm presented in this section was introduced to solve the problem in the case when the distributed system is composed of a linear array of processors (Lee et al., 1992). Similar to the two-processor case, the task interaction graph will be used as a representation of the program tasks. However, the distributed system is different in this case. It is assumed that the distributed system is made of m processors connected using $m - 1$ links such that P_i is connected to $P_i + 1$, $1 \leq i < m$. The idea used in this section is a generalization of the idea introduced

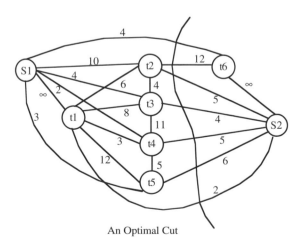

An Optimal Cut

Figure 10.11 Two-terminal network constructed from the task interaction graph of Figure 10.10.

by Stone in Algorithm 8. The solution to the problem is obtained using the max-flow min-cut algorithm. We first construct a related two-terminal network graph from the task interaction graph so that each cutset in the two-terminal network graph corresponds to a task allocation and the weight of the cutset carries the total cost for that allocation. Again the minimum cutset of the network will correspond to an optimal assignment of the tasks.

Algorithm 9

1. Construct a two-terminal network as follows:
   (a) For each node ti in the original task interaction graph, create $(m - 1)$ nodes labeled $vi1, vi2, \ldots, vi(m - 1)$, respectively, and add a source node S and a terminal node T.
   (b) Add an execution edge from S to $vi1$ with the weight ($xi1$ + some large quantity).
   (c) Add an execution edge between any two nodes vik and $vi(k + 1)$ with the weight ($xi(k + 1)$ + some large quantity), $1 \leq k < m$.
   (d) Add an execution edge from $vi(m - 1)$ to T with the weight (xim + some large quantity).
   (e) Add a communication edge between any two nodes vik and vjk with the weight equals the communication cost between the tasks ti and tj.
2. A max-flow min-cut algorithm is applied to the obtained network and a minimum cut C is determined.
3. An optimal solution of the task assignment problem is obtained from the cut such that a task ti is assigned to processor $Pk+1$ in the assignment if and only if the cutset C contains the edge (vik, $vi(k + 1)$). To make sure that each task is assigned to exactly one processor, the cutset must contain exactly one execution edge for each task.

Example 9 In this example, we show how to construct the two-terminal network for the task interaction graph given in Figure 10.12a on a linear array of three processors shown in Figure 10.12b. The vector shown next to each task provides the task execution time on the three processors. For example, task t_2 takes 5, 10, and 30 units of time on processors P_1, P_2, and P_3, respectively. Also remember that the value next to an edge is the communication cost between the two corresponding tasks if executed on two different processors. Let us assume that the large quantity used in the weights on the execution edges equals 100. The two terminal network is constructed as follows:

- Since we have three processors ($m = 3$), we will create two nodes v_{i1} and v_{i2} for each node t_i in the original task interaction graph. We will also add the source and terminal nodes S and T.
- We add the execution edges (S, v_{11}), (S, v_{21}), (S, v_{31}), (S, v_{41}) having the weights: 102, 105, 115, and ∞, respectively.
- We add the execution edges (v_{11}, v_{12}), (v_{21}, v_{22}), (v_{31}, v_{32}), (v_{41}, v_{42}) having the weights: ∞, 110, 125, and 107, respectively.

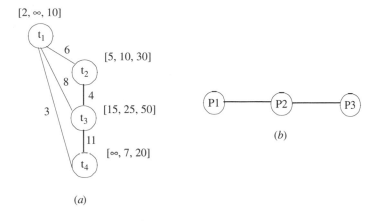

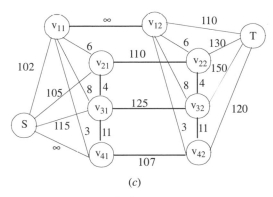

Figure 10.12 Constructing the two-terminal network of a task interaction graph on a linear array of three processors (*a*) task interaction graph; (*b*) linear array of three processors; and (*c*) two-terminal network.

- We add the execution edges (v_{12}, T), (v_{22}, T), (v_{32}, T), (v_{42}, T) having the weights: 110, 130, 150, and 120, respectively.
- The communication edges from the original task interaction graph are added to the network such that the weights of the edges (v_{1j}, v_{2j}), (v_{1j}, v_{3j}), (v_{1j}, v_{4j}), (v_{2j}, v_{3j}), and (v_{3j}, v_{4j}) are 6, 8, 3, 4, and 11, respectively.

The constructed two-terminal network is shown in Figure 10.12*c*. It is left as an exercise for the reader to determine an optimal and feasible task allocation by finding the minimum cut in the obtained network (see Problem 12).

10.7.4 Task Allocation Heuristics

The task allocation problem is known to be NP-complete. A formal proof that the problem is NP-hard even in the restricted case when there are only two values of communication cost between tasks allocated on different processing elements, zero and one, can be found in Ali and El-Rewini (1994). Again, the intractability of the problem has led to the introduction of many heuristics. A number of heuristics are based on Stone's algorithm for solving the problem in two-processor systems. These heuristics utilize the max-flow min-cut algorithm in solving the more general allocation problem. Other heuristics use graph theoretic approaches. Several related results and heuristic algorithms can be found in Ali and El-Rewini (1993), Bokhari (1981) and Lo (1988).

10.8   SCHEDULING IN HETEROGENEOUS ENVIRONMENTS

Numerous applications have more than one type of embedded parallelism, such as single instruction multiple data (SIMD) and multiple instructions multiple data (MIMD). Homogeneous systems use one mode of parallelism in a given machine and thus cannot adequately meet the requirements of applications that require more than one type of parallelism. As a result, a machine may spend its time executing code for which it is poorly suited. Heterogeneous computing offers a cost-effective approach to this problem by using existing systems in an integrated environment. Heterogeneous computing systems provide a variety of architectural capabilities, coordinated to execute an application whose subtasks have diverse execution requirements. One type of heterogeneous computing system is a mixed-mode machine, where a single machine can operate in different modes of parallelism. Another is a mixed-machine system, where a suite of different kinds of high-performance machines are interconnected by high-speed links. To exploit such systems, a task must be decomposed into subtasks, where each subtask is computationally homogeneous. The subtasks are then allocated to the machines (or modes) that will result in a minimal overall execution time for the task. Typically, users must specify this decomposition and assignment.

The problem of partitioning and scheduling in homogeneous environments can be considered a special case of the problem when the target computer is a suite of heterogeneous machines. For example, code classification is another objective of program partitioning in a heterogeneous environment. The code needs to be classified based on the type of the embedded parallelism such as SIMD and MIMD. Matching the code type to the machine type will also add more constraints to the scheduling problem. Scheduling in heterogeneous environments can be done at two levels. At the system level, each task is assigned to one or more machines in the system so that the parallelism embedded in the task matches the machine type. At the machine level, portions of the task are assigned to individual processors in the machine.

A parallel program can be modeled for heterogeneous environments as follows. The parallel program T can be divided into subtasks t_i, $1 \leq i \leq N$. Each subtask t_i is further divided into code segments t_{ij}, $1 \leq j \leq S$, which can be executed concurrently. Each code segment within a subtask can belong to a different type of parallelism (that is, SIMD, MIMD, vector, and so on), and should be mapped onto a machine with a matching type of parallelism. Each code segment may further be decomposed into several concurrent code blocks with the same type of parallelism.

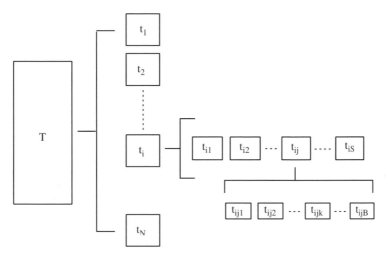

Figure 10.13 Heterogeneous application.

These code blocks t_{ijk}, $1 \leq k \leq B$, are suited for parallel execution on machines having the same type of parallelism. This decomposition of the task into subtasks, code segments, and code blocks is shown in Figure 10.13. Approaches to solve the scheduling problem in heterogeneous environments can be found in Chen et al. (1993) and Freund and Siegel (1993).

10.9 CHAPTER SUMMARY

In the era of network computing and grid computing, the problem of resource scheduling and allocation is gaining more attention. A computational job can be viewed as a collection of tasks which may run serially or in parallel. The goal of scheduling is to determine an assignment of tasks to computing resources, and an order in which tasks are executed to optimize some objective function. In this chapter, we provided a survey of the important aspects in this problem including modeling, optimal algorithms, and heuristic techniques.

PROBLEMS

1. Devise Gantt charts showing schedules for the task graph of Figure 10.1 on three and five identical processors, when communication is not considered. What is the minimum number of processors required to execute all tasks in five units of time?

2. Modify Algorithm 1 to handle the out-forest case. Apply the modified algorithm to schedule the task graph of Figure 10.1, after reversing all the arrows on the graph arcs, on four processors.

3. Show that a task graph is an interval order if its complement does not have any cycles of size four or more.

4. Write an algorithm to check whether a partial order is an interval order.

5. Provide an argument to prove, or a counter example to disprove the following: "Given a task graph with task execution time in $\{1, 2\}$ and two identical processors, Coffman and Graham's algorithm will result in a schedule whose time is not more than twice that required by the optimal schedule. (Note that communication is not considered.)

6. Write an algorithm to construct the augmented graph for an out-forest.

7. Assuming that communication is considered using Model C, do the following:

   (a) Construct the augmented task graph of the tree given in Figure 10.1.

   (b) Show the optimal schedule of the augmented graph on two processors without communication.

   (c) Construct a feasible optimal schedule with communication.

8. Given a task graph and a large number of processors, what is a lower bound on the length of an optimal schedule?

9. The problem of scheduling task graphs where communication is not considered and all tasks take the same amount of time on fixed $m \geq 3$ processors is still an open problem. Can you come up with an optimal algorithm? Can you prove its NP-completeness.

10. Devise a Gantt chart for each of the four clusterings shown in Figure 10.8 on two and three processors.

11. Given a two-terminal network, devise an algorithm for finding a minimum cutset of the network.

12. Determine an optimal and feasible task allocation for the two-terminal network of Figure 10.12c. (Find the minimum cut.)

REFERENCES

Ali, H. and El-Rewini, H. An optimal algorithm for scheduling interval ordered tasks with communication on N processors. *Journal of Computer and System Sciences*, 51 (2), (1995).

Ali, H. and El-Rewini, H. Task allocation in distributed systems: A split graph model. *Journal of Combinatorial Mathematics and Combinatorial Computing*, 14, 1993, 15–32 (1993).

Ali, H. and El-Rewini, H. On the intractability of task allocation in distributed systems. *Parallel Processing Letters* (1994).

Bokhari, S. A shortest tree algorithm for optimal assignments across space and time in distributed processor system. *IEEE Transaction on Software Engineering*, SE-7 (6) (1981).

Chen, S. et al. *A Selection Theory and Methodology for Heterogeneous Supercomputing*, Proc. Workshop on Heterogeneous Processing, IEEE CS Press, Los Alamitos, CA, Order No. 3532-02, 1993.

Coffman, E. G. *Computer and Job-Shop Scheduling Theory*, John Wiley, 1976.

El-Rewini, H. and Lewis, T. Scheduling parallel program tasks onto arbitrary target machines. *Journal of Parallel and Distributed Computing*, 138–153, 1990.

El-Rewini, H. and Ali, H. On considering communication in scheduling task graphs on parallel processors. *Journal of Parallel Algorithms and Applications*, 3, 177–191 (1994).

El-Rewini, H., Lewis, T. and Ali, H. *Task Scheduling in Parallel and Distributed Systems*, Prentice-Hall, 1994.

El-Rewini, H. and Ali, H. Static scheduling of containing conditional branching in parallel programs. *Journal of Parallel and Distributed Computing*, 41–54, 1995.

Freund, R. and Siegel, H. Heterogeneous processing. *IEEE Computer*, 26, 13–17 (1993).

Fujii, M., Kasami, T. and Ninomiya, K. Optimal sequencing of two equivalent processors. *SIAM Journal of Applied Mathematics*, 17 (4) (1969).

Gabow, H. An almost linear algorithm for two-processor scheduling. *Journal of ACM*, 29 (3), 766–780 (1982).

Gerasoulis and Yang, T. A comparison of clustering heuristics for scheduling DAGs on multiprocessors. *Journal of Parallel and Distributed Computing*, 16 (4), 276–291 (1992).

Hu, T. C. Parallel sequencing and assembly line problems. *Operations Research*, 9 (6), 841–848 (1961).

Lewis, T. and El-Rewini, H. Parallax: A tool for parallel program scheduling. *IEEE Parallel and Distributed Technology: Systems and Applications*, 1 (2), 62–72 (1993).

Lee, D. and Kim, M. Optimal task assignment in linear array networks. *IEEE Transactions on Computers*, 41 (7), 877–880 (1992).

Lo, V. Heuristic algorithms for task assignment in distributed systems. *IEEE Transactions on Computers*, 37 (11), 1384–1397 (1988).

Papadimitriou, H. and Yannakakis, M. Scheduling interval-ordered tasks. *SIAM Journal of Computing*, 8, 405–409 (1979).

Sarkar, V. Automatic partitioning of a program dependence graph into parallel tasks. *IBM Journal Res. Develop.*, 35 (5/6), (1991).

Sethi, R. Scheduling graphs on two processors. *SIAM Journal of Computing*, 5 (1), 73–82 (1976).

Stone, H. Multiprocessor scheduling with the aid of network flow algorithms. *IEEE Transaction on Software Engineering*, 85–93 (1977).

Ullman, J. NP-complete scheduling problems. *Journal of Computer and System Sciences*, 10, 384–393 (1975).

Advanced Computer Architecture and Parallel Processing, by H. El-Rewini and M. Abd-El-Barr
ISBN 0-471-46740-5 Copyright © 2005 John Wiley & Sons, Inc.